BLESSINGS

AT YOUR

FINGERTIPS

Much blessings to you!
11/21/2010

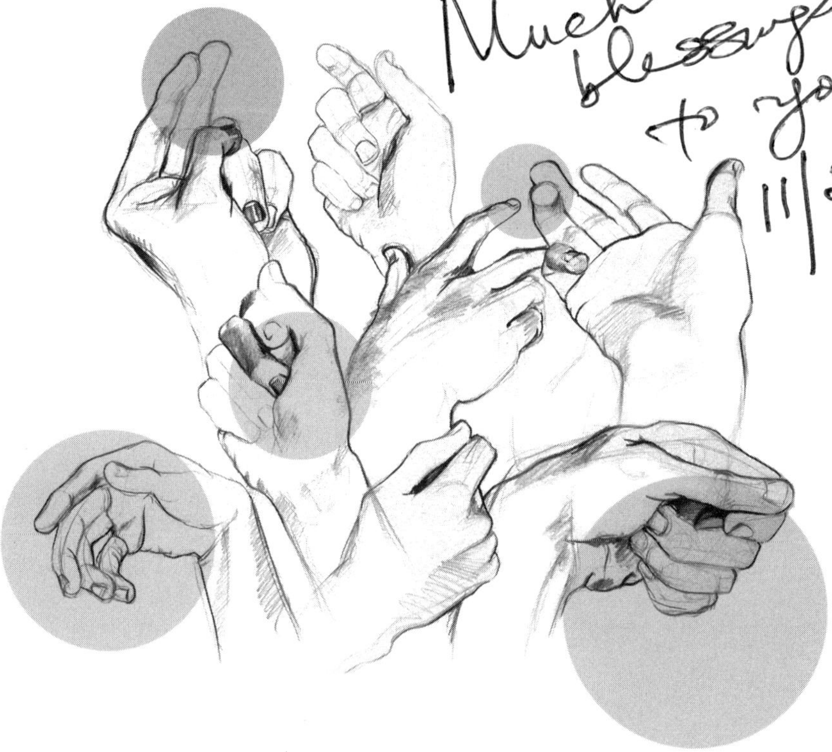

Nandell A. Palmer

Blessing
WRITE A
MEDIA

Seattle, Washington

ISBN: 978-0-9794565-0-3

Library of Congress Control Number: 2007925277

www.Writeablessing.com

Cover and Interior Design by theBookDesigners
www.bookdesigners.com

Cover drawing by Matt Moore

Printed in the United States

BLESSINGS
AT YOUR
FINGERTIPS

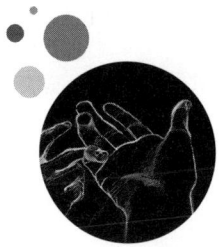

This book is dedicated to all the mothers and fathers, sisters and brothers, employers and employees, friends, teachers, doctors and nurses, pilots, paupers' daughters and rich men's sons. All those people who will find blessings at their fingertips to make their lives and those around them more impactful.

— CONTENTS —

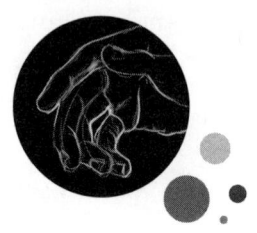

ACKNOWLEDGMENTS

I MUST DECLARE TO THE WORLD THAT THIS BOOK would not have been possible without the contributions of many hard working people. Indeed, I have been blessed to meet some of these very gifted and kind human beings throughout my sojourn, and I wish to introduce a few of them to you.

To Dr. Andre Sims, thank you for turning up the heat in your sermons, which has a way of burning off dross to reveal gold. Your $1 gift has changed my life forever!

To my father, Seymour Palmer. Thank you for sharing Napoleon Hill's book with me, the invaluable tool which jump started my passion. Thanks, too, for sticking around for us when greener pastures beckoned.

To my wife and best friend, Yvonne, for her unconditional support to follow my dreams. There is no doubt that you believe in me.

To my three dynamic sons, Jevoy, Jevaughn, and Jason.

Boys, you surely know how to inspire a father.

To my spiritual mother, Pearline Brown; you are a tower of strength! Keep on praying.

To Evangeline Martin, my fourth-grade teacher. You are still having an impact in my life today even after those many years.

To my birth mother, thank you for your breast milk; those colostrums have done wonders!

To all of my siblings, nieces, and nephews, especially to Rosemarie, for her dedication to loved ones and friends.

To Desrene Davis, Winston Lawrence, Sybil Thompson, Neville Williams, Joseph Ofei, Pastor Tony Moore, Sheba Makonnen, Pastor Herman Graham, Gayl Kirby, and Grady Smith. You've all motivated me to reach for the stars even when I was in doubt at times in finding them.

To Alian Design who designed the book, cover to cover; you make those pages sing! It is an understatement to say that you guys are a godsend.

To Debbie Bird, Jan Kendle, and Beverly Barker, three precious gems the Emerald City could not do without.

To Steve Preston, computer technician extraordinaire. Thanks for being the voice of reason while I navigated miles of bureaucracies.

To Jason Earls and family, Jennifer Brown and family, the Carters, Colemans, Freemans, Petersons, Crearys, and Akinlosotus, you guys rock!

To all the people who contributed to my $1 project, which inspired me for this book. You are forever blessed: Anita Rylander, Al & Lorna Coke, Ed Satterwhite, Shemiele DaBriel, Jason Fredericks, Garfield Knowles, Carmeta Francis, David & Diacy Thompson, Leon Turner, Phillip Green, Ruby Klaastad, and Deana Greene.

INTRODUCTION

It always amazes me to see the various types of people who buy newspapers. You will find that some people buy a newspaper for the sports section only. Others buy it to check up on how their stocks are doing in the market. Still others buy it for the latest gossip, and so forth. One way or the other, the publisher is a happy camper, because even though people buy the paper for different reasons, the primary goal of the publisher is to sell his newspapers. Whether the customer is young or old, short or tall, man or woman, boy or girl, the publisher does not discriminate in this regard.

It is no different in other aspects of life. Some people are very visual while others tend to be more ethereal. Some like to work with their hands and some prefer to work with their brains. All in all, at the end of the day, all those people will have worked for something common to both of them: money.

Dealing with spiritual matters, you can reach people by the

highly-spirited songs from a praise team or from the riveted words of a pastor's sermon. Some people prefer to hear real-life testimonies while others only can be reached by way of a Bible study or through a prayer meeting. The big picture here is the same result but different methods.

When I dubbed this book, *Blessings at Your Fingertips*, by no means I was trying to water down God's omnipotent power. But when I see how some of the simple things in life can be traced back to God's power, I could not help but to document a few of them in this book. We have seen how people's voices were used to bless millions through songs. How some people's taste buds have spawned culinary wonders; we have seen great sprinters by their mere feet, become a blessing to others. The hearts of benevolent people like Bill Cosby, Ted Turner, and Oprah Winfrey have birthed wonders in the lives of many of our unfortunate brothers and sisters in America and throughout the world.

So, as you can see, God can use many of our body parts to be a blessing to others. Even something as simple as our finger-tips can be utilized to become agents of blessings to ourselves, our loved ones, and even strangers. I just feel that those people who are not easily reached by their hearts or brains first could readily grasp something that they can see everyday – something tangible that they can work with or manipulate. But over time, those concrete matters will slowly sink in and find their way into the hearts and minds of those same people who you would not have reached were you to start them out with the matters of the heart approach. Flipped over, the result will be the same for the people who heard a sermon or read an inspiring passage somewhere, and later transfer it into something tangible in their everyday lives. Like cooking for the homeless or starting a business, which got them out of debt years later.

Similarly, some people are accepted into college with their high school diplomas, GEDs, SATs, and some through life experiences. But over time, all of those preliminary credentials can be realized into their getting a degree. Thus, there are different routes that lead to a common result. There are some medicines that are given topically, orally, and intravenously, but they all aim for the same result: healing.

My wish for you is that by the time you finish reading this book, you will have found complete healing in body, soul, and mind, by God's grace and mercy. You will no longer take yourself or those around you for granted. You will start appreciating the small things in life, being aware that through the little things, million-dollar companies can be founded. Through the little things, broken marriages can be restored, and sons will finally get the bond they've always yearned for from their dads. Daughters can talk openly with their mothers without being judged.

Believe that it can happen in your life today. King David slew the giant Goliath with something that was right at his fingertips — a sling and a marble stone; something that seemed so commonplace to everybody else. Joseph and Daniel, on the other hand, used dreams to find favor among men. Use what you have at your fingertips to advance you into greatness. Is it that book you have been putting off to write for the longest time now? Are they the salad dressing recipes you plan to market nationally from your kitchen counter? Is it the letter of apology you will write to your mother to wipe out years of bitterness between you and her? Only you know. Rub those fingertips together, say a prayer, and get the ball rolling!

I will warn you again that the seemingly infinitesimal things are the essence of this book. They are simple anecdotes and references, but if you apply them, you will see positive changes in your life. They will impact your life when you start taking notice around your surroundings.

Friend, we live in an era when we have pretty much everything at our beck and call — in other words — everything at our fingertips! It is a period when we can jet from Tel Aviv to Rio de Janeiro in less than 24 hours. We have instant access to current affairs all across the globe, with just one click of a computer mouse. From the comfort of our homes we can shop online and have our groceries delivered to us while we're lounging about, clad in our house robes. Hence, we ought to be thankful for all these opportunities and more in our lives. So, don't you deem it fitting that I label these things blessings at our fingertips?

We often wax poetic about major organs of our bodies, namely, the heart, the brains, etc. But seldom do we pause to celebrate some of our other body parts, which are never cast into starring roles. Some of those are none other than the fingertips. After all, the heart conjures up romances for which legends are made. There would be no *Romeo and Juliet*, *King Arthur's Court*, and *A Midsummer Night's Dream* – in other words – there would be no Shakespeare without the heart playing a central role in his renowned plays. However, whenever we think about the fingertips, they're merely relegated to picking and killing ticks, lice, and other pesky bugs. They are also the areas where felons are incriminated and sent to prison, sometimes for the rest of their lives. So I can understand why many of us don't readily celebrate them; the fingertips are not the darlings of our bodies. The eyes, lips, biceps, and legs are also some of the popular body parts that speedily get our attentions.

But have you ever stopped to wonder where our lives would be today without our able fingertips? What would a wedding march be without the organist playing Richard Wagner's bridal chorus, *Here Comes the Bride* so melodiously? What would the world do today without some of history's noted figures like Louis Braille and Helen Keller had they not employed their fingertips to change lives for millions of blind people? Where would worldwide companies like Microsoft and Boeing be without employing the fingertips?

You will read how a goatherd, Kaldi, picked the strange coffee berries and sampled them after his caffeinated goats feasted from the leaves and berries, and later ran amok on the bucolic

Ethiopian hillside centuries ago. This same coffee would later become the world's second largest legal export, making Howard Shultz' Starbucks a billion-dollar industry today.

You will also read about how a fourth-grade teacher blessed her students daily with one simple yet profound act of kindness. She did not give them money, gold, or shares in major stock options. All she did was used her fingertips to make each child feel special. Everyday, with dusty chalk, she wrote out a student's full name on the upper right hand corner of the blackboard. Many of those valued students have gone on to become scientists, actuaries, journalists, botanists, and professors.

Find out how a businessman who has made it his business to send out personal, handwritten thank-you notes to people for even the smallest deed, made a bundle from such gestures.

You will read about Michael Lee Chin, a struggling foreign student in Toronto, Canada, whose tertiary education nearly came to a halt until his country's government paid his remaining tuition to keep him in college. Today, that Jamaican-Canadian billionaire is a force with which to be reckoned. From that small contribution, he was able to invest millions of dollars into his country's economy years later.

The Bible says that God uses the simple things of this world to confound the wise. And, isn't that the truth!

I strongly believe that all of us are endowed with peculiar gifts and talents in some ways or the other. It is just a matter of time before they are unearthed. Many times you will not find those blessings at the fiftieth conference you will be attending. There will be no oracle to walk you through the enlightened path. Please know that all along those things were there – right at your fingertips. The execution of these skills and talents, enabled by God Himself, is what I call blessings. What a synergy. Have a lovely read.

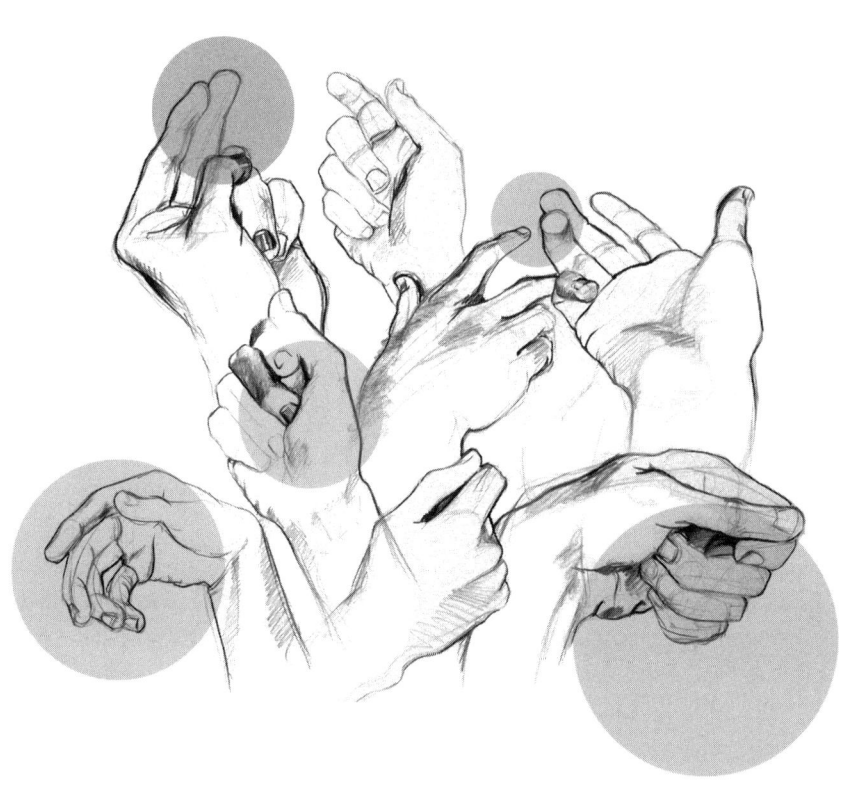

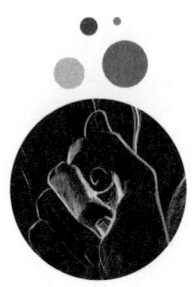

CHAPTER ONE

SEIZE THOSE BLESSINGS
AT YOUR FINGERTIPS

THE NEW WEBSTER'S COMPREHENSIVE DICTIONARY defines blessing as "giving favor and the invocation of it." If you can walk, consider it a blessing. If you are able to smell, it is a blessing. If you can read, it is a blessing. If you have the gift of making some people happy, that, too, is a blessing. The main source of those blessings comes from God Himself.

When I use blessings at your fingertips, I am not using the physical aspect alone but the spiritual as well. For example, while I can use my fingers to feed myself (physical), I could purpose myself to leave my house and travel a stone's throw away to attend a free seminar on "How to find inner peace in the time of storm." (Spiritual). Literally, that is information right there at my fingertips, which doesn't cost me money – just my time and effort.

The fact that my knowing about the seminar could potentially change my life and others in a more positive way, it would be foolhardy on my part not to take advantage of such a gathering. Hence, something so near – easily accessible – yet I refuse to take advantage of it.

According to physiologists, fingertips are specialized areas of the hand with highly developed sensory and manipulative functions. Large sensory and motor areas located in the brain regulate the precise and delicate functions of the fingertips. The fingertip is the site where extensor and flexor tendons insert. It is hard to believe, but fingertip injuries can result in amputation or tissue loss. Wow, so delicate yet so powerful!

Fingertips by themselves mean nothing. They need the body. In like manner, man by himself needs God before certain spiritual gifts can be made manifest. A body without life is a cadaver. A future canoe is a tree. A light bulb without electricity is a round-shaped glass without power. If you are able to write your son a letter, telling him how much you love and care for him, then you've got blessings at your fingertips. If you are able to pick up a telephone and give instruction to a newly-married wife 1,000 miles away on how to make peach cobbler, then you are exhibiting blessings at your fingertips.

If you have helped a stranded motorist by the roadside to recharge his battery, you did so with blessings at your fingertips. If you can tickle a drooling baby to laughter, you are reaping blessings at your fingertips. If you can stroke your husband's back after a hard day at work and tell him how wonderful it is to be married to him, you have blessings at your fingertips. If you are caught in bed with your ailing mother, propping her up to sleep on your chest shortly after the excitements of a New Year's Eve party, like my friend Beverly did, then indeed you have blessings at your fingertips. If you can dedicate an hour one evening to wash your wife's feet in petaled water and tell her that she's the glint in your diamond, then you have blessings at your fingertips.

God is working from the inside to show His work on the outside. Some Bible scholars have argued that the Book of Esther nearly missed being a book of the Bible because of the non-starring role of God. Not once was the word "God" mentioned in that book. But you don't have to go off in deep thoughts trying to fathom what role God played in Esther and her people's triumphing over the wicked Haman and his cronies.

Whenever I travel overseas and see the arts and craft for sale by local people, they just boggle my mind. The woven baskets, the beveled leather turned wallets, the wood and stone carvings. If you stop to think about it, majority of those pieces were handcrafted. The fingertips were very much at work.

During my relaxing time at home, one pastime for me is to just sit back and listen to a symphony, hearing those beautiful chords fill the space. I cannot help but see those nimble little fingertips at work. Some of the famous maestros like Bach, Beethoven, and Handel all used their fingertips to bless the world with their powerful music.

THE VITAL CONTRIBUTIONS OF THE FINGERTIPS

AGAIN, THE fingertips cut from the body are no use to themselves or to anybody else, for that matter. There ought to be a symbiotic relationship with the fingertips and the whole body for them to be functional. They need the hand. The brain. The heart. And blood. They need to know when to touch and when not to touch. Thus, making them dependent on the brain. They need to know when to caress gently and when to pull vigorously.

Combine all 10 fingertips and weigh them and they would hardly move the most sensitive scale. But those objects weighing less than a percentage of an ounce have the capability to provide something for the benefit of the entire body: Large comforters drawn to cover the entire body to keep it warm. They can produce megaton trains and skyscrapers. One fingertip can steady/steer a car on the freeway, if need be.

But many of us have never paused long enough to truly think about these powerful assets we take for granted on a daily basis. So, having been told about the myriad of blessings your fingertips can offer, would I be out of place to say that you can change a life with those fingertips? Would I be presumptuous if I were to tell you that you could start a million-dollar company with those fingertips right where you are today? If I were to tell you that the world is waiting for a bestseller novel from your hands, would you believe me?

If God could allow man to use fingertips to make megaton trains to run on lines, don't you think He could allow those same fingertips to push some new doors open for you to start a new business venture? Don't you think that it's possible for God to use your fingertips to write messages of love and hope to your loved ones to end four generations of hurt and pain?

You could write a letter right there in prison that will open the door for your release. You know that you are innocent all along, and the prosecutor ensured that you get the maximum time. Even your own defense attorney didn't buy your innocence. I am saying to you today, begin to write that letter. It will reach the right people, and you will be free. Find those blessings right at your fingertips.

Your only child is now strung out on drugs. You did everything as best as you could to raise him right. But over the last two years, he's been acting strange. He's not properly dressed as he used to carry himself. Instead, he's unkempt, hardly thinking about his appearance. Right now you are literally scared for your life, and you worry constantly about him. He has left home a month now without calling you. You don't know his whereabouts. But don't lose hope. In the meantime, find a drug rehabilitation center nearby and volunteer your service. Fast. There is something for you to do there. While you are helping somebody else's son at that rehab, God will send somebody to help your son, even thousands of miles away.

Picture that interaction like a space shuttle. NASA on earth can make wireless repairs to that shuttle hundreds or thousands of miles in space. And that shuttle can beam its satellite back to NASA on earth. They benefit each other. See the analogy as God at work in your life. So do the best you can by helping to ease somebody else child's pain. It will bless you both immensely. Start seeing your son being restored. It begins by putting those powerful fingertips at work. Stretch out your palms, look at them, and vicariously see those blessings working for you. God is doing the necessary repairs. Be encouraged by these words: "Your light will break forth like the dawn, and healing will quickly appear." – Isaiah 58:8.

When was the last time you sat down and examined those body parts that are not readily celebrated by you or others? How about the soles of your feet, when was the last time you took a look at them? Your fingertips are not the belles at the balls; they are not dressed up like mascaraed eyes. They don't quickly attract matchmakers like your pearly-white teeth, radiating 100-watt smiles.

Most of you depend on your fingers to eat a meal. Clean yourself. Caress your pet. Show victory. Plant a garden. But have you stopped to ponder a thousand other benefits you get from your fingers? And I am not talking about the one some of you give to drivers on the freeway who cut you off. What would music be without employing our fingertips? How could a barber possibly make a livelihood without his fingertips? What would become of great poetry and prose without our fingertips? Would we have a David in Florence,

Italy without the use of fingertips? What about DaVinci's Mona Lisa or Michelangelo's breathtaking Sistine Chapel? What about the monumental pyramids in Egypt or the majestic Space Needle in Seattle?

LOUIS BRAILLE AND HELEN KELLER

WHEN I first read the story of Louis Braille, a man who became blind at age three in France, and who would later create a system for the blind named for him – *Braille* – I was speechless. By age 10, little Louis surpassed his other blind peers in playing the piano and organ. With his invention of the raised-dot characters, the blind's world was revolutionized with one touch of their fingertips. What a blessing that must have been for those people.

In no time, because of this invention, the blind excelled in mathematics, world literature, and music. They would become a powerful force. Picture a world today without the vast contributions of the indomitable Helen Keller – herself a victim of blindness since early childhood. But it all started with one man who dared to dream dreams; one who wouldn't take no for an answer. In the true classical sense, he really found blessings right at his fingertips. Whenever you visit France, discover more about this great man at the Pantheon in Paris.

Only a few sights around today can compete with that of a serious, seasoned typist at work on one of those old typewriters. I am talking about the one whose head is cocked to the left while her fingers are tapping away on the keyboard at right. The speed. The dexterity. And, yes, the accuracy! There is hardly anything more graceful. Before the advent of computers, many of those ladies were a godsend. They bailed me out many times at the eleventh hour when those term papers were due, and my pre-typing days amounted to just picking one letter at a time. I will always treasure their memories. They indeed executed blessings at their fingertips for me and countless other satisfied parties.

THE FINGERTIPS PROBE FOR LIFE

AT THE doctor's office, a physician would first check his patient to ensure that certain vital signs are in order: blood pressure, pulse rate, reflexes, temperature, and the iron level in the blood. Combined, these tests would take no longer than seven minutes. But one feature that all of those tests have in common is that they must be employed by using the fingertips.

After wrapping that band around your arm, a nurse squeezes the bulbous apparatus with her fingertips to determine your blood pressure. The doctor puts his index fingertip on your wrist to determine your pulse rate. He uses a small mallet to tap your knees to make sure that you have the right reflexes. He uses his index finger to pull down on your eyelids to see if you are anemic. He uses his fingertips to check for lymph nodes on your neck. Further follow-ups include the physician's using her stethoscope to check your heart rate and lungs, and checking your body temperature.

Isn't that amazing? Running those cursory tests could tell a doctor a lot about you. That's the time when he decides whether or not you need further follow-up. Invariably, if all those tests proved favorable, the doctor could literally send you home sans the CAT-scans and MRIs. Notice again that all those tests require healthcare workers to use their fingertips in order to get the tests validated.

If those walk-in people's cases were to call for invasive surgeries, the primary instruments that would be utilized are the fingertips. To suture delicate veins and wounds, those physicians cannot depend on a machine to do the job.

Their fingertips are indispensable in those cases.

Thus, I find it quite profound to see, despite the advancement in modern medicine, how doctors still depend on something so commonplace as our fingertips to determine potential life and death situations. How then can I not say those things are blessings at your fingertips?

People who live with indoor pets have the best of both worlds. As the cat or dog sidles up to its owner, getting out those fingertips to stroke them is quite therapeutic for both owner and pet. Many of our everyday tasks, which we often take for granted, begin and end with our fingertips. Think about it.

CONTROLLING JUMBO JETS WITH THE FINGERTIPS

THINK ABOUT a pilot flying a jumbo jet or a captain navigating a cruise ship. They can maneuver those gigantic vessels with sometimes just a few touches with their fingertips. The plane could soar up to 37,000 feet in the air and cutting 610 miles per hour. In like manner, the ship can run several knots at a time, covering thousands of miles over treacherous oceanic waves. Those small pilots and sea captains can land those airplanes or anchor those ships at the nearest airport or port of call if they feel like it. What we see are these two individuals doing the required work to move or stop those vessels, but, collectively, there is a greater power at work. There is a larger network of engines and turbines and navigational compasses in place. Without those things in place, those men/women can do nothing.

That's how it is with God allowing you to create wonders with your fingertips. "He sets things into motion, and watches o'er us still," if I may borrow a few words from one of my father's poems. He sets you out there to accomplish great things under his guidance. He's already gotten the hard work and the kink out of the way. There is a large engine room behind you generating all the power that you need. The compass will take you to your charted destination. There is enough fuel in your tank to keep you going; so what else are you waiting for?

Whenever we do whatever is put in place for us to do in a positive way, we are merely putting on window dressing in comparison to what God has already done in the background. Don Wyrtzen, a noted musicologist and author of *No Loose Ends*, says it much more profoundly: ". . . I work with raw materials that he [God] created . . . and my creativity is derived from his. I put the wrapping paper and ribbon on his packages."

LOOK THEN TOUCH

Isn't it strange that two of the world's most invaluable inventions came about from the observation of birds? One being a barnyard fowl, up until that time, good for nothing else but for its eggs and meat. I was told that as a child, Thomas Edison had his "light bulb" moment after observing a hen sitting on her eggs. The heat that was transferred from the hen to her eggs was powerful enough to bring life 21 days later to her baby chickens, and that piqued his curiosity. Edison seized this concept and ran to town with it when he grew up. I'm certain that he did not only look at the hen and her eggs. Most likely he had to battle a fierce fowl as he inched his way closer to his discovery. Setting hens are known to be fierce. But perhaps he waited until the hen was on a meal break before he could pick up those eggs. That time allowed him to examine them, feel the amount of heat emanating from them, which nonetheless played a vital contribution for his hypothesis. But the biggest accomplishment for Edison's discovering the light bulb was getting his fingertips actively engaged in the process.

The other invention of note is the airplane. The stories that have been written about over the years, often linked aviation pioneers to the observation of flying birds or winged insects. After watching birds soaring through the sky, those pioneers came up with a way to imitate the birds. But before they could advance their observations, they had to somehow catch a bird, touch it, and examine it. They also had to find out which bone was connected to what joint, and so forth. But it started out that simple. The fingertips again were fully employed throughout that process. From those humble beginnings, today we have jumbo jets, beating out the fastest and most powerful birds ever.

What has been swirling around in your head for the last 10 years now, prompting you to put down on paper that invention, which will benefit the world greatly? Like Edison, which animal out there today has intrigued you enough that would merit your wanting to imitate its habits or forms in some inventions for the common good of mankind? Friend, it's all there waiting for you to make the move. Get up close. Grab it. Get those finger-tips working. Feel it, and come up with your own hypothesis.

Which tune have you been humming that's waiting to earn you a Grammy award? Flesh it out. Record it. But first, put it down on paper into words or musical notes. Get the key-board, piano, guitar or harp. Get to work. Make a telephone call. Make it happen! Seize those blessings. They are only a few fingertips away.

SPIDER WEB AND BLESSING

ANOTHER STUPENDOUS sight I can never resist is a beauti-fully-spun spider web. Seeing a spider crawling about our house, the first thing many of us would do is to find a shoe and kill it. Some would spray it. We just view them as good-for-nothing nuisance. But given a few hours, your doorway will have festooned with one of life's most intricate and glamorous sights – the spider web.

The same spider you thought was a nuisance was now bringing a work of art up front and in your face. Even if spider watching is not your bailiwick, many times you cannot help yourself but to admire the handiwork this insect produces. Yes, you can walk away inspired by a spider web.

And what about the little old lady who tats away daily with spools of wool, sitting at the same spot for hours? All most of you see is an old, retired lady who has seen better days, and now has nothing better to do with her time but to knit or crochet. Because you don't readily see her finished work, you push her aside. But one day, you are bowled over when out of nowhere, she presents you with a neatly-wrapped package, which later unveils the most beautiful sweater you've ever seen since your trip to Dublin, Ireland 20 years ago. Your eyes dart back and forth between the old lady and the sweater, as you still cannot bring yourself to believe that such exquisite work could come from a seemingly frail, old lady.

Samuel's mother made him a robe every year while he was living with Eli. See 1 Samuels 2:19. Those tasks, no doubt, were hemmed in with a lot of love turned blessings from Hannah's fingertips. Eli would pronounce blessing on her and Elkanah, Samuel's dad, after each trip to the temple. Joseph's coat of many colors – lots of fingertips burning for that one – but the blessing sustained, which later saw Joseph as the highest ranking official in Egypt after Pharaoh. Is that blessing or what?

Jesus spared an adulterous woman's life by writing on the ground with his finger. Was he writing her the blessing of com-passion? Of love? Of empathy? See John 7:53 and 8:11. That act was nothing short of blessings from his fingertips. Jesus also healed a blind man by putting his finger in mud and then applied it to the man's eyes. Again, he was exhibiting blessing of sight by way of his fingertips. When that woman with the issue of blood touched his garment, she received blessings by way of her fingertips.

The most visible and commonly-used body parts I've employed to bless others are undisputedly my fingertips: the recommendations I've written. The cash I leafed out from my wallet to send via money transfer services to pay for an elderly woman's monthly upkeep. The resume I helped type for the high-school senior. The baby I have steadied to take his first step. The inspirational message I forwarded to my friends via emails. The telephone call I made to say a prayer for the old lady who was due to undergo major surgery and was fearful to go through with it. My stroking the hands of an Alzheimer's patient, and getting a smile in return.

How can I pass on blessings via my fingertips? you ask. Well, how about doing some of the following: Cook a meal for somebody, unexpectedly; bathe an elderly person who cannot do so for himself; drop off meals from a Meals-on-Wheels organization in your city, if it's even for one hour a week; write a thank-you letter to your teacher, doctor, pastor, or to the person who loaned you money for books while you struggled financially in college; write yourself a love letter; plant a tree in honor of a loved one; put your forefinger to your idea and brainstorm about the business you've always wanted to start.

Help that handicapped person cross the road; give some-body a backrub for free; volunteer to play an instrument for the elderly in nursing homes at dinnertime; play videogames with your children for at least 20 minutes; comb the little girl's hair around the way whose mother died two years ago; pick some fruits from your tree and give them away to complete strangers; mow the lawn of your sick neighbor, and refuse to take payment even when he insists; shovel the snow for neighbors five doors down the street from you; write a check to pay somebody's light bill without her asking you; pick out a few cans of food from the pantry and drop them off at the food bank.

Husbands, run your fingers through your wives' hair; wives, play in your husbands' hair – if no hair, use your fingertip to write out blessings you want to see manifest in their lives via their bald pates; volunteer in pediatric wards at public hospitals to hug and cradle abandoned AIDS/HIV-infected babies; visit orphanages and touch a few children for the sake of it – this will mean the world to them; serve the homeless hot apple cider and cookies on a wintery day, long after the yuletide rush; knit something for somebody; teach somebody how to write his name.

The elbows, chin, ears, forehead, knees, etc. are all connected to the body, but they, on their own, cannot perform the aforementioned tasks. They humbly await those fingertips to do the honors, executing abundant blessings.

One little girl in the Greater Seattle area every December makes hats and mittens for homeless men and women. With her hand-drawn cart, she navigates her way around broken-down buildings, under bridges and viaducts, through alleys, on park benches, just to ensure that those people are warmly dressed for the winter. She works assiduously night and day – with helpers – to sew those items of value by hand. The kicker to all of this is that she has a noticeable physical handicap, and she has undergone a legion of corrective surgeries over the years for a cleft palate. She was teased in school, and had to be taken out and home-schooled, but that did not deter her from bringing blessings to others, conceived in her heart, and coursed down through her fingertips.

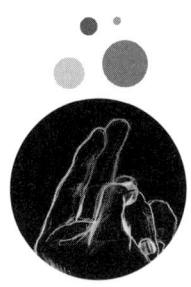

CHAPTER TWO

MY MILLION-DOLLAR LESSON
FROM A $1 GIFT

ON THE SUNDAY MORNING OF SEPTEMBER 10, 2006,
my pastor was handing out $1 bills to congregants who could tell
him some of the criteria necessary to be *Blessed and Highly Favored*,
stemming from his month-long series. He was in the second week
of the series, and he wanted us to recall some of those principles he
had taught on the week before. I answered that obedience was one
of the key principles to being blessed and highly favored, and I was
rewarded with a $1 bill. Two more people, including my wife, came
up with the other criteria, and they, too, were rewarded with $1 bills
for their input. The pastor's gestures were part serious and part
comical, as when he told us to go out and treat ourselves to hamburg-
ers or chicken nuggets with the $1 he gave us at some of our fast food
places around town.

Reading from Genesis 26:1-5; 12-15, the pastor was extolling
the virtues of obedience. There was a famine in the land, and God

appeared to Isaac and said to him not to go down to Egypt, but instead should live in the land where He will bless him. Naturally, when there is a famine, it is caused by drought, a lack of water. So to the average man in the street, it would be utter nonsense for someone telling him to plant a crop. I could just hear that irate man asking, "And where the water is going to come from to water the plants?" But in Isaac's case, he didn't ask such questions. He felt that if God was doing the talking, all he needed to do was to obey what was being said to him. Thus, he overlooked the obvious and trusted God at His word. And as we read in verses 12-13:

"Isaac planted crops in that land and the same year reaped a hundredfold, because the Lord blessed him. The man became rich, and his wealth continued to grow until he became very wealthy. . . ."

Now, do you want a clearer definition of what being blessed and highly favored look like? Isaac was the epitome of what being blessed and highly favored looked like.

In all of my life, I have never felt so empowered with one sermon so concretely fleshed out from the Bible. I was so fired up! I felt that my body and spirit were transformed into that of Isaac's. I felt that the same thing that happened to Isaac could happen to me. I was prepared to start breaking up those crusty, sun-baked, parched lands in my drought-ravaged life. I longed for springtime and abundant harvests. So, I continued to reach out. My faith was maximized to the zenith.

Shortly after the pastor handed me that $1 bill, something strange happened that morning, which I can hardly express in words. It felt as though I was in a swoon, and after I snapped out of it, a voice said to me to keep that money separate and apart from my other money. I meticulously kept it aside in my pocket and then in my Bible. My thoughts kept asking what was the reason behind the money given to me. What was so special about getting $1? I have collected thousands of dollars through business transactions time and time again, so why should I set aside a mere $1 bill? I was able to follow the sermon in its entirety, but as soon as the service was dismissed, I felt driven. I cut out of church so fast that it was a surprise to many people. As my family and I drove home, my thoughts became pregnant with ideas. Upon reaching home, I said a prayer, asking God to reveal His purpose for me, and what exactly I should do with that money given to me.

It was revealed to me that the money was a seed money; that I was to increase it a hundredfold. As Yvonne prepared the Sunday dinner, I sat around the dining table, going over countless possibilities as to how I was going to get $100 from $1. I soon grabbed a piece of blank paper and began to write down 10 potential areas I could go to get this money. The boys were quite agog as well, and they, too, chipped in with their ideas. Sometimes I can be a very literal person, and since the pastor said that we could buy hamburger and chicken nuggets with the money, I settled on the latter. But before I left out for the fast food restaurant, I called my friend, Anita Rylander. She was about half-hour away from her home.

"Anita, I am selling some chicken nuggets and looking for buyers, would you care to buy a few from me?" I shamelessly asked.

"Oh, yes, how much are you selling them for?" Anita inquired.

"Well, I will have five of them, and they will be a dollar each," I chimed in.

"Bring them over, and I will decide," she said. "See you when I get home."

As soon as our telephone conversation was ended, my middle son, Jevaughn, and I dashed out from the house and into the car. We headed to one of the national office supplies chain stores to photocopy the $1 bill as proof after the money was spent. Why was I doing this? I couldn't tell. For all we know, a dollar is a dollar is a dollar. The only thing that distinguishes one from the other would be clean or dirty; old or new. All dollar bills have the same size; they are printed at the same place; they share all the common characteristics of another bill. So I had no clue as to why I was drawn to this.

I was about 10 feet away from the copier when a store employee walked up to me.

"Don't you know it's illegal to photocopy U.S. currency?"

"Balderdash!" a small but rebellious voice countered.

"Oh, it's okay," shouted another employee to me across the room, as he sidled beside us at the machine.

"As long as he increases or decreases the size of the bill and keep it in black and white, then all will be well," the older man assured us.

Wow, I felt as though I was in grade school all over again. I felt cheated – feeling as though my finance class was not up to par for having something as simple as this slip through my brains. I thought I knew a lot as they relate to civic duties, protocols, basic laws, etc. But I left that store feeling grateful for learning something I didn't know before. Again, I felt empowered. If for nothing else, at least I can answer one more *Jeopardy* question correctly, I said.

The most interesting thing about the money-copying incident was how those two store employees got involved, I would say, needlessly. First, I was shocked at what the man was saying to me because before that time, I had not heard about any such thing. I was also doubly shocked when he accosted me since I had not gone to the machine directly to do so yet. All I had was the dollar bill in my hand. How could he have known that I was going to photocopy it? I had been to that store more than a hundred times over the last five years, and not once had anybody ever stopped me before or after that encounter. If I needed help, I had to go in search of an employee to help me. So, again, it was strange that a dialogue was going on about something that was so "trivial." But in hindsight, I think it was divinely planned. It was a setup – a very rewarding one at that.

As planned, I bought a 5-piece chicken nugget with the $1 the pastor gave me, and pretty soon, I was at Anita's house. I told her about my project, and she was eager to oblige in supporting my cause. She took the five nuggets and gave me a $5 bill in exchange. I recall telling her that she would be reaping a hundredfold or more on her $5 before the month was over. After I left her house, I immediately went to a dollar store and bought some more items with that $5. I traded those items for cash and bought more goods with those proceeds. Since I still didn't know exactly the full outcome of what was going to happen, I prayed again, asking God for clearer directions and insights. Yvonne and I talked about it, too. But before the week was out, I knew exactly what to do with that money once everything was in: Give it back to the pastor – his seed money of $1, along with the hundredfold money, which is $100.

I strongly believe that his sermons needed to go beyond the periphery of our local church and reach thousands or millions more people out there. It was not okay for me to sit Sunday after Sunday gorging on those rich messages, while others were getting lean from not hearing these life-changing words. That man has about a dozen books inside of him ready to be birthed, and so, I decided to aid him in his project to make the balls start rolling. I consider it a drop in the bucket, but at least the money could buy stamps or stationery to send him in that trajectory.

I had projected to turn in the money in 30 days' time, but by the first week, I had received a little over $34. I bought books, packaged vegetable and flower seeds, avocados, picture frames, just about anything I could find. I made a few telephone calls to some of my friends out of state, and before long, they, too, wanted to be a part of what I was doing. Some of them wanted to just send a donation, but I insisted that they receive something in return for their money, and so, I mailed them packets of flower/vegetable seeds. Three local barbers also gave to the cause. Can you imagine paying $20 for a packet of seeds? Yikes! But they did so with pleasure. After I reached my quota, I stopped collecting. I even had to ask people to stop sending money as the project was over. Just before service on Sunday, September 24, 2006, I presented my pastor with a thank-you card, containing $101, along with a giant-sized photocopy of the dollar bill he gave me. He was astounded, to say the least. I gave him another $40 the following week that was delayed in the mail.

That night I went to bed a little earlier than usual, and at about midnight, I found myself tossing in bed. I just couldn't sleep. All of a sudden, ideas started welling up in my head. A project that I had been praying about two years prior to that night, all of a sudden began taking shape. I could see the blueprint as clear as day. I told myself that I would write down those ideas when I woke up in the morning, but it was as if someone was pushing me out of bed to write them down that minute. I was obedient, and the same dining table that I sat around to brainstorm about things to do with that $1 two weeks earlier, was the same table I used to write down about five pages of ideas.

Crystal-clear ideas were flooding my mind as I had never experienced before. When I wrote, there was no pause, no hesitation. It was as if somebody was holding my hand to help me write. I wrote texts relating to better relationships among fathers and sons, mothers and daughters, wives and husbands, orphans in orphanage who need to be adopted by loving parents; employers and employees, friends, among others. And that's how my new company, *Write A Blessing Media*, was born.

On Monday, October 2, 2006, at about 9 p.m., I got a call from Anita. Remember the same lady who bought my chicken nuggets? She was excited, talking so fast that I could barely hear a word as to what she was saying. I started to think the worst as she has three sons, one of them being a teenager.

"Calm down, Anita, what is the matter?" I asked. ·

"You, you, you, . . . you will never believe this," she stuttered. "When I didn't get my paycheck in the mail, I went to payroll to inquire as to the delay, and today I got my paycheck, and I saw $475 extra on it. . . I am still in shock. To top it off, a hospital bill that I owed for $1,400 for more than a year, is now forgiven. The hospital wrote to tell me that I have a zero balance."

She went on to talk about how her coworkers were saying that the extra money on her check was a test, and that her employers would be looking to see if she was going to report it. But after she again went to payroll, they told her that indeed the money was hers and that she should not worry about any misappropriation. In other words, as far as they knew, she had earned the money. Anita to this day, cannot explain how that extra money came to be. For the hospital bill, she said she was constantly inundated with bill collectors dunning her for payment toward the outstanding debt. She got several warning and threatening letters, but she could not find the money to make the payment. Thus, she was quite surprised to get a letter in writing telling her that her debt was forgiven and that she would not be penalized.

I told her that if in case she had called up friends, complaining to them about how this lowdown man ripped her off by selling her $1 worth of chicken nuggets for $5, then she needed to call them back and tell them about her remarkable testimony: How $5 has earned her nearly $2,000 in less than a month for being obedient. Anita has grown leaps and bounds from that point onward. And you will read more about her in the coming chapters.

Because of my newfound quest to ferret out information and to seek out more of what God has in store for me, the weeks that followed had me going into my neighborhood libraries getting books and downloading materials on finance. Currencies, stock and bonds, etc. Before long, my three boys got curious as well and wanted to learn more about money matters. And because Jevaughn was there with me that Sunday afternoon while I photocopied the dollar bill, he was being schooled at the same time with me, witnessing everything live and direct. Our heightened quest for monetary knowledge was untamed. We pored over everything meaningful about money. I wanted them to appreciate it, and not take it for granted.

On the last Saturday of September 2006, we were settling in to watch a few DVDs or whatever was showing on TV, but that evening, the boys all shunned the newly-rented DVDs, and asked instead to learn more about money matters. I soon set up the chalkboard in the center of the living room, outlining the basics of a balance sheet, and so forth. They came up with dummy companies, applying real-life scenarios to their deals. On Sunday, October 1, after our family devotion, I used the occasion to kickoff the inauguration of their individual business. I presented them with three pennies, and told them that they had 100 days to turn each penny into $100, and by Sunday afternoon, they came up with their own company names, logos, business cards, etc. I told them that I could have easily given them $20 each to start their business, but I chose to give them the penny because a penny can be viewed as a beginning and an end at the same time, depending on who is looking at it. You can allow a penny to keep you locked in to a corner or you can choose to push it forward and allow it to work for you.

Jason, our youngest son, and I were driving out one Saturday afternoon, and I asked him how he had planned to make his penny work for him. First, he was saying that the idea was inane, and that nobody could possibly move a penny to make an increase in profits. But within three minutes of our conversation, it was as if he saw the light.

"Oh, I know what I am going to do. I am going to trade my penny with you for $1 and then I can use that $1 and do some of the things you did to get a hundred," he said confidently.

"The ball is in your court, Jason," I said to him. "The sky is the limit. You can be anything you want to be if you put your mind to it."

I went on to tell him that if he and his brothers needed any help, they should not hesitate to call on me. I gave him a few pointers as to how he and his brothers could earn money. I encouraged him to write poems and sell them to their grandfather, aunt, teachers, and other people that they were familiar with.

Because I had a lot of children's book directed to their learning, I found myself getting deeper understanding from complex materials found in "grownup books." And I had no shame reading those elementary-level books. In one of the books I checked out was a large-sized copy of the one-dollar bill breaking down what every emblem, serial number, and so forth stood for. Every seemingly idle word was brought into perspective. Suddenly, everything had a meaning for me. I would later categorize these items into areas I deemed relevant in my life:

EQUITY

THE LATIN term, "*E Pluribus Unum*," meaning "Out of Many, One," pretty much spells out equality for me in this great country, boasting a population of 300 million people, from every walk of life. What a joy it is to be a member of the human race and the opportunity to live in the United States of America.

FAVOR

WHEN I read the term, "*Annuit Coeptis*" – another Latin phrase which means, "He has favored our undertakings" – I was comforted. It says to me, even with a $1 bill in my possession, I have the potential to be blessed because I am favored. I can use it to start a business, amassing millions of dollars in the process, in these United States of America because He has already favored my undertakings. What could potentially hold me back now to blaze new trails?

HOPE

I AM really liking these Latin phrases. Another one that drew my attention was "*Novus Ordo Seclorum*," meaning "A new order of the ages," which stands for the new American era. Even though those words were giving hope to earlier settlers who had shaped the American landscape, they are still lighting a path for the refugees from Cambodia, who look to America as a beacon of hope. It is for the single mother in Santa Fe, New Mexico, struggling to feed her family. It is for the D student in Brooklyn, New York, grappling with thoughts about staying in school or quitting.

TRUST

WHEN THE bills pile up and you don't know where to turn, it's hard to trust. But when I see the phrase, *"In God We Trust"* strategically placed in the center of the bill, I am reminded that I am cushioned on all sides if I only trust God. When the demons of your past taunt you that you will never make it in life, all you need to do is just trust. When you have to forgo a trip to the doctor in order to put food on your table for your family, still trust. When the dream house fails to materialize on your request lists for the last 10 years, take another look at that dollar bill and say out loud, "In God I trust."

GUIDANCE

THE UNBLINKING eye peering through the sun's ray reminds me of God's guidance – His omnipresence and omniscience are with me. He will shed light through all the nooks and crannies of doubt. It reminds me of Psalm 23: ". . . Though I walk through the valley of the shadow of death, I will fear no evil. . . ."

STRENGTH

THE PYRAMID symbolizes strength for me. I will not be moved by the winds of doubt. I will not crumble when things are not going my way. I will always look to the Rock that is higher than I.

CONFIDENCE

LIKE A lot of people in our Western frontier, I have bought into the negative connotation with the number 13, while not doing so overtly. Frankly, if I had a choice to choose three numbers and 13 was one of them, I would not choose it, even if it meant inconveniencing myself to reschedule an appointment. But after studying my dollar bill, I found out that 13 was a very symbolic number represented on the note. There could be more, but I counted seven from my observation: The phrases *E Pluribus Unum* and *Annuit Coeptis* both have 13 letters; on the right hand seal, the eagle, which represents the original 13 colonies, holds an olive branch, which carries 13 leaves and 13 berries. In the next talon it carries 13 arrows; the shield has 13 stripes, and 13 stars above the eagle's head.

On Friday, October 13, 2006, for the first time in my life I went against all my preconceived ideas about the negative connotations associated with Friday the 13th and sat for a rigorous 4-hour examination. I passed with flying colors. What a breakthrough for me! When I shared my former fear with a friend of mine, he flatly mocked me on the spot, telling me that I should have renewed my mind a long time ago by overcoming *triskaidekaphobia* (fear of the number 13). I said aye to that, but at least I was honest in talking about that fear. I thought about those people who were crippled with this number and others. I know people from all faiths whose account numbers start with 666 or those who live in areas where their zip code ends with 666. Many of them have closed out their accounts or moved away from that community altogether just in order not to associate with that strand of digits. And even if you are giving away a room for free, many people would never stay in a room with 666 emblazoned on its door or stay on the 13th floor. Thus, I was not alone in coming to terms with this universal fear of certain numbers. I recall Jesus, along with his 12 disciples, numbering 13. I also thought about how special it is for a customer to get a baker's dozen — when he receives 13 items instead of 12. All in all, I can truly say that I am completely free from the fear of the number 13.

HUMILITY AND APPRECIATION

TWO OF the biggest lessons that I've learnt in all of this new awareness are humility and appreciation. As I have mentioned before, I have handled thousands of dollars in the past, but it had never dawned on me to look at them – to appreciate those bills. All I wanted to do was just to spend them. I learnt that knowledge is power, and that it doesn't matter who or where the source of that knowledge comes from, as long as it's positive, moving your life in the right direction, then accept it. I am now willing to be taught by my 10-year-old son or a 99-year-old great-grandfather. Because of this one-dollar bill. I have understood a greater concept of finance and economics, which had seemed "teflonic" in the past (they just couldn't stick). Thank you, Pastor, for giving me a gift of new beginnings through your $1 largesse.

And just like how the dollar bill is the least of its denominations, so, too, I can learn from a lower-ranked employee or child. I have passed the test!

Right now, a penny cannot be too green for me to pick it up from the sidewalk. There is no such thing as a stray dime or nickel.

The greatest strand throughout this whole lesson, again, is obedience; it is the one criterion that is repeated over and over here. When my pastor gave me the $1 bill, I was obedient – albeit in a childlike manner – to buy what he said to use the money to buy: fast food. When I asked Anita to buy the 5-piece chicken nuggets, she was obedient to my request, and she was rewarded with nearly $2,000. Because of my obedience, I was catapulted into an area that I had never dreamt I would go – trading the foreign exchange market, or *Forex*, for short. Because of my obedience, my children are more financially savvy today. I would not have gone to the library to rent books or to download materials online about the forex market had I not been stopped by the store employee for copying that $1 bill. It is amazing!

CHAPTER THREE

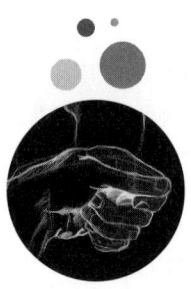

THE DISTASTE
OF FINANCIAL DEBTS

I WAS STRANDED IN THE VOLTA REGION OF GHANA,
West Africa, some years ago, and couldn't get back to my hotel in
Accra. I was too happy when a kind family hosted me for the evening.
That night at dinner, we had fufu – a staple of cassava and plantain
– along with a peanut-beef stew. The food was tasty, but while eating with my fingers, as was the custom, I noticed that people were
smirking. And before long, I found out that I was the object of their
amusement. Somebody was brave enough to educate me about the
protocol in eating fufu. "Nobody in Ghana chews fufu," my host
informed me. "You must swallow it – not chew it."

That was quite a shock to me. How else that glutinous mass was
ever going to go down my throat without my chewing it? I pondered.
Considering myself quite adaptable, I soon followed suit, much to
their satisfaction. Nevertheless, I felt as though I was swallowing
vitamin tablets, where I was not interested in the tablets themselves but their nutritional properties. My observation from that

experience taught me a big lesson. I proved that eating without chewing and savoring one's food will only produce a full stomach without any enjoyment to the diner. It also has the potential to make you ungrateful.

Since it was a communal eating setting, everybody took turns helping himself to handsome portions. The biggest insult you can make to an African hostess is to refuse her food or eat small portions thereof. Because I had foreknowledge of the culture, I wasn't going to make myself a social pariah on that trip. Therefore, I swallowed that food with much alacrity. Not feeling full, however, I decided to suspend eating. But it appeared as though the hypothalamus was not keeping track of what I was downing because when I decided to rise from the dinner mat on the floor, my stomach felt as though it had a ton of bricks in it. Never before had I eaten to such satiety. Hence, I had never felt that way before. I have eaten fufu several times after that, but I had to break with tradition and masticate my fufu before swallowing it, even at the expense of great derision among my fellow Ghanaian friends here in America.

Some of you are perhaps asking, what does fufu have to do with finances? Yes, the analogy between eating fufu and spending money is quite a stretch of the imagination for a number of you. But I am trying to flesh out the similarities between the two modes of action: Eating without tasting can balloon your stomach without your knowing it, and spending without sensing can bankrupt your finances without your realizing it.

FINANCIAL CONSEQUENCES AND BLESSINGS

LIKE THE fufu, many of us have had a difficult time enjoying our hard-earned money. We have lost the joy that comes with money. And with more people using debit cards for a big chunk of their purchases and payments, actual cash is playing second fiddle to those ubiquitous plastic currencies. We swallow the bitter pills of paying our bills with hardly any time to enjoy the good taste of our money.

INFORMAL BANKING

THROUGHOUT THE Caribbean, the local people have in place an informal banking system called *partner* or *box*. In the French islands like Haiti or Martinique, it's called *Sou-sou* (susu). It's a system where money is pooled together on a weekly basis, say, from 20 people, and the lump sum is given to one person weekly. A set amount like $100 per week was required by participating members, and each week, that pooled amount would go to one person. Thus 20 people giving $100 weekly amassed to $2,000 for each party, interest free. The recipient of that *draw*, the lump sum amount, out of courtesy, would give the banker a small portion of cash for his or her service.

That informal banking system has found its way to many large cities like New York, London, and Toronto. People to this day rely on partners to make down-payments on a house or to purchase a car. Still others use them to start a business or for a wedding reception. Since a lot of people were not disciplined enough to save $2,000 on their own, they gladly welcomed this gateway to financial freedom.

I was talking with a young man from India recently, and he told me that in India most people don't take out loans to build houses. They save their money and then buy a house or build from scratch. I told him that people in the Caribbean did the same thing years ago. If you were to run an informal survey throughout the Caribbean today, I would postulate that more than 80 percent of the people who owned their homes, say, 30 years or more, did so without the aid of a bank. It was hard-earned cash by way of selling, trading, partner, etc.

I recall as a child when my dad would come home days before Christmas with a big wad of cash. What a pleasure it was for us as children to take turns around the dining table counting those bills! There was something about feeling paper money. With sparkling eyes and darting fingers, we captured all the essence of what hard-earned money was all about. We were practicing millionaires in our own little world. I also remember how excited the entire family would be when that mother or father received a partner draw. Again, parents who were not financially conservative, would allow their children to spread that bundle of money out on a table and count it.

Even if the children were never to get a red cent from that money, they would walk away feeling very privileged for having been allowed to touch it. I am sensing now that those moms and pops were giving their children a real lesson in money appreciation.

But in this day and age, when you can make your monthly payments of basically all your bills online, and the vast usage of ATMs, you could go for weeks without ever having the need to go inside a bank for direct transaction with a teller. You can also go for a very long time without handling live cash. Frankly, I miss the feel of real cash in my hand every now and then. That's why sometimes I go out of my way to change a check just in order to feel and see the money I worked so hard for. Then deposit it.

As a result of many of us not having live cash placed in our hands, I believe that we have lost the intimate touch of money. There is no gauging mechanism in place to monitor over spending. And so, a $1,000 on plastic doesn't feel like $1,000 in cash.

THE PULL OF MONEY

In Brooklyn's Flatbush Avenue commercial district, it used to amaze me to see how a salesperson would be hypnotized by cash. If a pair of shoes were selling for $150 and you flash a $100 bill in front of that salesperson, mark my word, you would not leave that store without that pair of shoes for $100 – tax and all. On the other hand, try using your credit card for that same purchase and you would be met with frowns. Now, don't try that in Seattle or Salt Lake City, as I doubt it would ever work. Cash can do magic, whereas credit cards and checks dance to second fiddle.

When the appreciation of money is gone, the true joy of spending is abated. The people with no credit cards who have $200 to spend during the holidays on their families will gladly find gifts to match that $200 budget and walk out of stores feeling good about their purchases. But for some of the families with $10,000 credit limit cards, come Christmastime there's no limit in sight to stop the spending spree. And most likely they will not be satisfied with their purchases even after spending a whopping $5,000 on gifts.

There is that temptation to get just one more item. After all, it's not cash; it's only plastic. Your fingers are no longer inured to counting out bills. Your appreciation for money slowly drifts away. This feeling is exacerbated when the monthly payments on your multiple credit cards far exceed your monthly income. Therefore, instead of money being a blessing, it's now become a curse because you earn it with your sweat, blood, and tears. And before you can cash that check, it's already spent. What a vicious cycle.

You no longer get happy about seeing money or hearing about it like you used to. Thus, if you are not careful, ingratitude could dominate your life. For example, if someone were to give you $50 for a birthday gift, you can hardly get excited about that "chump change" when your burgeoning debt is hovering past $50,000. It's a drop in the bucket, you would murmur, and it's a far cry from solving your dilemma. Since that $50 will not go for its intended purpose: treating yourself to a shirt or a perfume, you become even more bitter, having to use it to make up the gas bill or to pay an outstanding parking ticket.

If somebody gives you $5,000, the excitement would still not last as you would have preferred $20,000 – or $50,000 for that matter – to clear you out of debt once and for all.

Despite your wallowing in debt, don't ever lose the appreciation of money. Every now and then, take your eyes off that mountain of bills and get down to the valley of pennies. Perhaps you need to start looking at a penny again and appreciating it. If somebody sends you a dollar bill, go out of your way to write that person a thank-you note, telling her how thankful you are of it. Little by little the portal to financial independence will swing open. The penny could open bigger doors for you one step at a time. How else do you explain a former millionaire who lost everything, and had to start collecting empty soda cans in order to get by? Over time, with a new and improved appreciation for money, that same cash-strapped man will have become a millionaire again. But the second time around, his attitude about money will be different. Friend, understand that in order for money to abide with you, you have to purpose yourself to be in good standing spiritually and mentally.

I like the way how Napoleon Hill in his classic, *Think & Grow Rich*, compares money and poverty: "Poverty and riches often change places. When riches take the place of poverty, the change is usually brought about through well-conceived and carefully executed plans. Poverty needs no plan. It needs no one to aid it, because it is bold and ruthless. Riches are shy and timid. They have to be attracted."

Many of us cannot seem to get any break from our escalating bills from every which direction. With our trying to catch up and to please this credit card company and that, we drive ourselves insane. Lucy and Ethel of *I Love Lucy* fame had nothing on us. Do you recall that episode where both women were working in a chocolate outlet, packing candies as they tried in vain to keep pace with the conveyor belt?

We have many Lucys and Ethels today playing that balancing act. We wake up with that pressing problem every morning, racking our brains as to when the bills are going to be paid off, and go to bed feeling the same way. But that is no way to live.

I will admit that I was once caught up into that vicious cycle as well. After living in Seattle for a while, I went back to New York City for a month to do contract work with one of my former employers. The money was great. But as fast as I could earn it, there were several credit cards statements waiting to gobble up that money. The minimum payment on one of those cards was a whopping $650. Thus, I was only swallowing that big salary, but I couldn't taste the mouthwatering flavor of it. After paying my bills, there was hardly anything left for me to enjoy.

FIRE LIKE MONEY

I LIKEN appreciation for money to that of fire. You don't truly value a stick of matches until you are stranded somewhere. On rainy days. When the woods are damped. And where there's no kerosene or gas to start a fire. No old newspapers. And where there seems to be no second chances.

You would gingerly gather together bramble or straw or lint in a strategic spot. You don't bargain to miss once that match is struck. You will then gather all those dry items and put them on little by little. You'll ensure that the big piece of log is not there to snuff out the life of the nascent fire before the time is right. You then put on smaller dried branches and then the logs. In your time of urgency, the log is not king but the wood chip. However, in time of plenty the log is king and the chip is peasant. But whatever you do, you first have to treasure the chips before you can treasure the logs.

Even though you have the potential to reach out and get a large chunk of logs, if you don't spend time appreciating your chips, then all you have is potential. Once the fire is up and running, you can use logs of all descriptions to get the blaze going. Mahogany logs, peach logs, oak logs. Logs of stocks and bonds. Logs of real estate investments. Logs of foreign exchange trading.

It is impossible to pay a million-dollar debt with $5 to your name. But starting to build up that payment of bramble with $1 at a time can build a sustained fire that could burn off those log debts overtime. Don't snuff them out with the logs of impossibilities. Take your time to build your small fires of payment.

You will never truly miss water until the well runs dry. You will never fully appreciate a fire until you are down to your last stick of matches. You may never know the value of a dollar until you are financially bankrupt, where mounting debts loom.

Since you have survived your ordeal, you will now make certain to always be found with more than one stick of matches. It will serve you well, too, to have backup flashlights, flint, or extra kerosene and gas at hand.

Transferring that analogy to money, if you have truly learned your lesson, your finances will definitely be in better order. You will start to appreciate even a common penny you found on the sidewalk. You will not be caught without vital dollar logs to advance you to a bigger financial fire. You will not readily smother your small fire with ultra risky investment logs. You will do so with caution. Never again will you have difficulties treating $1 and $1 million equally and with respect, because by then you will have been sensible enough to know that they both come from the same source. A U.S. $1 bill is the same size as that of a $100 bill. They are the same color. They both answer to the same boss. They are made at the same place. The only difference is that one has two zeroes while the other has none.

DEPORTED WOMAN FOUND SUCCESS

I RECALL a woman who was deported from Canada to Jamaica in the early 1980s with only the clothes on her back. It was said that she had a very cushy life in Toronto: a nice home, car, and a wonderful group of friends. But she lost every earthly possession there. She had been away for years, so returning to Jamaica without any money was the biggest shame she could ever incur. It cut away at her pride, but she decided to sell mangoes out of a basket at the roadside. Whatever fruit that was in season, she would sell it. She later rented a shop and started selling grocery items. There was a burnt-out supermarket sitting idly for the longest while, and within a few years, she purchased the building, renovated it, and reopened that supermarket. She seemed to be expanding exponentially, as she was buying up every building that was for sale close to her business place.

Today, she is a very proud woman, with her head held high. She was able to send her children to some of Jamaica's prestigious schools. I strongly doubt now that she ever regretted being deported from Canada.

Many times when we begin to take things for granted – primarily money – there is a spiritual pull. And it is in our best interest to align that gap before it turns into a chasm. I will not second guess that woman's fall from a moneyed lifestyle in Canada, but somewhere, somehow, she sat herself down, humbled herself, and started to appreciate money from the bottom up. There was no big profit to gain from selling a few mangoes from a basket, but she had faith, believed in herself, and God gave her the financial wherewithal.

You can find financial success again. Just pray and ask God for direction. Remember, start to appreciate the little things around you. Start giving money away – however small – in the form of sowing seeds. Believe that you will get out of debt. Strive to be fiscally responsible. Resist the urge to spend every dime you receive. Deliverance is on its way.

Get back to being that 5-year-old who smiles ear to ear when given a $1 bill. Get excited about money again without it ever controlling you. Read more books on finance. And as you leaf through those pages, may you find well-deserved blessings at your fingertips.

SHUN THE GET RICH QUICK MENTALITY

A LOT of us have been buying into the get-rich-quick mentality, which over time dims our deep appreciation for the myriad blessings already at our fingertips. There are millions of people who cannot eat a hot meal today because of deforestation. They simply have no firewood in place to make even a cup of tea. But all you need to do is just touch a few buttons on a microwave and, voila! You have dinner or that cup of tea. You have a four-burner stove or an electric kettle, but not for a minute have you ever stopped to think that, indeed, these things are part of the streams of blessings.

I am not inferring that you should feel guilty for your successes in life. Quite the contrary. It is God's will for us to be abundantly blessed and prosper in everything we do, but not at the expense of being ungrateful. You say, "Well, those things only affect suffering people in Africa, Asia and Central America." But please understand that those people are part of your family as well. Remember we are all God's children in the Creator's sight?

You want to be Rachel Ray, yet you are unwilling to do some of the things Rachel did to get where she is today. You want to be like my real estate broker friend, Kennedy, who currently owns a sizable financial portfolio, but nobody is willing to work fulltime on a minimum-wage salary, while simultaneously putting himself through college. Only a few quotations on the subject can rival Longfellow's: "The heights by great men [and women] reached and kept were not attained by sudden flight, but they while their companions slept, were toiling upward in the night."

Look around you and see how blessed you are. If you are homeless, thank God for the stranger who bought you a cup of coffee this morning or last week. If you are a child in school, thank God for your teacher. A popular chorus goes: "Count your blessings, name them one by one. Count your blessings see what God has done. Count your blessings, name them one by one, and it will surprise you to see what the Lord has done."

Many of us can only see no more than a 10-foot distance at a time. We say, "Well, by the look of things I would say God has passed me by. He has blessed my neighbor with a fancy car and my coworker with her third house." But instead of being in the dumps about other people's successes, rejoice for them. If you can believe it, you can conceive it. Sometimes whatever you are believing for is two weeks down the road. Sometimes it won't happen for the next two years. But as Jesse Jackson often says, "Keep hope alive." The fact that you have the gift of seeing what everybody else has, minus yourself, you should use that gifting and channel it into other avenues to encourage yourself. How about this other quote? "All I have seen teaches me to trust the Creator for what I have not seen." – Emerson.

If at 50 you see your daughter making twice your salary, then trust that in due course God will make it up to you. That line is worth repeating: "All I have seen teaches me to trust the Creator for what I have not seen." A lot of what you have seen already is just a tip of the iceberg that is waiting for you. But don't ever compromise your values to gain things.

We are frothing at the mouth, gorging ourselves with "stuff" that we cannot even pause to mumble a semblance of thank you to the source of our stuff. You work three jobs back to back trying to get more stuff, but you can't even feel a sense of achievement. Why? Because you are doing it for the wrong reason. You have never met your son's third-grade teacher, and the school term is coming to a close, all because you want to upstage your older brother, Jeff, at the next family reunion with your new wheels. You are raking in big money now, but your health is of paramount importance as well. Actually, your health is rapidly failing without your even realizing it. But just as a reminder, in a lot of cases, wealth cannot buy health. I alluded to this earlier, but there are millions of people around the world today with large bank accounts who cannot even exceed drinking four ounces of orange juice from money they have so assiduously worked for. Doing so would kill them on the spot. If a health aide doesn't turn them from one side to the next, they cannot move. It is just that stark a reality.

Friend, while you are busy watching your shares in the stock market, continue to love somebody. While you are prospecting for the next multimillion-dollar deal, take some time to reflect on how blessed you are. Don't get so preoccupied with competition that you have no time to truly enjoy the taste of success.

ENJOY TODAY

I RECALL another incident on my African trip where I videotaped every length and breadth of the country. I videotaped everything in sight. I accumulated so many hours of filming than I would ever be in need of. I took multiple shots of even the common toilet without realizing it, for which I am still embarrassed today. The most profound thing that struck me, however, after the tapes were edited, was the way how a lot of the things that I had videotaped – by myself – were new to me. I went to an underground slave museum, but at the time, I didn't know that people around me were sobbing. I was just too preoccupied with videotaping. Those spontaneous moments of feeling someone's pain had passed me by. I was trying to get connected with the pictures I so laboriously converted onto VHS, but I couldn't enjoy them as much. I blamed myself then for spending so much time living for future moments instead of the moments at hand.

From that day, I pledged never again to be the guy behind a camcorder recording anything beyond 10 minutes – especially when they relate to travel. Granted, I would spend hours at a time watching a lion charging after its prey or a volcanic eruption on the nature channel, but as long as it's not me doing the videotaping, it's okay. I truly have a deep appreciation for cameramen/women, and for the proud parents who taped away at christenings, bar mitzvah, debutante balls, etc.

Too often the preceding scenario of videotaping is evident in our lives. Like those lenses that eagerly try to capture every sight and sound, so are we trying to capture every dime, nickel and penny in sight. Finally, when we have accumulated great wealth, we can barely enjoy it. We need to turn over the videotaping at times to others so that we can enjoy the spontaneity of the moment. Hear the laughter and the sob; hear the birds sing and the frogs croak. Not later but now.

One drawback to videotaping is that you run the risk of losing countless hours of precious tapes, based on poor quality or damaged reels. Sometimes sounds and pictures don't turn out the way you would like them to be. This now turns into regrets. "I should have spent more time at the party enjoying myself like everybody else, and not going crazy capturing everything in sight. But alas!"

SMALL BREAKFAST BRINGS SIZABLE CONTRACT

A FEW years ago I was contracted to do a business breakfast for 12 people on a Saturday morning at 8 o'clock, and I nonchalantly took up the offer. Naturally, the last place anybody wanted to be on a Saturday morning was a breakfast, barely yielding a decent profit. Nevertheless, we went along, and somebody from that breakfast liked the food and our presentation of it, and decided to book us two weeks later at another early morning breakfast. As we prepared to leave that function, a well-dressed lady walked up to us, and matter-of-factly asked, "What can you do with $X,ooo for our upcoming holiday party?" I must have blinked a thousand times in one minute through utter shock. That account turned out to be the highest paid ever for a few years in a row. And the client is one of the most benevolent, selfless women I have ever come across. I am tempted to write out her name, but for the sake of corporate privacy, I will refrain from doing so. Because of this woman, I got to meet many of Seattle's luminaries – mayors, sports bigwigs, law school deans, high-profiled CEOs and doctors, just to name a few. Whenever I am challenged to make decisions on seemingly low-profit earnings, I am always reminded of that incident because a few bucks might just catapult me into thousands more around the corner.

A CHILD'S JOY EVAPORATES

ALL THE children were having a jolly, good time at the weekly after-school Tuesday meeting. Midway through the session, one of the leaders paused, and called out a very pretty girl to the stage. He asked the kids to sing her happy birthday in the most unconventional way ever. Under the strains of siren-like wails clashing with subdued soprano, the girl stood in place listlessly. It was evident that she was not having fun! It was not that kind of a party.

As the program drew to a close, the leader went over to her and said that he would see her next week. Her hands couldn't keep pace with drying her tears, as they streamed down her beautiful face. He promised her that everything would be alright. The sadness emanating from this innocent blond girl was hard to witness. So I probed into the matter a bit further. The leader told me that the girl was sad because she couldn't find the money to pay for the uniform the other kids were wearing for the simple reason that her parents had recently filed for bankruptcy, and they had no discretionary money to toss about on something as trivial as a uniform.

As she muttered her financial woes, it was as if she was carrying the world on her tiny shoulders. My heart went out to her and her family. This 12-year-old should not have been burdened down with the cares of life so early. But again, that's how crippling monetary debt is. It doesn't stop at parents alone. It can have lasting ramifications on generations to come. It has the power to drag its rank self through the peace and quiet of a stable home. It can wreak havoc on a seemingly stable marriage. It can turn loved ones against each other.

When I got home that evening and related the story to Yvonne, immediately she was touched with the girl's plight and was ready to write a check for the child's uniform and other accessories. I felt very proud of that leader, and I complimented him for doing a fine job encouraging that young lady. He was so transparent with her that he even told her about his personal story of filing for bankruptcy a few years ago, and how he and his family weathered the storm. Again, he assured her that everything would be alright, and that there was a way out. Her tears were slowly drying up, and before they parted, he hugged her and she radiated a smile that rivals the sun. By the next week, she was in top form, being carefree in her uniform just like the other kids.

The lesson I walked away with from that story is that despite the bleakness of your overwhelming debt, the sunshine will one day peer through. You will smile again. Sing again. Live again. Don't lose hope. Don't suffer in silence. Start today by finding those blessings at your fingertips. Use those fingers to write your creditors letters from the heart, in lowering your interest rate or your minimum payments. Use those fingertips to get you up and running in a new business, which will help you to defray some of your overhead costs. Seize the moment and find those possibilities.

CHAPTER FOUR

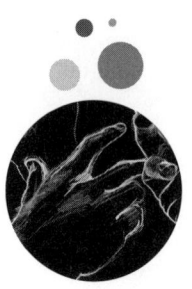

DON'T UNDERESTIMATE
THE LITTLE THINGS IN LIFE

A QUOTE, DRILLED HOME BY DOCENTS FROM kindergarten to military schools for more than two centuries, is still current in this day and age. It was made popular by America's first millionaire, Benjamin Franklin, when he published it in his Poor Richard's Almanac:

> *For want of a nail the shoe was lost.*
> *For want of a shoe the horse was lost.*
> *For want of a horse the rider was lost.*
> *For want of a rider the battle was lost.*
> *For want of a battle the kingdom was lost.*
> *And all for the want of a horseshoe nail.*

It doesn't take Einstein or Thoreau to explain the aforementioned quotation. All this is simply saying is that many times something of great importance may only warrant minute details to get the ball rolling. So, do not underestimate the little things in life. Example after example abound where men and women use the little things of this life to make a fortune.

Opportunities can be disguised as unsolvable problems and chaos. They can shield themselves in the mundane things of life. Often times blessings are right at our fingertips if we are just more aware. Many of us have values laced between our harried lives. We all have some form of worth. In the Bible and in the corporate world, anecdotes abound where small-town "nobodies" metamorphosed into world-acclaimed titans: Moses, Gideon, Henry Ford, Thomas Edison, Oprah Winfrey, just to name a few. Again, do not underestimate the power of the seemingly insignificant things or people around you. A powerful saying goes, "Don't look down on a man unless you are trying to pick him up."

God can still sort through your spiritual wastebaskets and find pearls. Don't ever think for a minute that you've been so far gone that you cannot be of value to somebody. Turn those tests into testimonies and trials into triumphs. Yes, it's true that you've been shipwrecked, tossed overboard, washed up, and left for dead, but millions of people can benefit from a blessing (seed) years from now because of the blessing you sow today.

In the sage words of Jim Rohn, "Human beings have the remarkable ability to turn nothing into something. They can turn weeds into gardens, and pennies into fortunes."

THE DISCOVERY OF COFFEE

IT IS said that the discovery of coffee happened out of sheer chaos. A brilliant Pakistani friend of mine gave me a copy of a travel magazine he wrote for in that country many years ago, and I was rather thrilled to learn the humble beginning of the coffee bean. According to legend, a goatherd by the name of *Kaldi* was out with his goats one day on a hillside in Ethiopia when he discovered that his goats started acting strange. A few of them even died as a result of the high level of caffeine they ingested, when they tumbled downhill and broke their necks. He soon found out that the goats had eaten leaves and berries from a strange tree. Frightened, the young man didn't know what to do. But after he got home, he reported the strange behavior of the goats to his master. He was asked to collect some of the berries and leaves from the strange plant, which the goats had feasted on.

It was said that fire was a means of ridding food of poison – a mode of purification. Therefore, his master set to work and tossed the bush and berries inside the fire with the express intention of sampling the taste after purification had taken place. But to everyone's amazement, minutes later the sweetest aroma emanated from the fire. And as they say, the rest is history.

The mere thought that goats could stumble upon a coffee plant to showcase coffee to the modern world still boggles my mind. Just think about it. Coffee is merely a berry with two pods, which split when processed. For centuries now, those simple beans/berries have dominated and shaped cultures, economies, and social structures in many parts of the world. Some of the best stories are told around coffee. Multi-million dollar deals are sealed over coffee. Wars and truces are often brokered around coffee. Besides oil, coffee is the second largest exported legal commodity around today.

From its humble beginning in Africa, coffee has spawned its way into an economical powerhouse, a force with which to be reckoned. Coffee exports have been the lifeblood of sundry economies, employing more than 30 million people worldwide. From its hilly terrains of Guatemala to the tony cafes of Seattle, coffee has demanded our attention in one way or the other.

Howard Schultz, Starbucks' CEO, bought Starbucks for $4 million and turned the company into a billion-dollar corporation. Today Starbucks can be found in many countries around the world. Again, I need to drum home this message: Don't ever underestimate the little things. Even goats can teach us a thing or two if we are observant enough to heed their message. What is in your coffee pod today? Find out from those blessings at your fingertips. Remember, what started out as a freak of nature or utter confusion on a verdant hillside in Africa, is now a multibillion industry the world over. Again, don't take the little things around you for granted.

Many times what seems like chaos and confusion could be blessings cloaked in the commonplace. Sometimes, all we need to do is smell it; get close to it; touch it, and if need be, later on, taste it.

Blessings are intertwined between those seemingly confusions.

Writing about this chaotic discovery, I am reminded of another. While trying to make a Jamaican-flavored salad dressing/marinade, a Seattle chef decided to blend his regular herbs and spices together, but for some strange reason, the dressing took a turn in another direction that the chef had never gone before. It tasted nothing like his original sauce. He decided to go ahead and serve it up anyway, and it became a hit among his customers. He retraced his steps to replicate that concoction and today that chaotic blend is known to the world as Jamaica Mistake, a very mouthwatering product indeed.

Richie Nicholson many years ago was ironing his brand new pants he had just picked up from the tailor. The iron, however, was too hot, and it burnt out a big patch of the cloth on one of the legs. Not wanting to part with his pants, Richie decided to take it back to the tailor. He requested that the tailor put in a patch with a different color cloth, and he also cut out a piece of cloth on the other leg and patched it with a piece of the same cloth. Overnight Richie became a fashion sensation. People would literally stop him on the street to ask him where he had gotten those unique pants. Many of them descended on his home *en masse*, borrowing his pants to take to their tailors to "catch the style," he said. And before long, most of his friends and acquaintances were wearing the same one-of-a-kind pants.

Many of you thought that you have taken the wrong turn in life. After all, you got married too early; you went to a local college instead of the Ivy League school your SAT scores merited. But all that was divinely planned. Those *mistake* are actually blessings today. You were hooked up with the right professors, and you were more focused than if you had gone to the Ivy League school.

You were fired from a job and have threatened your boss ever since. But truth be told, had you not been fired from that job, you would not be where you are today in a more positive sense. It was no mistake. It seemed chaotic at the time, but that chaos has proven that God was always involved. What you need to do now is to release that bitterness and claim those blessings waiting right at your fingertips.

MERE NOTES OF THANKS
CAN OPEN DOORS FOR YOU

OUR FAMILY started this thing at home where we would collectively
write thank-you letters to somebody who has made a difference in
our lives – may it be a pastor, politician, teacher, doctor, bus driver,
etc. One Friday evening, Jevaughn wrote a letter to his school bus
driver and Jason wrote one to his teacher. Both boys delivered
their letters to their respective parties on Monday morning. When
Jevaughn got home from school that evening, he was overjoyed.

"Dad, Dad, it works!"

"What worked?" I asked.

He said that he gave the bus driver the letter, and when he was
coming back in the evening, she stopped him, with tears in her eyes,
and said that she had never received anything so precious from a
child. She showered all the kids on the bus that day with chocolate
and other delectable candies. I could tell that made him feel special
and grateful, too. He could not wait to write his next letter.

I was overjoyed once more when he came home a month later
to tell me that a little girl, spurred on by his gesture, gave the
bus driver a thank-you letter as well. They were showered with
candies yet again, and the bus driver was touched just the same.
Remember, all it takes is to be nice. Many times you will have to
be the one to initiate it.

A friend of mine lives and breathes thank-you notes. He can
tell you story upon story about how simple thank-you notes have
transformed his life over the years. Some years ago, he was eying a
piece of property to build his dream house, but before he purchased
the land, he had to face a curmudgeon of a man. The man became
difficult as can be. He later met with the man's son, who also proved
difficult to work with. But after their brief contact, my friend sent off
a handwritten thank-you note to the man's son, telling him thanks
for meeting with him. Within a few days later, the wheels of negotia-
tions had begun turning. Not long thereafter, my friend was made
the proud owner of that piece of land. Not only that, he got the land
at a discounted price. Today that plot of ground boasts one the most

palatial homes in his neighborhood.

He also told me about sending a thank-you card to the woman at a government-run office after meeting with her for something to be done to a new property he had purchased. What normally would have taken six months to do, because of his thank-you note, it reduced the timeframe to merely a few weeks. The woman told him that in the 15 years that she had been working at her job, no customer had ever done anything for her remotely to what he did. Because of this simple yet kind gesture, my friend stands to gain more than $100,000 from this one project in the not-so-distant future, all because of a note-from-the-heart investment.

Remember here, folks, he did not give her money or gold, all he sent to her was a stamped, miniature thank-you card, valued less than $1. And the woman was not doing anything illegal in granting him special privileges, but that's what doing the little things many of us take for granted can do for you. Doing the simple things for people many times will grant you favors when you least expect them. Why not make it a habit today? Practice becomes perfect. Just get into the mindset of doing more of the little things. It starts by using those blessings at your fingertips. Writing somebody a thank-you note is freeing up blessings at your fingertips. You bless others, and they in turn will bless you.

THE POLICEMAN AND HIS BUSH REMEDY

SINCLAIR, A former police officer who later became a coworker of mine while we worked together at a major point of interest in Kingston, told me a story that I've held dear ever since. He said that shortly after he and his wife got married, she started suffering from irregular bleeding, which later turned into hemorrhaging. It took a toll on the nascent marriage, but he decided to hold true to his vow: For better or for worse. Every doctor they went to, none of them could accurately diagnose his wife's suffering. She popped multiple pills and swigged bottled medicine daily, but the bleeding persisted. He feared the worst for his wife, since she had lost a lot of weight. He worried about becoming a widower and single dad at such a young age, at the time he was no more than about 25.

He said that after the bleeding got worse, he was so frustrated that he flushed every capsule, pill and liquid medicine down the toilet. One night he said that he found himself running to a nearby field, and he started gathering leaves from all kinds of trees and shrubs. He went back home with two handfuls of bushes and placed them in a pot where he boiled them for about an hour. When the concoction was cooled, he strained it, said a short prayer, and gave it to his wife to drink. She didn't even question him as to what she was drinking as she was too far gone. By the next day, the bleeding stopped. They couldn't explain it, but her health had returned. She was hale and hearty and back to work. And Sinclair was back to his old self: jocular and talkative.

While I would not recommend anybody to do what Sinclair did – boiling sundry leaves for his wife's elixir – I will say this. Sometimes when we're faced with the throes of life, when darkness seems to pervade every cubit inch of light, when we're at our wits' end, that's the time when you begin to start thinking creatively and critically. That's the time when you'll get a breakthrough. He was sick and tired of seeing his wife suffer, and by faith, he believed that she could be made well with his brew. Looking back, I doubt the mixture itself had anything to do with his wife's healing. It was his dogged faith, to stand in proxy for her healing. Water with oil perhaps could have done the job, as well as salt mixed with sugar. But it was sheer faith.

Other coworkers would later learn of Sinclair's story, and everyone all wanted to hear from *Dr. Sinclair* as to what his potion was comprised of, but he could not recall which leaves made it to the pot that night. Who knew, they probably wanted to pass on that information to an ailing relative or friend, or even for themselves. I remember telling the story to an elderly lady and by the next day, she wanted to tear down every bamboo leaf and other leaves from various plants in sight to make her brew. She wanted to try it, but I forbade her to do so, telling her it could potentially be detrimental to her health. While that method worked for Sinclair, it's not for everybody. One thing was for certain, he thought about using herbs for cure way back from a great-grand parent, and he was willing to piggyback on what was taught to him. Thus, he became proactive and reached for those blessings at his fingertips. He was a believer that out of the little things, great things could happen in his life.

If you are a husband or wife undergoing burgeoning problems, don't give up. There is a way out. Wade through the darkness and reach for those blessings at your fingertips. Here is another story that I believe will make you take another look at the little things in life.

ONE SLAP BROUGHT HER BACK

I RECALL family members repeating an incident that occurred in London, England, in 1970 involving a beloved relative. It is said that after giving birth to her seventh and last child, she fell into a coma. Doctors postulated for a few months as to what could cause her to go into a coma, but they couldn't help her. The medicine seemed to do nothing. But one morning one of the attending physicians took it upon himself, broke medical protocol, and decided to do the extraordinary. While other doctors and nurses looked on, he slapped the woman as hard as he could with the palm of his hand on her face. In a few minutes, the comatose woman sprang back to life, and within days, she was released from the hospital to be with her baby son and loving family.

There are many people who have died from the blow of a punch or even from a powerful slap. But to think that something like a slap could be this fierce a method, and in the end bringing forth restoration, is unfathomable. Like Sinclair and his medicinal potion, I doubt the slap on its own could have brought about this transformation. There had to be some divine intervention, and with that divinity, that doctor exuded blessings at his fingertips through healing to bring this woman back to life. Ms. Pearl Brown went on to live for 35 years after that miraculous day. She was grandmother and great-grandmother to legions of offspring until her passing in June 2005.

A drowning man will grasp after a straw, the saying goes, to get him to safety. When your back is against the wall, there are myriads of blessings coruscating in front of you. Grab them. Own them. Make them part of your life. We hear cases time and time again of mothers lifting up 2-ton vehicles off their children, when in a normal cir-cumstance, that would be quite a Herculean task for them to even consider much less lift off.

SHIRLEY'S CAFÉ

LITTLE THINGS turned out to be big things for Shirley Lai, a noted Chinese restaurateur on the island of Guam. A gentleman who worked for that family many years ago, told me how Shirley started out in business, with just a small café. Apart from the lunch counter, she had about three tables and a few stools for her faithful customers. From that humble beginning, Shirley was instrumen-tal in turning a profit, over time sending her sons to prominent universities in America, two of those schools being MIT and Texas A&M. They returned to the island with civil engineering degrees and MBAs, he said, where they started new businesses of their own. While she was branching out, the new cafés were simply known as Shirley 1, Shirley 2, Shirley 3, and so forth. Today, Shirley's Café is now a chain restaurant throughout the island, amassing millions of dollars in profit annually, said the source. And the Lais are one of the richest families on the island today. The grandmother is so popular that even Spam™ printed her fried rice recipe on one of their brands. That gesture alone is saying a thousand words.

WE HOSTED ANGELS IN DISGUISE

A KENYAN delegation was in Seattle to do business for their govern-ment a few years ago. I met the group at church and a week later, Yvonne and I invited them for dinner, about 10 people in all. Less than five months later, Yvonne and I attended a wedding reception for our friends. We may have searched for that reception hall for more than two hours before we found the place. We made several attempts to go back home, but something inside of me told me that I should persevere. I was really mad, but I persisted, and finally, we found the place. When we arrived, all the "elite" seats were taken, and we were forced to linger in the back with two other couples. We introduced ourselves to them, and they tried to make small talks with us, but I was not in the mood to talk. Over time, the initial sangfroid was cut through with warm conversations.

I noticed one of the men from the group was eying Yvonne and me, but I didn't make anything much of it. "I know you . . . I swear I have seen you guys before," he said. You could see he was having a hard time deciphering where he had met us. It was as if he was going through one of those labors, yearning to give birth to his curiosity. About 45 minutes later, he said, "Ha, ha! I know where I know you guys from now." I was just waiting for his comment.

"Do you know a lady by the name of Joanne from Kenya?" the man asked, his expression now fixed with confidence. After many hems and haws, I finally realized who he was talking about.

The MIT graduate, who has held a very coveted position with a major Seattle corporation, went on to tell us that he had just come back from Africa. And while flying from Kenya to South Africa on a business trip for his company, he struck up a conversation with a young woman about 38,000 feet in the air on a jumbo jet. She went on to tell him that she and her colleagues were in Seattle a few months earlier on business, and they met a couple who hosted them for dinner. She showed him photographs of the people who hosted them, telling him how nice the couple had been. Joanne even went as far as telling him all the menu items they had for dinner.

"So, do you know what?" the man stammered, "you are the people the woman was telling me about . . . now the names are coming back to me. You are Nandell and Yvonne, right? . . . She spoke so highly of you both."

Every time I think about that *chance* encounter between Joanne and that man, all I can allow myself to say is "wow!" What are the odds of going halfway around the world where two complete strangers sitting in the same row of seats, striking up a conversation across the African sky, talking about a good deed some other strangers did for them on another continent? Think about the millions of people in Africa. Why he had to meet Joanne? Was it coincidence? Could there be a deeper meaning in that? I may never know.

Coming back home that night brought me so much peace and

confidence. I thought about how mad I had become when I couldn't find my way to the reception hall. Look how many times I tried in vain to turn back and could not bring myself to do so? I strongly believe now that it was destined for that man and us to meet that Friday evening. I am so encouraged by what he related to us. It just goes to show that God is concerned about every detail of our lives. And the little things we do for each other, can someday open big doors for us.

BLESSINGS AS SEEDS

IF YOU want something positive happening in your life, put out a seed somewhere. A cup of dried beans could do several things: they could become somebody's dinner at one sitting, they can be planted and yield a hundredfold come harvest time; they could be for decoration in a bottle sitting on somebody's windowsill, and they could be props to help toddlers learn how to count. Depending on your purpose for those beans, they can work for you.

If you put them out in the open, migrant birds could snatch them, and 500 miles away, those beans could start a new family on their own, say, even in a new country. But you first have to declare your purpose. I use the analogy with beans/seeds to writing. If you want something or want to be at a place in the future, write it down and declare it.

It's so funny. One Monday evening after dinner, I sat around the dining table and started to write out some of the things I would like in the money department. Well, by 10:30 a.m. on Thursday morning, I drove up to a store. As soon as I alighted from my car, I saw a red purse on the ground in the parking lot. Nobody was around. When I opened it, I counted some crisp $20 bills. But too nervous to finish counting, I stopped somewhere around $140. I looked for an ID and found one.

I went straight inside that store, and asked a store employee to page the woman. True to form, the owner came forward about 10 minutes later. She wanted to reward me, but I refused her offer. She eventually pushed a $5 coffee gift card in my pocket. Prior to that day, however, the largest amount of money I had ever found was

$20. I knew that the money was a test, and I passed it. My faith grew stronger as a result. It has paved the way for bigger money down the road. My belief is intensified: Seemingly impossible things can happen when you put your mind to them.

"Don't underestimate the power of a simple act of kindness. It can really brighten someone's day." That was another sage quote I read somewhere years ago.

One of the happiest moments in life is to just sit back with your family at home and do nothing but beam love among each other. Some of the best meals you'll ever eat will not be from the chef at a 5-star restaurant but from the hands of your 10-year-old daughter.

Sometimes when the spiritual atmosphere is charged, all a minister ever needs to say to his congregation is hush, and there's no room large enough to contain the power. At other times, all a praying mother can do for her wayward child is to prostrate on her floor, not say a word but uttering intermittent grunts. But don't underestimate those grunts. They are saying a thousand words.

As human beings, many of us have a penchant for searching out the hard things in life. We harbor no hope for the so-called small things. Thus oftentimes while we are scanning the scenes in search of solutions, our ready answers are staring us right in the face without our ever realizing them.

So often many of us looking for positive things to happen in our lives tend to discount the commonplace things around us. Instead, we all aspire to see Moses' burning bush. And like Gideon, we challenge God over and over again to show himself with sleet on fleece.

A very classically-trained musician once told me that if I wanted to learn music unhindered, I should start out by using children's books. Too many times, he said, colleagues feel compelled to write technical jargon to uphold the status quo. In doing so, many laypersons are left out in the cold. Hence, if you can get down to the level of a child's quest to learn about timbre and plainchants, you would grasp it much easier than the $80 book written for adults. If you are having a hard time being convinced about the power of the little things, take this advice from a man who knew: "When the solution is simple, God is answering." – Albert Einstein.

WHEN POTENTIAL CAN LAUNCH
YOU INTO PROSPERITY

SOME YEARS ago I read a newspaper article about a drug bust where cops seized millions of dollars in cash. The irony of the story was that the money was held inside a run-of-the-mill storage, kept secured by a $2 lock on the door. Just think about it: $20 million secured by a $2 lock?

That analogy is not too far off from what potentially so many of us are doing day after day, year after year and decade after decade with our lives. Why do we continue to secure our potential fortunes with cheap locks? Why do we shortchange ourselves from God's richest blessings?

Have we stopped to think that we are potential millionaires riding the bus when we should be driving Porsches? Do we realize that we are company CEOs trapped inside a just-getting-by-to-feed-my-kids body? How many of us can sing our way to stardom yet we hold onto those dead-end jobs year after year feeling miserable?

How many of you have the gift of expressing the written words, where you could potentially earn thousands of dollars for your work, but are being held back by a $2-a-page proofreading mentality? Your quality work is worth much more than that paltry $6.50 an hour you now earn. Secure your wealth today with some expensive locks. Spiritually and mentally invest in some state-of-the-art security systems to guard your potential wealth.

"When you do the common things in life in an uncommon way, you command the attention of the world." – Anonymous.

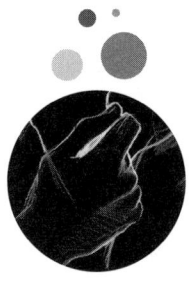

CHAPTER FIVE

WRITE A BLESSING

". . . AND ALSO BLESS ME."

Those four little words were not uttered from the mouth of a down-and-out, cash-strapped sharecropping landlord. They were not from the lips of a destitute wife, begging her estranged husband one more time to bless her as he leaves the family home for good. They were not said by the also-ran politician, hoping to be anointed by the powers that be from the steps of city hall. No. Those words belonged to one of history's most powerful and influential men the world had ever seen – Pharaoh.

When I read that passage recently in Exodus 12:32, I was dumbfounded. It was the time when the children of Israel were getting ready to flee Egypt and Pharaoh had had enough and was shooing them away for them to get out. But in that network of confusion, he made one last wish – "bless me." Now, picture this. The world's richest man begging Moses, a seemingly displaced leader, for blessing? Well, if that is not the mother of all ironies, then I don't know what is.

If the renowned and all-powerful Pharaoh could beg for blessing, then we ought to find out more about this blessing thing. Remember, he had money. Fame. Prestige. Influence. He had everything money could buy and enough fame and influence to last from generation to generation, yet he was *begging* for blessing. Uh, that has a nice alliteration to it, which is worth repeating – *begging for blessing*. What is so special about this blessing? About being blessed?

The term blessing has become so clichéd over the years that many of us have taken it for granted. We generally *bless* others when they sneeze, but outside of that we have no other use for the word. For a quick second, let's think about it; all of us could do a little better with a blessing or two in our lives. Just ask a Pharaoh when in doubt. Hence, to be blessed is no small wonder.

I was filling up a pan with water a few months ago, when an object fell inside of it, sending ripples outside of the pan and all over the place. I got a light-bulb moment there and then. I deliberately tossed a few pebbles into the water to observe this fascinating lesson. I likened it to how blessing could potentially work in our lives. I saw those ripples acting as blessings whenever you throw a blessing seed into somebody's blessing pool. Those ripples can go in any direction – east, west, north and south – before they settle down. Thus, your blessing won't necessarily come back from the person whom you have just blessed. One of those ripples could go out 5,000 miles away to somebody in another country. So don't believe for a minute that blessing others, especially your loved ones, is in vain. You will be blessed one way or the other. Notice how the ripples always settle back in place, to the source.

God intends for us here on earth to love and bless one another. There are several relationships in which we ought to engender, and when those relationships are not in place, a vacuum ensues. No man is an island. No man stands alone. We need each other. And the sooner we realize this, the better our lives will be. I strongly believe that every living, breathing human being in his or her sound mind, has a profound yearning to feel appreciated and loved by another human being. And when that takes place, it has the potential to change lives in a positive way.

MY FATHER WROTE ME A BLESSING

THREE YEARS ago, my father visited us in Seattle. He wanted to spend his 75th birthday with me and Yvonne, and what a joy that was for us to host him and celebrate his life for those 75 years of his birth. I was heading home from an early morning errand, when I tuned into a radio station and heard Luther Vandross' lilting voice longingly begging to dance with his father again. His pleading was palpable, a memory tinged with hope, love and loss. I may have listened to this song more than 30 times prior to that morning, but after listening keenly to the lyrics on that particular morning, I couldn't help myself. I had to pull over to the shoulder from the highway and bawled my heart out. I later said a prayer for him and for the millions of people out there who had lost a mother or father, and now yearning for what Vandross was importuning.

The day was March 4 – my father's birthday. A special kind of joy enveloped my being after I realized that I had another chance to dance with my father again if I wanted; I had another chance to tell him how much I appreciate him, and how much I pray for God's blessings on his life. I couldn't wait to get home. And as soon as I entered the house, I hurriedly dashed to his room and found him sleeping. I watched him as he breathed in and out in solitude. My thoughts drifted back to the days when he would check up on us as children, when I would occasionally spot him sneaking up on us and lingering around while we drifted in and out of sleep.

I immediately set to work making breakfast for him. That breakfast was fit for a king. Looking back now, the portion I gave my father that morning could have served five people. I realized I had been carried away – trying to use up everything in sight from the refrigerator and the cupboard just to show my love and appreciation for my daddy. He helped himself heartily from the cornucopia of food set before him, but there was no way under the sun he could have finished it. We joshed about this spectacle. And I did not hesitate to tell him how much I truly treasure him for the next hour or so. That same evening at a surprise birthday party at my friends' house, I read a tribute, which I had penned days earlier, telling him my thanks for all the positive influences he created in my life, amid many misty eyes. What a blessing it was on that birthday for all of us. Months later, I felt as though there was some unfinished business that needed to be done from that visit, but I kept on delaying it until the appropriate time. I try my best to stay in touch with him as often as possible. But sometimes the east/west coast time difference is not always agreeable for both of us.

On Sunday, September 24, 2006, I called my dad in New York City after not hearing from him in about three weeks. I was calling from my car, parked up in a supermarket's parking lot. It was an evening that boded well for me, evident from what happened that night after I went to bed.

"So, how did you like the book?" he asked.

"Which book?" I said.

"Oh, I thought that is why you are calling me. . . ."

My dad went on to tell me that he sent me a book a few days earlier, which he thought I would enjoy reading. He gave me a synopsis of what it was all about, and the most astounding thing happened. For months prior to our conversation, I had entertained the thoughts of starting a new business, and wanted some direction as to where I should go. My father was right on target with his counsel. The next day I checked the mail and found the package he sent. In it was the book, *Think & Grow Rich* by Napoleon Hill, with certain pages dog-eared for me to take notice of. A check for $300 was between the front cover. And I couldn't put down that book. It is still strange how that happened, because my dad and I hadn't talked about this particular book ever, and he did not give me a head's up that he was going to send me this wonderful keepsake. Reading that book has given me the mental stamina I needed to push forward. It debunked a lot of my fears. I cannot say enough about it.

That Sunday evening, after we chatted at length, a wonderful feeling swept over me, and it prompted me to ask my dad for a father's blessing to his son. I was as bold as they come. I had gotten that urge several times in the past, and refused to ask my dad, but this time I was ready. I have never heard of a son asking his father for a blessing except for the Prodigal's son found in Luke 15, and for many of us, we know very well how that deal turned out. Nevertheless, I was undaunted. I felt that there was some greater spiritual connection to be made between me and my dad. There was something missing. I knew that my dad loved me, but connecting the dots was quite a task. How should I ferret out that father-son love?

Whether or not I had sounded silly, I could care less. I wasted no time worrying about the what ifs when I thought about the power of asking. I wanted to be proactive. I also believed when the Bible says, "Seek and you will find; ask and it will be given; knock and the door will open." This line I also took to heart: "You receive not because you asked not." What would it take from me to ask? The worst thing that could potentially happen was my dad saying no to that request.

In the classic example where Jesus said if you ask for bread, which good father would give you stone instead? Hence, I had the confidence to ask for whatever I wanted without fear and reservation. I tried to find other scriptures to bolster my newfound confidence. "This is the confidence we have in approaching God: that if we ask anything according to His will, He hears us – whatever we asks – we know that we have what we asked of him." – 1 John 5:14. That's all I needed to read to set me into high gear.

"Dad, can you write me a father's blessing?" I said.

"How do I go about doing something like that?" he chuckled.

"Well, you can put it into a letter format," I said.

A few days after I had that conversation with my dad, I wrote him an unsolicited "a son's blessings for his father" and later I wrote "a father's blessings for my son" for my three sons. I also wrote "a husband's blessings for his wife." Before the week was out I was flabbergasted when my 14-year-old son turned around and wrote me "a son's blessings for his father." That was followed by his reading out aloud his letter to me, and then placing his hands on my head and said a most powerful prayer for me. That boy made me look as though I was in beginner's class the way in which he articulated his written blessing to me. He framed his, and I will be looking forward to framing mine or putting it in a certificate holder.

What a joyous day when I received a handwritten "a father's blessing to his son" from my dad in the mail a few weeks later, signed and dated! I felt as though somebody had given me a million dollars. There's no greater high than to have that synergistic feeling of being blessed by your heavenly father, earthly father and son simultaneously. I couldn't wait to get my mother's blessings, so in the meantime, I excerpted some sage words from some of my spiritual mother's letters over the years and typed them up into a nice document. And I want to tell you, I am feeling mighty fine. Sometimes I feel like writing a blessing to everybody I've come in contact with. I want them to feel that same joy and that natural high I get from this synergy.

Many of us would think that a person who pronounces blessing on his child is brazen. Some old folks would say, "You're flying into God's face." But from reading many accounts in the Bible, by no means is it anathema to bless our children and grandchildren. The tradition of passing on blessings from parent to child should not be taken lightly. There is power in a father's blessing to his children. There is power in a mother's blessing to her children. The biblical patriarchs passed on blessings from one generation to the next: Abraham to Isaac, Isaac to Jacob; Jacob to Ephraim/Manasseh, just to name a few. So don't go away curling your toes when the thought arises to bless your children. It is your God-given rights to do so.

When a pastor pronounces a blessing for your new house or business, he's drawing from that high-powered reservoir of blessings – God. That person pronouncing the blessing is acting as a liaison through God the Blessor. At a baby's christening what does a pastor do? At a Bar Mitzvah/Bat Mitzvah, what does a rabbi do? If those words were to be written out, they would be "written blessings." I strongly believe that as parents, we have a certain charge to keep. By virtue of your being parents – whether you're a 14-year-old mother or a 70-year-old dad, God has endowed you with special privileges. If you're a parent via adoption, it doesn't matter. There is a certain spiritual commission that comes with the package.

DAVID BEGGED HELP FOR SOLOMON

AFTER READING how David put pride aside and asked for help, I felt as though I was in good company. Friend, there is no shame in asking for help or favor. Like other powerful and wealthy officials, historically and otherwise, making your request known to the right people can only spell more blessings for you. Winston Churchill did it in England, so did John F. Kennedy in America. And even though Moses did not grant Pharaoh's request, we read in other books of the Bible how asking changed a nation and a dynasty.

For a lot of wealthy fathers – not to mention kings – the last thing you would hear coming from their lips in public is asking or begging for help. But David, the influential king of Israel, possessed no such hang-ups when he publicly begged for help on behalf of his son, King Solomon. Again, that was another passage in the Bible which nearly had me gasping for breath.

"My son, Solomon, is young and inexperienced, and the house to be built for the Lord should be of great magnificence and fame and splendor in the sight of all the nations."

Those words were uttered in 1 Chronicles 22:5. He further went on in the chapter to ask able-bodied stonecutters, masons, carpenters, as well as other men skilled in every kind of work in gold, silver, and bronze to rally around Solomon, aiding him with skills, talents, money, and hard work, in advancing the work of the Lord in building the temple. The appeal amassed unprecedented gold and silver, lumber, etc., for that cause. Now, that spoke volumes! And all David said to Solomon were these encouraging words, "Be strong and courageous. Do not be afraid or discouraged. . . Now begin the work, and the Lord be with you."

I could just see many of us pumping up our 18-year-old son or daughter's credentials when we show him or her off to the public. "Well, Tyrone is a genius. He started college at 11 years old, and has excelled in civil engineering . . . Martha has three degrees, all from Ivy-league universities." But notice that David didn't do that even though he had more than enough clout to lavish on his son. He did not sugarcoat Solomon's nascent skills because he knew that the young king needed all the support he could get from his people. So why don't we take an example from David in furthering our quest for greatness?

Asking can position you for great favors. If you truly ask your friend to say a good word on your behalf to the HR director at his or her job, oftentimes you could get a foot in the door, provided you are qualified for the job. If you didn't know anybody or if you didn't ask that friend to say something positive about you to the employer, most likely you would not have gotten that job. So don't underestimate the power of asking. We gladly ask for recommendations from our professors, former employers, colleagues, among other relations, with the expectation that they would come through for us. Many times, if you don't ask for those letters you will not get them. Armed with those recommendations, you are looked upon with favor by prospective employers, deans, registrars, etc. It is a nice feeling when somebody can write something good on your behalf. In Proverbs 16:24, Solomon said that pleasant words are a honeycomb, sweet to the soul and healing to the bones. Now picture the spiritual application the same way.

GOD BELIEVES IN WRITING THINGS DOWN

"THE LORD gave me two stone tablets inscribed by the finger of God. On them were all the commandments the Lord proclaimed to you on the mountain out of the fire, on the day of the assembly." – Deuteronomy 9:10. It is also written in another chapter, "And you shall write very clearly all words of this law on these stones you set up." – Deuteronomy 27:8. In Exodus 17:14, it reads, "Then the Lord said to Moses, Write this on a scroll as something to be remembered, and make sure that Joshua hears it."

While it is good to get verbal blessings, I think it is more poignant when the written words are utilized. God could have orally given Moses the Ten Commandments, but instead he wrote them down on a tablet. Even after Moses smashed the tablets in vexation, God rewrote them again. So there is power in the written word. We see cases after cases in the Bible where the written words have withstood the test of time.

When Jesus spat in dirt and used his finger to write in it, indirectly he was writing a blessing. With those blessings from his fingertips, that frightened woman who was about to be stoned to death by her accusers for committing adultery, was saved when Jesus told her to go and sin no more.

Writing is a very powerful instrument for posterity. A marriage without a contract is no marriage. Well, in America, that is. Every real estate agent or even neophyte investor knows that purchasing a house without a title would be a bad move. Things have to be written down. Abraham was promised free acres of land, but he insisted in buying that property so that records would be in place for future generations, where they could inherit those holdings without a hassle. Writing things down again is crucial.

A restless King Xerxes was able to dig up old records in his palace from way back when, after he stumbled on Mordecai's contribution in saving his life years earlier. That one act alone, fully documented, was the catalyst for saving a people.

"Write down the revelation [your vision] and make it plain on tablets so that a herald [whoever reads it] may run with it. – Habakkuk 2:1. Again, I strongly believe that God inspired men to write the written words. Could you imagine most of us recalling scriptures from memory today? Write blessings into your life, your child's life, your husband's life; your parents' lives; your friends' lives, etc. What better impact can words from a mother, grandmother/father do for a child who's away from home! The feeling will be more synergistic.

UNDO OLD INSULTS WITH NEW WORDS OF AFFIRMATION

THE WRITTEN words can also bring greater credence to erstwhile insults. For example, the mouth that once spewed condemnation on your young sons and daughters sometimes has a hard time convincing those same sons and daughters when they become adults, telling them, "I love you." Some of you parents ought to take another route – writing a blessing to your children – in order to make a paradigm shift in your relationship.

Marsha, you have long forgotten the blowout fight you had in the schoolyard 20 years ago with your classmates who jumped you until I bring it up now. But when your own mother told you that you were too fat and ugly and not attractive as your sisters, you are still in search of her revoking those words. Remember folks, death and life is in the power of the tongue, according to the Bible.

You forgot about Jeffery who went behind your back and dated your girlfriend. Actually, they're now man and wife. The amazing thing is that you are good friends to both Jeffery and his wife. You totally forgave them. But for some strange reason, you cannot erase your dad's pointing his finger and scowling his face across the living room that Saturday morning, telling you, "Boy, you are a good-for-nothing bleep, bleep, and you will never amount to anything good in life!"

You have immersed yourself in studies, gaining a Ph.D., an MBA, before the age of 30, and you're on your way to getting a JD. You are the life of the party. Your colleagues adore you; you live in the right neighborhood. Your children attend the best schools in town, but somehow you still hold on to that lie your mother told you when you were three years old: "You are just like your daddy; and if you don't change someday you'll end up in prison just like him." You have long proven her wrong, but you cannot get Mama's words out of your head.

Parents, picture the joy when you swallow your pride and give your hurt son or daughter a written blessing in his/her hand that you have labored long and hard to write for them. Yes, specifically to him or her! I cannot foresee Marsha or Byron hating you for long. Those words of affirmation have the power to foster greater relationships between you and your estranged children. They will love you and adore you for life. Envision them reading it over and over again until it reaches to that point of acceptance. I could just see Sarah and Josh waking up at 2 o'clock in the morning, like eager 10-year-olds, tiptoeing to the family room to read those affirming words Mom or Dad wrote to them a month ago.

"Did Mom really mean this?" "Did Dad think this highly of me? Is he serious?"

With those words beginning to slowly seep into their psyche day after day and week after week, that one little note alone could be a spiritual elixir to broken hearts and flagging confidence. Let healing begin today.

THE PROXY BLESSING

WHEN I started out writing about parental blessing, I somewhat ran into a trap. My wife listened intently, and after a long pause, she asked, "So what about somebody like me who has lost both parents?" Immediately I got an answer: "You can always find a mother/father figure to do you the honors," I said. "And remember, God is always your ultimate parent." I could see the blood starting to come back to her pallid face. I went on and on, and even the next day, more and more revelations were flooding my thoughts on this subject. She was very much assured that she would not be left out.

The Bible is also replete with many references where God looks out for those motherless or fatherless sons and daughters. He gets involved in parental roles mainly when those mothers and fathers have shirked their responsibilities. So there is no excuse for anyone not getting a taste of this universal love and attention. In Psalm 27:10, David said, "When my father and mother forsake me, the Lord will receive me." There is provision for the motherless. Isaiah 49:15 said, "Can a woman forget the baby at her breast and have no compassion on the child she has borne? Though she may forget, I will not forget you!"

Yvonne's mother died when she was 18 years old, and she had never met her father. My own mother left Jamaica for London, England, when I was three years old. And I never laid eyes on her again until I visited her there a month after my 28th birthday. Nevertheless, I have been drawing a ton-load of love from the mother I "adopted" when I was 19 years old. She means the world to me. Her letters – yes, some folks still write them – are always chock full of encouraging words. I consider her the mother of mothers. I honestly don't know where my life would be today hadn't it been for my adorable spiritual mom, Pearline Brown.

With most important documents involving children, whenever they call for signatures to be signed on the dotted lines, most often than not, you will see parents or guardians. And the guardian's signature carries as much weight as the parent's signature in this scenario. Furthermore, if it were to be summoned in a court of law, then the judge would rule favorably on the part of a guardian in lieu of a parent or in the absence of a parent. Therefore, I strongly believe that God will honor those words from proxy parents in the form of blessings.

Naomi was a proxy mother and grandmother of sorts to Ruth and Ruth's son Obed. That child started the chain for one of the most powerful royal dynasties in the history of Israel, from which David and Solomon hailed. Mordecai was a proxy parent to the orphaned girl, Esther, among other proxy relationships in the Bible. Parents, what you write to your children today will affect many generations to come. Hezekiah was delivered from his enemy because of the covenant God made with his great-grandfather David. Timothy was blessed because of his grandmother, Lois' faith. When you give blessing to your loved ones, it will allow them to live out their dreams. Joseph was living out his dream of being a blessed man even when he was in prison, working as a cleanup man.

STEPS OF WRITING A BLESSING

IN MARK 10:13-16, mothers brought their children to Jesus not merely because Jesus wanted to jump rope or play baseball with the children. They were brought there for him to bless them. And parents, I strongly believe, have been given the tools for them to bless their own children, with the constant supervision of God himself.

I have been sounding this alarm for parents to become more proactive in their children's lives for some time now, and one mother who has swallowed my words, hook, line and sinker, is Anita. Yes, the same lady who bought the chicken nuggets for $5. She has three sons, and she decided to write each of them a "mother's blessings for my son." Anita was looking forward to the perfect time to give her sons these letters. But she couldn't wait. However, on her second son's birthday in January, she excerpted a part of what she had planned to give him in a greeting card. While reading the card, the 20-something man was awash in tears.

According to Anita, the man's girlfriend quipped, "Well, I don't know what is causing him to cry, but it surely has me crying." Before long, Anita joined in that lachrymal party, and they all hugged and cried themselves some more rivers. What was interesting, Anita reported, was that shortly thereafter, she started seeing marked changes in her son. His struggling days took a hike. She attributes those changes to the powerful words she has sown into his life. The young man landed a well-paying job with lots of benefits, among other good things. His earlier employments were all dead-end, seasonal jobs; they were a shadow in comparison to his new job. I am just listening out now for more updates about the others.

My friend, Joe, in Clearwater, Florida, took a different approach. He wrote "a father's blessings for my son" to his two sons, who are both under the age of five. He wrote them in a letter form and took them directly to the post office to get them stamped and sent to his address. Once he got them back in the mail, he carefully put them away. And whenever the boys are old enough, he said that he will have them open the letters and read them aloud.

BLESSINGS AT THE GRASSROOTS LEVEL

I'VE OFTEN heard celebrities say that after receiving multiple Oscar or Grammy awards, some of the most meaningful awards they've ever received are from their local neighborhood high schools, or civic associations. That's when everything truly sinks in, when these grassroots-level people take the time out to honor them. As it is said, a king has no honor in his own country. So any community which goes out of its way locally to honor one of its homegrown celebrities, it truly speaks volumes. Indeed, it is saying a thousand words.

There are certain things that have to take place from the bottom up before true acceptance can of itself take place in an individual. Therefore, even though those same celebrities are wined and dined, and are fussed over by admiring fans regularly, what is of real importance to many of them is the love from the people around their base: mother, father, wife, husband, children or good friends. Not being fed from that source is equivalent to doing calculus without first knowing the basics of algebra.

Many people are looking for the burning bush or the big band striking up a fanfare to declare their grand entrance into greatness, but most often than not, it will be nothing that dramatic. You can start with those blessings right at your fingertips. Friend, don't take your daddy or mommy's blessings for granted. Like the celebrity who comes home from Hollywood to receive that special plaque, your father and mother can make you feel important as well before you even get on the road to Hollywood or Broadway. Understand that they're endowed with blessings from their own Big Daddy, God Himself.

When my dad wrote me a father's blessing to his son, it made me feel validated. My being a new dad, I wondered whether or not he would step up to the plate and love our sons or any other children we adopt, as his bona fide grandchildren. Based on his written words to me, I found out that he would love all of us unconditionally.

My father's blessing gives me confidence. It gives me love, even though he didn't say it. His words tell me so. It makes me want to get even closer to my super dad. My earthly dad assures me that he will be there whenever I need him. And so far, he has lived up to his words.

PARENTAL ROLES
ARE GOD-GIVEN COMMISSIONS

GOD INTENDED for us to have solid, earthly relationships with our fathers and mothers, even though He is the ultimate parent. When parents find it in their hearts to give love to their children, those children in turn will give love back to their parents. Over time, that same unadulterated love will find its way among siblings, friends, teachers, coworkers, etc. That strong love is good enough to convert arch foes into lifelong friends. He doesn't micromanage our relationships with our earthly parents or leaders. Picture a school district. A principal reports to a superintendent. The superintendent reports to a mayor, but one indispensable person in this line of relationships is the classroom teacher. She is queen in her class. She gives A's and also recommends suspensions, most often than not, sanctioned by the principal. It is the same with God. He doesn't dabble into the day-to-day things we can handle, but if you call on Him, He will be there to aid you.

Parents, do you know why you are so trusted? Because from infancy, you had to care for your children. Whether your children liked it or not, long before they became that top surgeon or corporate VP, you were the boss/es. They trusted you to change their diapers, monitor their food intake – well, minus the Brussels sprouts and spinach. When they tripped and fell, guess who was the first person they were looking forward to run to in order to soothe their pain? Therefore, that's the reason why when David is 68 years old, he still values his parents' words and counsel because he's drawing from that groundswell of trust.

I was talking with Garfield Knowles, a Seattle businessman, some time ago, and he told me a story about his boyhood days in St. Thomas, Virgin Islands. He toyed with the idea for awhile of becoming a professional boxer. And at the arena, fans would scream out his name before the fights begin. He appreciated his fans, but the only voice that mattered among those crowds wasn't his best friend or faithful fan. That voice was his mother's. He would listen keenly to hear Mama screaming out his name above the din. And that was enough to get him to trounce his opponent – Mama's voice and presence made the difference. And it is no different for countless adult "children" today.

I found that yearning for approval even among my own children. Going to some of the boys' performances, I am often amused, whether it's a soccer match or choral recital, how they – especially Jevaughn – would constantly crook their necks to see if we're watching them. Thus, children never get tired of their mother or father's approval.

Children, don't be afraid to ask your parents for love, and parents, don't be reticent in asking your children for approval. For a lot of parents, they've started out becoming parents in their teenage years and often times they second guess themselves, wondering, "Did I really do a good job of raising my child/children?" There is still that vacuum that never seems to go away. Children, please reassure your parents that they are/were the best parents in your eyes – even though you had to get inside the house before 6:30 in the evening, leaving your friends Ray-Ray and Kimani still playing on the street until they felt like stopping on their own.

CORPORATION GIVING BLESSING

FOR A number of years now, I've purposed myself to pray for large corporations and their leaders: Microsoft, Costco, Starbucks, Coca Cola, along with mom and pop startup companies around the world. But some skeptics have assailed me for praying for mega corporations. "Why do they need to be prayed for?" they argue. "God knows that Warren Buffett doesn't need another dollar passing through his fingers; therefore, you are wasting your prayers. Pray for the poor in India or Haiti instead."

What a lot of people don't understand is that the gargantuan-sized companies we see today were only a prayer and a dream years before. Those founders had to navigate dissenters' muddy waters who constantly told them that it couldn't be done. Sometimes their own doubts showed up, questioning whether or not they were doing the right thing. But you know what? They persevered.

Folks, millionaires are still breathing human beings. They still require the same amount of oxygen and nitrogen like all of us in order for them to stay alive. They still dab a tear or two at funerals, and coo along with their toddlers who are just learning to say da-da or ma-ma. So perish the thoughts that once a man or woman has a few more zeroes to the right of their digits, they're automatically transformed into unfeeling, uncaring beings. That they don't need added blessings.

It is no wonder then why some of us can easily commiserate with our grieving neighbor who lost her only daughter through abduction but can laugh along with late-night comedians when a Jon-Benet Ramsey tragedy switched from sadness and empathy to jokes. I actually stopped watching a late-night show days after the tragic passing of Princess Diana. I could not believe that while sons, husband, siblings and other loved ones and friends were mourning, this person decided to make the tragedy a laughing matter, re-enacting the accident without showing an iota of grief. I didn't get it and I still don't get it.

While our private lives should be respected, public figures' lives should be grist for late night talk shows. I strongly abhor that stance. Celebrities and rich people do have feelings, too.

It would appear that when it comes around to public figures, we're given carte blanche as to how far we can criticize and castigate them. There's a feeling that allows us to say anything about them without our feeling any forms of guilt. After all, they're celebrities so they're insulated from our stinging vitriol. Celebrities are held to a different order; therefore, what we say about them will not do anything to us – affect us, you say.

Let us move away from the mindset of consigning noted people in the news as untouchables. Oftentimes many of them are agents of blessings. Some of the people I've most admired over the years are Billy Graham, Martin Luther King, Jr., Oprah Winfrey, Bill Gates and the late Mother Teresa. With their economical and celebrity power, they have transformed the 21st century leaps and bounds. They have written blessings for countless millions of people around the world, giving away much needed supplies.

In the case of Oprah Winfrey and Bill Gates, they could be easily content with piling on millions of dollars to their ever-growing estates, but quite often, they seize the moment to better the lives of their fellow human beings.

I live in the Greater Seattle area, and every time I walk into one of the King County public libraries, I'm in awe! Never have I seen a public library system so well run and so up to date. And a lot of credits go to the Bill and Melinda Gates Foundation for spearheading the financial wherewithal. As soon as any change comes about in computer, you can rest assured that it would be implemented at our local libraries. It's a joy to see 5-year-old children getting on Microsoft Publisher or PowerPoint, navigating their way through that program with aplomb.

Bill Gates has selflessly given himself to humanitarian causes, especially as they relate to AIDS and Africa. Giving away millions is one thing, but being up close and rubbing shoulders with the downtrodden is another thing. Gates could have easily shifted this role to many of his proxy agents, but touching the people while imparting his blessings to them is paramount to his quest in changing people's lives for the better. Blessings at the fingertips don't get better than this!

When I look at the myriad contributions Oprah Winfrey's Angel Network has done to bring back hope to people who were out on the fringes, I can hardly find words to describe my feeling for this powerful woman. How many company executives fly their multitudinous employees and their families to exclusive vacation resorts? She also never forgets her past. She realized that she stood on the shoulders of others to get where she is today and she never fails to acknowledge that. One example is her time-stopping gala affair she had for her "Legend Ladies" at her "Legend Ball."

Who can ever forget the horde of children being touched and hugged by the benevolent Winfrey in South Africa? Some might argue that she does it for the camera, but there are thousands of ways one could show off via celluloid. I could sense the altruism. She uses power to uplift instead of tear down. Where would some of those Katrina-ravaged victims be today without the generosity of an Oprah Winfrey? She gladly gives back with her generous heart, fused with blessings at her fingertips.

Mother Teresa. What can I tell you about this indomitable woman what you have not already known? Surrounded by abject poverty, Mother, as she was affectionately called, owned nothing except two chairs and a wooden table that dotted her Spartan dwelling in Calcutta, India. Ironically, this diminutive woman, who had no earthly possessions, had world leaders ingratiating themselves to her. But her sole mission in life was never to address the General Assembly at the UN or the U.S. joint Congress but to change poor people's lives every chance she got. Because of her years of contribution to the outcast, she had spawned awareness among young people that cut a swath from Mexico to Istanbul. Only a few people who have graced this earth ever amassed the kind of respect and integrity accorded Mother. Everywhere she went her wrinkled hands dispensed fingertip blessings. One thing I have noticed with genuinely-blessed people over the years is that once they have been blessed, they cannot keep it to themselves.

Corporate blessings are not so far afield. It has a biblical heritage. When we look at Boaz in the Ruth 2:4, we see how he would greet his employees in his field: ". . . The Lord be with you." And they in turn would say, "The Lord bless you."

And who could ever forget these wonderful words said by Levite priests found in Numbers 6:24, used in many churches today as benediction?

"The Lord bless you and keep you; the Lord make his face shine upon you and be gracious unto you . . . The Lord turn His face toward you and give you peace?"

If you are that business tycoon reading this today, you can personally send your executive assistant a handwritten note, telling her/him what a great job she/he is doing. In like manner, if an employee has benefited from the generosity of his boss, do the same thing. Write a note/card telling your boss what a blessing it is to have him as your director. You would be surprised to see the drastic change this act of love can bring about. Don't be mindful of what your coworkers will say. Some will perhaps call you names like "Brown Nose," "Kiss Up," among others, but as long as you know you are not kowtowing and using puffery/flattery to gain your boss' favor, then you'll be fine.

When I think about the thousands of workers who benefit from a corporation, all I can do is just to pray for their management. Where would Oral be today had he not received the stock job at Costco when he got out of prison five years ago? When Bettina wanted to get off public assistance but nobody would give her a chance, another one of those giant corporations came to her rescue. Many major corporations that dot our cities and towns are actually the lifeblood of those communities. If they had ceased to exist, hundreds of thousands of homes and small businesses or lives would be disrupted. Foreclosure, depression, lassitude, and mass exodus are some of the negative things that are often associated with large corporations closing their doors.

Many times why good fortunes pass us by in life are simply because we are so steeped into believing that the things from which good fortunes are made are off limits to us. We fail to travel the unbeaten path. "Well, if nobody had ever tried climbing that hill, then I am not going to take the chance," you say. "I grew up hearing my grandparents and great-grandparents saying it was dangerous, and I am not going to try now."

There are places in rural Jamaica where people have considered off limits for centuries. By the time a child was two years old, he was trained enough not to visit those places. Even as he matured to the ripe age of 70, he would not dare to climb on top of that hill or swim in that river. Many times it would take tourists from distant lands to come and dispel some of those myths. The thing is, they harbor no such fears. For them, rivers were made to swim in and hills were made to climb. They would climb those hills and ford those rivers and come back hale and hearty for all to see.

Which mental river or hill today is bombarding you from reaching your goal? Because Daddy didn't write you "a father's blessings to my son" doesn't mean that such a bold step would not be sanctioned by God. You could be that bold tourist today dispelling the myths, and bringing freedom to your young sons and daughters' lives. The folks who change the dynamics of the family are the ones who are hungry for change. They are the ones who hate poverty. They will try anything, to the point of death, to forge a new path for positive change. A common saying goes, "A drowning man will grab after a straw." And if you are drowning in debt, a bad relationship, enmity, why not try grabbing after that straw of deliverance today? It may seem to be of no help, but you may never know. That straw might just be stronger than what you originally thought.

By faith, write your children a blessing today. You can do pretty much anything if you believe it can happen. The saying goes, if you can conceive it, you can do it.

A FRIEND'S BLESSING

"ONE LOYAL friend is worth ten thousand relatives." – Euripides. Good friends. What can I add to those words to make them richer? The sheer essence of *good friends* is purer than gold. What would we do without them? I have been very fortunate to be blessed with a number of people I call my good friends. A number of them are like brothers and sisters, and my life would be lacking desperately had it not been for these selfless human beings. A lot of my successes in life can be attributed to friends. For many of us, the older we get the more discriminating we become; therefore, it is much harder to make friends now than when we were in our twenties. But for those friendships that have weathered the storms of life, don't, for a minute, take them for granted. I am imploring you to write a blessing to your friend(s) today. The relationship will take on more gusto. More oomph! It will be worth it.

THE QUALITY OF PAPER DOESN'T MATTER

MANY YEARS ago, I saw a man chasing down a paper note while the wind whirled fiercely. Every time he caught up with his money, the breeze would send it a little further. Finally, just as he was about to lay claim to it, a stray goat out of nowhere was just in time to make itself a meal out of the note. Needless to say, the man was livid! He watched helplessly as the goat noshed away on the piece of paper. That goat was a walking bank.

To the goat, it was just another ordinary piece of paper blowing in the wind, but to the man, it was valuable. Writing about this incident forces me to question what makes a piece of paper valuable to one person while it is of no use to the next person. Had the man been chasing after a check valued at $10 million, the goat could not have distinguished between value or worth because all it sought was a quick meal – a pick-me-upper until it reached some green meadows for supper. Again, when does a piece of paper become valuable? Is it when some notable figure signed it? Is it the amount of zeroes preceding the first digit? Is it the nice feel of it?

The stack of checks in your checkbook means nothing until somebody puts a figure in place and then endorses it. And you can write a check for $.32 or $32 million. It's all about the value and the signature. Without those things, the check will be non-negotiable. Even if the money is available in the account.

When you write a blessing for your loved ones and sign it, you are doing a wonderful thing for those people's future. You are planting a seed. And when seeds are planted, they don't stay stagnant. Given the right climate, they will grow. They will produce more seeds. Some of those seeds will eventually turn into big trees with spreading branches. Some will shade you, while some will feed you, but eventually, they will come to benefit you.

It is my wish to have every father and mother write a blessing to their children. Whether it's on a ripped out piece of ketchup stained, greasy note pad, saying 50 words of affirmation, do it. Some of you will perhaps use fancy stock papers, etc., but bottom line, the words will go forth. I can assure you that no meaningful son and daughter would ever shy away from such potent force of reckoning in their lives. They will hold on to it until their dying day. Try it.

Signing your child's blessing gives authority. Doors will be opened just like how clearance of a check is valid when the correct signature is verified. Again, it doesn't matter how flimsy a piece of paper you write it on, it's not the paper that matters, it's the content.

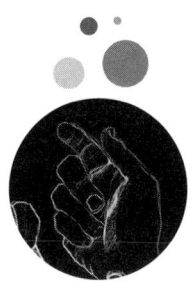

CHAPTER SIX

TRUST YOUR INSTRUMENT PANEL—NOT YOUR EARS

I AM AN AIRPLANE AFICIONADO, AND TO GET MY undivided attention, just start a conversation with anything to do with planes. Planes downright just fascinate me. Thus, it was music to my ears when I met a student pilot a few months ago, and he started telling me about the intricacies of flying. We sat down for more than four hours, and most of our conversation revolved around aviation until we were able to discuss what we met for in the first place.

One of the most striking things I learned from that conversation was the role each sense plays when a pilot sits inside that cockpit. Kevin told me that a major lesson every prospective pilot learns early in aviation school is that he/she should never always rely on his/her ears as the ears will often times deceive you.

He told me about the first time he went flying with his instructor, and how as the plane soared to the sky the man told him to close his eyes. All Kevin could feel then was a myriad of sensations. He felt as though the plane was going backward; other times he felt as though it was going sideways, and still other times it felt as though it was going to crash. But within minutes, his instructor asked him to open his eyes and look on the instrument panel. He was shocked to see that indeed the plane was traveling as normal as could be.

The instructor told him never to trust his ears when flying. For example, when flying through heavy clouds, your vision is taken away; therefore, your sense of direction will be compromised. And that's the time all of the senses and your body are jockeying to take over. Your inner ears will try to take over your eyes, which can make you feel as though you are going backward. At that time, he said, all you need to do is to ignore those senses and look at your instrument panel. You have to fight those urges and believe what the instrument panel is saying to you in those crucial moments.

He learnt a big lesson that day, which has crossed the boundaries of aviation into everyday life. Despite the negative things others are saying about you, don't believe the lies. Remember, God says that you are blessed and highly favored. You are the righteousness of God. You are a peculiar person, and that you are bought with a price. So whenever naysayers come to tell you otherwise, just be reminded to take another look on your spiritual instrument panel and read what it says.

BELIEVE THAT YOU ARE AN OVERCOMER

BE PREPARED to get fired from a job for incompetence on the eve of a monumental breakthrough in your life. You have been cited with numerous awards in children's services over the years, and now that you have gotten the green light to open your 4,000-square-foot daycare center, you've been accused of child abuse. My encouragement to you is to just press on. You will be vindicated. You will shine in your role as owner/director of your new enterprise. Persevere. Be faithful. Take these wise words from 2 Chronicles 20:15, ". . . Do not be afraid or discouraged because the battle is not yours but God's." And He has the last word.

You are considered one of the best up-and-coming designers this side of town, and have recently been contracted to sell your label to a major department chain store. Now your closest friend tells you in your face that your fashion is not all that. Normally, you are not moved by everybody's criticism, but this one really rips you up. I say laugh in the midst of adversity and challenge. Stay the course. Don't lose sight of your dream. Remember, not everybody dreams your dream. Therefore, don't expect him or her to feel what you feel or see what you see.

Don't get weary en route to fulfilling your dream. The same thing that landed Joseph into the pit (his ability to interpret dreams), is the same thing that elevated him to the palace. Of the three major *P's* that affected his life – Pit. Prison. Palace – he didn't get discouraged and say that since two-thirds of his *P's* resulted in his apparent downfall, he wasn't prepared to see what the next one has to offer. He had enough faith to believe that not all *P's* are negative. With the other remaining *P*, it has more than compensated for his two earlier ones. That's when he hit the jackpot of myriad blessings.

We could learn a valuable lesson from Joseph and his determination. How many of us have given up a promising relationship just about the time it started to take a turn resembling the one you terminated a year ago? How many business prospects have we jettisoned overboard because we thought nothing would come out of them once the feasibility study is done? Had we stuck with it, it could have gotten around the curve and resulted in a blissful marriage and a multimillion-dollar corporation.

For every lock, there is a key. Make sure to unlock the last door to your entrance into greatness. You have been successful so far in opening the others, but you will need to open one more in order to claim your prize. This time calls for you to be focused. Find the right key.

Friend, like Joseph who told his dreams to his brothers and was hated for it, it behooves you not to tell your dreams to everybody. Not everyone is excited about your dreams. Not everybody can look past the dark horizon of yesterday and see the city on a hill tomorrow. Don't try to convince some people that when it is summer in Australia and South Africa, it is winter in Germany and the United States. Don't ever try to tell them that when it's noon in Seattle, Washington, it is 8 p.m. in London, England. Would they believe you if you were to tell them that Chinese is the most widely spoken language in the world? I think not. To them, their world has one time zone. Their world speaks one language, for all they care: English. French. Tagalog. Hindi. Farsi. In their world, they say you cannot rise above your caste, and that you should stay in your place. But you know otherwise.

You will be wasting your time because they will not be convinced. Therefore, don't try to tell them that 10 years from now you will be a fledgling entrepreneur, pulling in millions of dollars in profits. Because even when those dreams are festooned with klieg lights all about them, they would still be blinded to your dreams.

In a climate of uncertainty, God told Jeremiah to buy a piece of property, while the children of Israel were being taken captive by the Babylonians to a bleak future. Many of those people who had been around long enough could tell Jeremiah a thing or two about being captive, albeit from a source that spanned 10 generations. They could tell him that what God was saying to him didn't make sense as when you buy property and leave, there's no guarantee that it would be yours later on. The status quo was that if you will not be there, then don't buy! So all along Jeremiah was right in heeding God's words. Even though it followed the popular thoughts of doubt inch for inch, Jeremiah took God's sage advice, and took a turn in the right direction. One big factor: God was in the picture.

Every woman who has ever suffered a miscarriage or a stillbirth knows the difficulties of carrying a baby full term. Life is truly a paradox. A young lady told me some years ago that when she found out that she was pregnant with her first child and realized that emotionally and financially she couldn't take care of her baby, she did everything possible to terminate the pregnancy: She jumped from trees, tossed herself on hard surfaces, thumped her stomach, among other things. But all those things seemed to only make the fetus grow stronger. At age 16, she gave birth to a bulky, healthy 9-pound baby boy who later became a bundle of joy to her life.

Meanwhile, I had an aunt who had several miscarriages with just the mere twisting of her shoe heel, or a slight slip on a banana skin. Finally, after giving birth to her one and only child, Hilary, she was most elated. While many of her miscarriages had the same symptoms, she persevered to make Hilary's birth a success. What a

bittersweet moment for many women. The excitement of the expectant mother is deferred as she's scolded by family and friends not to
count her chickens before they're hatched. Many of them have had
to take bed rest long before their due dates just to ensure foolproof
safety. They fail to get excited because they have felt many a heart
beat before; they have witnessed many sonograms; they have seen
their babies up close and center, but one little glitch, and that fetus
would be history. Once again, that mother must undergo the pain
and disappointment of not giving birth to a child.

Recalling those scenarios, I'm reminded of the many times life
throws a curveball at people. The successful businessman who would
later close his business through bankruptcy, sometimes is adamant
in starting a new business. After all, many argue that the business
plan will mirror the original one. Everything in the new business
would be a dead-ringer for the old. Sometimes the only change
would be one minute detail, but being cognizant of that detail could
spell success where failure runs rampant.

By the time the new business is up and running, he will have had
the right bookkeeping in order, the right advertising and insurance,
a steady flow of customers. But somewhere deep down inside that
man, that gnawing feeling of failure beckons. The feeling is even
more intensified with the fast approaching anniversary date when
the former business folded. But what a joy to overcome those pangs
of failure and believe God for the seemingly impossible things to be
made manifest! Many times, after minimizing doubts, businesspeo-
ple who faced daunting challenges in the past can rebound to even
heightened greatness. Look at Donald Trump, for example.

KEEP ON PUSHING THAT ROCK

I WAS told about this parable some years ago, and it is not my
intention to embellish it. So here it is as it was told to me. There
was an African village that possessed a lot of gold, and people time
after time would carry pots full of gold to the king of a neighboring
village in lieu of money. However, the practice of toting gold to the
king became very risky over time as robbers would waylay the gold

"carriers" and rob them of every ounce. Before long, the villagers got discouraged and stopped their trade altogether.

One brave man decided to take the risk of selling gold to the king, and after a few successful trips, one day he discovered that his journey was made impassable because of a huge rock blocking his route. Therefore, he no longer had a shortcut to ply his trade, but instead had to travel the longer road. He prayed and prayed, asking God to remove the rock, and God told him to just push the rock away. The thought of pushing away that rock seemed impossible; nonetheless, he tried and tried and tried, and still nothing happened.

About nine months later, just when he got exhausted with pushing and seeing no results, he discovered that there was a narrow road leading away from the huge rock, and he saw the opportunity to now bring gold once again to the king. But alas, his elation was short lived. As he meandered down that narrow trail, lo and behold, the robbers were there to greet him. They pounced upon him, demanding him to strip from his clothes and give them every ounce of gold in his possession. As he began to strip down, the robbers became amazed on seeing his Herculean biceps. Never had they seen bodybuilding of such magnitude. They began to feel fearful and threatened, commenting that with a man bearing those biceps, it would not be in their best interest to interfere with him. In no time, they all took off and left the man by himself with his pot of gold untouched.

All that rock pushing finally paid off for that man. What he thought was punishment from God actually turned out to be a blessing. By simply pushing on that rock daily, he gained enough strength and body mass to put those disgusting thieves to flight once and for all.

The moral of this story is: Sometimes you will feel like you are going through hell, but in that time, while you think you are going through drudgery, indeed you are building courage, faith, perseverance, endurance and fortitude. In other words, you are building mental "biceps" to withstand the cares of life. If you are one of those people who feel like God has asked you to do the impossible like pushing on rocks without your seeing any breakthrough, don't give up. When things seem like they're not going well, that is the time when God will unleash his favors and blessings on your life. Is that rock a bill you cannot pay? Is it a marriage that has run its course with divorce as the only option? Is it rock of a bitter enemy? You, like that African villager, can overcome. Just push one more time. An escape route is not far away. Be blessed today. Remember while pushing on that rock, the exertion will feel the same, but one day you will see the breakthrough if you persist.

THE WHEAT AND THE TARES

MANY OF us have heard the biblical parable of, "Let the wheat and tares grow together until the day of harvest," but for many non-wheat growers, that proverb is quite a stretch for their imagination to comprehend. It is said that the wheat plant looks exactly like the tare plant, and that the distinguishable feature for both plants can only be determined at harvest time. Both wheat and tares grow to the same height, they have the same leaves, stalks, and flowering. Therefore, no sane farmer would ever run the risk of uprooting his crop with the hope of getting rid of the good-for-nothing tares because he cannot tell the difference. Hence, he has to wait until the day of harvest in order to make that decision. Many times it is to his chagrin that he reaps because those tares have only usurped his precious field, shortchanging his yield in the process. There's no shortcut around it. Then, and only then, can he tell the difference. One will be the real wheat while the other will be fake wheat.

Many of you have gotten married with the hope of mirroring your marriage to that of your parents'. And for awhile, things were rosy. But come harvest day, you realized that you were reaping tares of infidelity instead of wheat of trust. Sometimes it was tares of abuse instead of wheat of compassion. But unlike the literal tares of the field, which are readily tossed out, the spiritual tares pose even a bigger problem; they have to be tempered. There is no regret in ferreting out and dumping the tares of the field to their nearest dunghill, but when those tares are matters of the heart, if you are not careful, they have the potential to choke off every living fiber of your emotional and spiritual wheat field. But don't lose hope. The wheat invariably outnumbers the tares. So it behooves you to carefully gather your wheat a bundle at a time and then trample over those useless tares.

You decided to move to a new country, a matter in which you have prayed about, and now felt led to go. Your only obstacles, however, are your friends who warn you about the danger of going there permanently. They recall every negative story in the book where people just like you who went and had to return home in less than one year's time. Here's a wheat and tares moment for you. Don't start prematurely plucking out your tares because they could very well be valuable wheat. Follow your heart.

You are not alone. Many people who went to Hollywood had to weave their way through the wheat and tares field as well. People told them that they were too short or too plump; too dark or too tall. They told them that they, too, would become permanent waiters and waitresses among the thousands, waiting to be discovered, but they were not affected the least. They did not run about trying to make sure that their field was all wheat. They weathered the storm. Actually, some of those tares lent themselves as buffers to the wheat in turbulent times. All in all, those aspiring actors and actresses waited until the day of harvest and today they are some of Hollywood's leading men and women.

We have seen the wheat and tares scenario play out itself as well in churches, synagogues, corporations, and academia.

You have the grades and the qualifications to enter medical school, but you have gotten cold feet after hearing your dad saying how hard it was for him when he entered med school some 30 years ago and had to drop out after two years into the program. You want to forge ahead but somehow, Daddy's failures have now become yours. What makes it even more eerie is that you are approaching his age when he enrolled, and the fear is too much to bear. Your dad even tried to discourage you in no subtle ways about entering the medical field, but I am saying to you today, go the distance. Don't shortchange yourself.

Your lives perhaps are parallel in many ways. You find yourself doing some of the same things he did when he was your age. You may share the same DNA like your dad; you may be the spitting image of him, but realize that you are two different people. Don't let fear keep you from realizing your life-long passion. Overcome that fear and you will be the doctor you have always wanted to become before long. Find the strand that differentiates you from Dad, and use that to your advantage.

THE DOCTOR
WHO OPERATED ON HIMSELF

I WAS talking with a Seattle nurse recently when our conversation drifted to one of history's most stellar pioneers – German-born, Werner Forssmann. I was awestruck with the brief history of Dr. Forssmann. He was interested in researching a catheter for the heart, a method which calls for putting a catheter through the arteries, probing to see if there are blocked veins present. Liquid dye would then be squirted into the artery to guide doctors in pinpointing any blocked arteries. He tried on several attempts to convince his superiors to allow him to perform the technique, but nobody budged. As a matter of fact, his superiors at the small clinic even forbade him to investigate anything so dangerous. Over time, he became a laughingstock.

In 1929, when he was 25 years old, he tried yet again to get somebody to volunteer for this procedure, but nobody budged. Undaunted, he decided to go ahead without his bosses' approval. One drawback presented itself, however; he did not have access to sterile instruments without the permission of a nurse. The shrewd Forssmann was able to convince a nurse to get him those instruments, telling her that he would use the catheter on her. The compliant nurse agreed to let him perform the technique on her. While she was lying on the operating table waiting to be operated on, the doctor strapped her down so that she could not interfere with him. He anaesthetized his arm, then slid a 26-inch catheter up a vein and into his heart. Well, in case this is not coming together for you clearly, he performed the operation on himself. X-rays later proved that the tube was actually inside his heart. He would go down in history as being the first man to ever perform angioplasty. It is said that Forssmann was fired from that hospital, but within a few years, his superiors begged him to come back and perform his techniques. It is known by doctors throughout the world as angiogram. Cardiology would be nothing today without that determined doctor's contribution. In 1956, Forssmann was awarded the Nobel Prize for his work.

It just goes to show that even when folks laugh at you and tell you that whatever you are doing is nonsense, if you believe in yourself you will have the last laugh. Take a walk in Dr. Forssmann's shoes today and silence some doubting Thomases. Take a look at the instrument panel and resist whatever you are hearing.

THINGS ARE NOT
ALWAYS WHAT THEY SEEM

MANY TIMES situations will look the same. Cookies will smell like other cookies you have smelled before, but most likely they will not taste alike. Just be mindful that things are not always what they seem to be. For example, water flowing over a waterfall will only pass that way once. You'll see the mist, and you'll hear that body of water thundering forth, but each drop of water will be different in the sense that it will only pass that way once. You will not be able to tell the difference because water is water, and all you see is water. And sometimes in life, we are unable to tell firsthand what is success and what is failure. The couple that seemed so incompatible while dating is the marriage that lasted for 50 years. On the other hand, the ones who could not get their hands off each other during courtship, were divorced after five months of marriage. Things are not what they always appear to be.

Don't just go about making haphazard comparisons and shortchange yourself of some great successes. If you failed in one business, learn from your mistakes and start a new one. Stop constantly comparing the two. You can get more from your relationship when you stop comparing your partners and start seeing them for who they are.

You are perhaps a top CEO, and Dennis – the object of your affection – is a carpenter. Start seeing him through the eyes of love. You are seeing Bridgette, a very attractive receptionist privately but you are somewhat apprehensive about going steady with her. After all, you are an attorney and you constantly worry about what your peers would say if you were to introduce her to them. In both cases, each party treats the other with the utmost of respect. They are gregarious;

they are kind, and they are thoughtful. The only downside for you is the job status thing. Yes, you want to be compatible both intellectually and otherwise, but don't overlook those great qualities for the sake of pride. Realize that you've got wheat all this time in your field and not tares. Therefore, start enjoying a bountiful wheat harvest even with a few scattered tares. Find them among those blessings right at your fingertips.

Sometimes good news and bad news come in the same package. For example, the parent who tried to save his child's life in a drowning accident but lost his own. It's good news that the child's life is spared but bad news because the father perished.

Again, sometimes things look alike but have different purposes. Take, for instance, sugar and salt; kerosene and water; honey and glue. Many times you will have to smell or taste them to determine the purpose. Just looking at an egg, one is unable to tell whether or not it's from a chicken, duck, turkey, snake, goose or turtle. Well, unless you are an expert. Based on its size, however, one can deduce that it's from an ostrich or a pigeon. But most likely, for a lot of us, we would not know what is inside that egg until it's hatched. Do you recall the story, *The Ugly Duckling*?

"Enjoy your own life without comparing it with that of another."
– Cordorcet.

We tend to have the bad habit of always comparing ourselves with others, and a lot of times, it's not the positive stories we walk away with but the negative ones. We seldom hear about the story of the mother of eight who juggles college work and full-time motherhood. But we readily identify with those people who started college for a semester and dropped out, never to return. We heard of 35-year-old Pablo who didn't get his book published, having been turned down by 27 publishers, but we didn't hear of 17-year-old Brian who was publishing his second book.

Many of you have refrained from having children not because of reproduction abnormalities. It's simply because you fear that your children will turn out like you, a sibling or a grandparent. But that is not true. Frankly, I, too, was in that boat for a long time. Despite your rough side on the mountain, bouncing around from home to home, you would make an excellent mother or father. What you have been through has already paved the way for you to raise some great kids.

If a parent died of lung cancer at 50, there's no way it's set in stone somewhere that you, too, will die from lung cancer at 50. Because of that, you have slowed down your life immensely. But not so fast. You have that children's book to publish. Some of you have a few schools to build. True, Denise didn't make it, but you will. There is a generation out there waiting to hear your story, Pastor Elect Michael Brown. Don't be setback by the tares. Continue to grow your wheat unhindered. If you don't arrest those fears, they can cripple you mentally and spiritually. What you are running away from could just be what you'll end up becoming, save for God's grace.

In Chinua Achebe's *Things Fall Apart*, the central character, Okonkwo, fought a similar demon. He tried in vain to stay clear of the things his late father stood for, and in the end, he turned out just like his dad and even worse. But my word to you today is, don't believe the hype. Just take one more look on that instrument panel, and soar into greatness.

CHAPTER SEVEN

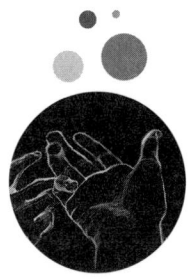

SHE WROTE MY NAME
ON THE BLACKBOARD

WHAT WOULD THE WORLD BE TODAY WITHOUT teachers? I have had some wonderful teachers, and yes, I, too, can recall memories of those who did not evince the true characteristics of great docents. I should just get out the bad one at the get-go. And focus on the positive aspects of those teachers who have played a pivotal role in my life.

In college I had to do a core class in music, and thank goodness music was not my major because somewhere around the world a conservatory would be mourning a loss. My teacher would have killed that ambition for me. I learnt everything from General Cornwallis' role in the Civil War and Picasso's paintings than from what I learnt about Gregorian chants, Bach's symphonies, or recitative. Five minutes before the class would end, when students started packing up, he would remotely touch on something relating to music. Students whiled away their time catching up on their other classes' assignments. Well, I guess I shouldn't complain too much about that class as I have gained a groundswell of knowledge in history and art at the expense of music appreciation. But for the most part, the majority of teachers are called to this avocation. Whether they're paid $500,000 or $50 per year, they would still teach. And I am happy to report that I was blessed with most of those teachers.

One particular teacher who has stood out from among the many is Miss Martin — my fourth-grade teacher at Balmagie Primary School in Kingston, Jamaica. It has been a little over 35 years (Phew! Time flies.) since I first set foot inside her classroom, but for some strange reason, which I can never seem to explain, it feels like it was just yesterday. I can still see the blackboard and the wooden desks; I still smell the rain beating down on the dusty playing field, while I daydream and look outside through the slatted windows. My preoccupation with that class is so acute that I still remember every student's full name today from memory.

Here is the list in no particular order: *Arlene Noble, Arlene Gordon, Lurline Grant, Janet Lee, Janet Forbes, Avril Rainford, Pauline Oragia, Pauline Grant, Pauline Mason, Roxie Carty, Sharon Thomas, Jean Walker, Evelyn Garrick, Beverley Clarke, Beverley Ranger, Angeline Welch, Eunice Walsh, Marjorie Brown, Claudia Robinson, Leonie Morrison, Charmaine Morris, Yvette Wade, Sandra Persaud, Andrea Johnson, Sonia Moodie, Miriam Joseph, Marcia Douglas, Dawn Rhoden, Hyacinth Wheeler, Nelson Holland, Vincent Sutherland, Harold Thompson, Michael Murphy, Aneft Budhai, Derrymore Lyon, Everald Crawford, Everald Gallimore, Adin Haye, Shorne Service, Lancelot Fray, Glester Muschette, Dwight Perry, Clive Francis, Owen Williams, Robert Gordon, Claude Cousins, Glenford Findlay,* and *yours truly, Nandell Palmer.*

I have not seen many of those classmates since we parted company in fourth grade, except for about five. I wouldn't know what a lot of them look like today. I wonder, too, as to how many of them would remember me. One came out to Seattle in November 2001 to visit me, and we had a great time catching up on Ms. Martin's class.

Don't ask me why I do remember this class in its entirety, when I would have to scratch my head several times to recall 10 names from the list of my college classmates, which came much later in life. My memory of fourth grade is intact, to say the least. Could one reason be that Ms. Martin's class was the only class I attended for the entire school year during my elementary and secondary education? I did not attend fifth or sixth grade, thus I leapfrogged my way to seventh grade.

I can remember lists of spelling words, poems, and math problems. Oh, by the way, Ms. Martin, I have finally grasped the concept of the term *addend*, short for the word addendum, which you so valiantly drummed home to those students who were a bit challenged in math. Like me. Miss Martin's class was seen as the envy of the school. Everybody was a somebody when it was announced that he/she was a student of Grade 4A. We were unique in many ways. When other classes were doing social studies, we were doing *Environmental Studies*. How could I ever misspell that "big word" again? She would schlep her record changer (portable stereo unit) around to teach the girls dance moves from Aretha Franklin's, *Rock Steady Baby*, among other popular dance music of the day. She vicariously took us to Ireland with our practicing some of those lilting tunes. And from my recollection, we were the only class setting aside time for PE, apart from the schoolwide races.

Looking back now, I am still trying to fathom what was so different or so special about fourth grade as opposed to my other classes. What was the catalyst for my constantly going back to Ms. Martin and fellow classmates? But I think more and more I'm making some headway to determine why that class, and no other, made such an impression on my young mind. For one thing, Ms. Martin was more than a teacher to many of us. Also, I basked in a kind of love which I had never felt anywhere else prior to my entering that class. The respect with which I got or gave was akin to nothing that I had ever experienced, again, prior to Ms. Martin's class.

As mentioned earlier in a different chapter, my mom and dad separated when I was three years old. She soon emigrated to London, England, where she later started a new family. My two sisters and one brother – ages 4, 2, and 6 months' old – were raised by my father, but spent a few months here and there living with other relatives off and on with many aunts and uncles scattered throughout the island. I come from a culture where, for the most part, it is still not manly for a father to tell his son, "I love you." I felt very love starved for a number of years because, even though I knew that my father loved me, I did not hear it from him, and my mother was certainly nowhere around to say those words to me. I felt unimportant.

"If you were worth anything your mother would not have left you," a constant voice would whisper to me over and over again. It took on new life when a neighbor, Ms. Thelma, a woman who could be my grandmother, said those same words to my face. After changing several schools because of the constant interruptions with our moving from one relative to the next, I finally settled for good with my dad when I was 10 years old.

There is absolutely no doubt that Ms. Martin was a godsend to me. I consider her a large-scale, over-the-top blessing! My life was destined to be touched with hers. She acted as the mother figure I didn't have at home. Granted, she was perhaps a mere 12 years older than her charges. She doled out love by the ton load among her students. She drew from her treasure trove of compassion to make everybody feel special. One of the first things I observed about Ms. Martin was her sense of equality, and that meant a lot to me then. It was a time when preferential treatment was done most flagrantly in the home, among friends, and among neighbors without anybody batting an eye on those left out.

The first thing she did each morning when she entered that crammed classroom was to choose a pupil's name at random from her lengthy register and write it on the upper right hand corner of the blackboard. With bated breath all of us would fix our eyes on the board to see who would be *king* or *queen* for that day. And that person would be celebrated by his or her fellow classmates for that entire day.

There were students with green eyes and some with brown eyes in my class. Whether you had nappy hair or long, flowing tresses, your name would get on the board at least three times for the school year. Some were driven to school by their parents, while others walked to school barefooted. Whether you dressed right or wore patchy clothes, it didn't matter; your name would be emblazoned on that board. Once you entered Ms. Martin's class, you became one with everybody else. Egos got checked at the door. All of us, at one time or another, got slapped with that thick leather belt. There was no partiality once you stepped out of line.

The name for the day would remain on the board for the duration of class until she replaced it the next morning with another celebrated student's name. Writing about this now makes my body convulse with joy! Seeing your name on the blackboard is equivalent to seeing it in neon lights in Times Square. It was such a natural high. I can still feel the goose bumps that took over my body the first time she wrote my name on the blackboard.

The interesting thing about what Ms. Martin did was that it was not mandated by Balmagie Primary School. There was no bureaucratic edict from the Ministry of Education for schools to do that. It was not part of the school's protocol to write students' names on the blackboard to build self-esteem. The last time I checked, Ms. Martin was the only teacher who did that, I would postulate, throughout Jamaica. Because in all the other schools I have attended both in Jamaica and abroad, I have never seen it done anywhere else, whether from the elementary level on to the tertiary level. Whenever I tell people about this, they would tell me that they, too, have never seen nor heard about such a thing in place. Well, no wonder why we felt so special in that fourth-grade class. Absenteeism was hardly a problem in our class as no student wanted to be left out. You never knew when your name was going to be on that blackboard. So rain or shine there was a full class. Lunch money or not, there was a full class.

After the first month in Ms. Martin's class, my confidence level soared tenfold because of her sense of fairness and her exceptional teaching skills. She has blessed my life in so many different ways. Every time she wrote out my name on the board, she was also writing a hundred blessings on my heart. Indeed she gave out daily blessings to her charges that seemed insignificant to many at that time. I am wondering out loud now how was she able to accomplish such great feats in a class peopled by so many students?

Did she know ahead of time the profound effect her kind gestures would have brought? Did she realize that each time she wrote a child's name on the board she was also shaping a generation? Did she realize that she was investing in a multitude of blessings? Has she pondered about her great investments paying dividends to millions of people because of her initial deeds, germinating seeds? My ultimate dream is to one day give out substantial scholarships to needy students or build a school in honor of this nonpareil educator and philanthropist, Evangeline Martin.

Ms. Martin truly raised the bar for me. Inside or outside of her classroom, I read voraciously, anything I could get my hands on. In fact the first Spanish term I learnt to write, "¿Qué color es el zapato?" ("What color is the shoe?") wasn't from a Spanish textbook or in front of a class but from a discarded notebook I found on the street belonging to one Veronica Walker. Similarly, my learning basic accounting, balance sheet and simple inter-est, were not from a formal class in accounting but from the soggy pages of another discarded book belonging to a student of Immaculate Conception High School. I taught myself from those basic lessons. That's why I cannot resist the theme, blessings at your fingertips. As I have mentioned earlier, I skipped a few grades during elementary and high school, and I wanted to do something to remedy those lapses.

I had long entertained the thoughts of acquiring a solid education. I vowed to put myself through college. And that dream came true when I took the high school equivalency exam, which I used to enter col-lege. Through rain or shine, snowstorms and beach-like days, I went to school, never skipping a day until graduation. Working fulltime and attending school fulltime was quite a challenge, but I persevered. I was on the dean's list every semester. I was inducted into various honors societies like the Golden Key National Honor Society. I graduated *magna cum laude*, garnering a 3.77 GPA with a bachelor's degree in journalism. That day when I received my degree, I thanked Ms. Martin and the other great teachers along the way, because they've all made it possible for me to see that day. I felt as though my name was again on the blackboard. Being the first person to graduate from college in my family, today I believe that I have more than made up for those miss-ing days from school. Here's hoping that this will not come across as bragging; all I want to do is to write to those who felt that life has dealt them a bad hand. I want to encourage them that there is a way out. So the last thing I want to do is brag and boast. But for God's grace, I could easily be some vagrant on the street in some city somewhere.

Thank you, Ms. Martin, for giving me blessings at your finger-tips. Every time you took those chalks between your fingers to write a child's name on the board, you were doing the most profound act of love. You were building confidence; you were championing equality, and you were instilling perseverance. I salute you today.

I have long pondered how I could show my appreciation to Ms. Martin without monetary gifts. That reality came about a few months ago when I launched a personal campaign to collect letters from every continent of the world. I received heartfelt letters for her, glowing with congratulatory messages from Queen Elizabeth, Nobel Peace Prize Winner, Archbishop Desmond Tutu of South Africa, the governor and senators of Washington State, mayor, school-board officials, college president, principals; scientists in Antarctica; educators in Canada, Australia, Thailand, Peru, just to name a few spots around the world. At a reception in Kingston, Jamaica, to honor Ms. Martin, I read excerpts from a few of the letters, and then presented the large portfolio with all the laminated pages intact to her. I also presented her with a personalized plaque for her sterling service to students. You could just feel the love wafting throughout the hall among her colleagues and well-wishers.

Here is an excerpt from Archbishop Tutu's letter: "Dear Ms. Martin, Nandell Palmer has told me what a remarkable mentor you were to him and others when he was at primary school. I, too, as a barefoot township urchin, had the tremendous blessing of an exceptional teacher and mentor in my formative years, the Revd. Father Trevor Huddleston. I do not know if I would be who I am today if it were not for him. Teachers can be the most powerful influence for good or the opposite on the lives of young people. You have been a mentor, a guardian angel, a guiding light, a source of understanding and compassion and have been a profound positive influence on the lives of your pupils. Thank you for being such an outstanding representative of a profession that too often is not given the status nor recognition it deserves."

THE OTHER SIDE
OF NAME ON THE BLACKBOARD

I AM so conditioned with that name on the blackboard phenomenon that whenever I visit a classroom, it's like second nature, I look around to see if a child's name is written on the board. But there is not always glee associated with a student's name on the blackboard. I would find this out decades later among my own children.

Our second son, Jevaughn, was sent to his bed early one evening as a form of punishment. He started to cry, saying that he needed to do an overdue school project, and that if he didn't turn it in the next day to class, his teacher would punish him by writing his name on the blackboard. He was not prepared to have his pride decimated in front of his classmates. His incessant pleas were more than a father could bear, and I finally relented and granted his request. But that got me thinking, "How could one's name written on a blackboard be a punishment?" In my fourth-grade class, when your name was written on the blackboard you were royalty. You hardly want to leave the classroom for that day. You didn't feel hungry. Your cares seemed to all flutter away into the heavens. How things and times have changed!

GIVING BACK TO TEACHER AND SCHOOL

OVER THE years, so many teachers have sown seeds of blessings into my life, and for that I will forever be grateful to them. Some that readily come to mind are Profs. Manbeck, Martinez, Catto, Trumbach, Brown, and Breen. Ms. Taylor, Mrs. Watts, Mrs. Grayson, Mrs. Smith, just to name a few.

Great teachers have not only been influential in my life but in my sons' lives as well. They tell their stories of how teachers sowed into their lives in a very big way.

Jevoy, the eldest boy, recalls a story when he was about six years old. One morning when he did not show up to school, and while sleeping in bed, he felt taps on his body. He awoke from sleep to find two of his classmates standing over him. They were commissioned by their teacher, Ms. Green, from the Tavares Gardens Primary School, to get him. He had a quick wash, put on his school uniform, and headed to school with the two "detectives." Upon his arrival, without saying a word to him, the teacher bought him breakfast, paid for his lunch for the day, and gave him pocket money. She knew that he didn't show up for school because he perhaps didn't have money for lunch. And instead of having a future great mind waste away, she became proactive, as most great teachers would, and filled those needs. Writing about that act of kindness is overwhelming; it makes me again choke up with a sense of gratitude and pride. It makes me believe again in the beauty of one selfless human being helping another for the common good. It makes me believe that people are not all bad. God has provided wonderful people in our lives, and some of those angels who walk this earth are called teachers.

If you were a student whose life was changed as a result of a good teacher, you can do your part to give back your time, energy, or money to a student, teacher or school. Whether you are now living in Dublin or Dar-es-salaam, but attended school in Denver, you can still do your part by contributing locally to a school and its causes. Some of you need to drop by your former schools whenever you are in town and let your teachers know how appreciative you are of their unique pedagogy. Send a thank-you card to him or her 3,000 miles away, extolling their praises.

How many of those teachers scrimped from their meager salaries to supplement your going on that field trip, which changed your life for the better? When you couldn't rely on a mom or dad to make pertinent decisions, your teachers were always there. Today, some of you are movers and shakers in your respective fields. Therefore, it behooves you to give back, passing on blessing in the forms of scholarships, mentoring youth, being a big brother or big sister to a child who's bereft of role models in his/her life. Go back to a school and give a pep talk to inner-city school children; donate to a local PTA. Those gestures would seem small now, but they have the potential to launch many future careers.

MAILMAN AND GIVING BACK TO STUDENTS

THE STUDENTS at the elementary school where two of my sons attend are very blessed indeed. A mailman for the area buys popcorn the last Friday of every month for all students of the school. That's a stupendous contribution, and I know that some little kid will remember those freebie popcorns years to come.

We read stories over and over again about poor people making a difference in the lives of children. A few years ago, a washing lady gave her life's saving to college-bound students. Now, here's another example of blessings at your fingertips. After scrubbing some of those clothes by hand to make a living and in turn giving that money away, that woman was able to be a blessing exponentially to hundreds of people because she invested in their lives directly or indirectly.

MY UNCLE GIVING MONEY TO SCHOOLBOYS

MY UNCLE told me of a story about a group of children who used to walk a 3-mile journey to school daily. As a pastor, many of these children would look to him for occasional treats as he drove past them several mornings. He gave lunch money to quite a number of them who would not otherwise have eaten for the day.

Many years later, he was driving on the same road he gave out his gifts and he had a puncture on one of his tires. Within minutes, after getting out of his car, a police car drove up beside him, and out came a robust police officer. The policeman, before long, got down on his knees, not mindful of his immaculate-starched uniform getting dirty. He ordered my uncle not to do anything, and after the tire was changed, my uncle was overjoyed. He thanked the officer profusely, and proceeded to give him some money for his kind deed.

"What are you doing?" asked the stunned officer.

"This is just a small way of showing my appreciation," said my uncle.

"This would be an insult to accept your money," thundered the officer. "Do you know how many mornings you provided lunch money for me as a child? I should be the one giving you money."

And with that said, the policeman took out a few crisp hundred dollar bills from his wallet and gave them to my uncle, who was reticent in accepting the money. But the cop insisted that he take them. It just goes to show how blessings can multiply a hundredfold over time when you sow into somebody else's life. My uncle did not remember that schoolboy he used to give money, but that boy grew up to remember that kindness, and it came in quite handy when my uncle needed some help. So if you are that teacher, student, farmer or custodian, do your part in sowing into a child's life. You may never know what lies on the horizon 10, 20 or 30 years from now. Did that story play a part in my uncle's son becoming a police officer? Today my cousin is one or two promotions away from becoming a commissioner of police.

What I like about all the examples I have listed so far is the simplicity with which each person employed to make a difference in a young person's life. Nobody else was writing students' names on a blackboard, but Ms. Martin became proactive and started blessing her students in this simple way. The mailman couldn't buy every child a pair of sneakers but he could treat each child to a bag of popcorn once a month. My uncle's few pennies perhaps would mean nothing today to someone making a six-figure salary, but it sure made a difference 30 years ago in a needy child's life.

PUTTING MISS MARTIN'S
METHOD TO THE TEST

I WAS teaching a small group of boys at church, and wanted to use Ms. Martin's approach. I spoke with my director about it, and he was all excited. But there was one reservation: he suggested that we give each boy a gift to go along with his name on the blackboard. My director is one of the most amiable and giving persons you will ever meet, but after pondering that thought for a few days, I pretty much gave his recommendation thumbs down. There can be merits from the simple things. Not everything has to be festooned with frills and money for it to change lives. What I remember about Ms. Martin was the sheer essence of her benevolence. I am wondering now had she given her students money, would we think about the money minus our names on the blackboard? Would one gesture beat out the other? I don't recall ever getting a red cent from Ms. Martin, but what she did for me is worth much more than silver or gold to date.

WHAT TEACHERS MAKE

MY COUSIN, Hope Palmer-Bruff, a former schoolteacher who currently lives in Connecticut, sent me an email, entitled, *What Teachers Make*, which I found very interesting. There is no attribution given in the email for this piece; therefore, it is cited anonymously. Perhaps this will cause all of us to look at those who choose the teaching profession in a different light.

The dinner guests were sitting around the table discussing life. One man, a CEO, decided to explain the problem with education. He argued, "What's a kid going to learn from someone who decided his best option in life was to become a teacher?" He reminded the other dinner guests what they say about teachers: "Those who can, do. Those who can't, teach." To stress his point he said to another guest: "You're a teacher, Bonnie. Be honest. What do you make?"

Bonnie, who had a reputation for honesty and frankness replied, "You want to know what I make?" She paused again and looked at each and every person at the table.

I make kids wonder.

I make them question.

I make them criticize.

I make them apologize and mean it.

I make them have respect and take responsibility for their actions.

I teach them to write and then I make them write.

I make them read, read, read.

I make them show all their work in math.

I make my students from other countries learn everything they need to know in English while preserving their unique cultural identity.

Finally, I make them understand that if they use the gifts they were given, work hard, and follow their hearts, they can succeed in life.

CHAPTER EIGHT

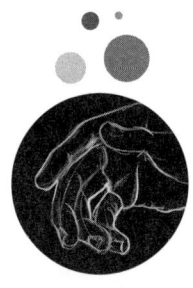

A LOVE COMES
OF AGE IN HARLEM

*ABOUT TWO WEEKS BEFORE MY UNCLE'S 80*TH birthday, I called him one Monday morning in New York City. I enjoy talking to him each time because, more than anybody else in the family, he is a walking repository of our family lineage going back many generations. I consider him the Alex Haley of our family. He could tell you the scholars and the scoundrels of our clan. I spoke to his wife, too, and she informed me that she was getting ready to go to the doctor to schedule an upcoming hip surgery. Wow, this poor woman has seemingly had more than her fair share of surgeries over the last 10 years. Before her sickness, she was a very spry woman who walked a mile in a New York minute.

Always one to glean something new from every conversation about the family from my uncle, I seized the opportunity to yet again learn more from him. After all, he is 80, and my father is never one to go back in the past. I was back and forth with both my aunt and uncle on the telephone, when I asked my uncle what kind of a father and husband his dad was, and he was too happy to oblige.

"Three things I remember my father telling me as a child," my uncle said, beaming with pride. "Number one, he said, don't ever question the birth of your child if it's not obvious. Number two, never move in with a woman; make her move in with you. And number three, never tell a woman that you love her – show her love, but never tell her that you love her."

The stories I've been told about my grandfather were always sweetened with praises. The consummate provider for his family. A devout Christian who would give the shirt off his back to a stranger. I surmised that it was the era he grew up in. He couldn't help it. He also had to bury two wives, then tried love again, which resulted in a third marriage. So I will not be too hard on this man. I was only taken aback by that last line.

Wow! I was speechless. That was quite an earful. I felt a kind of pity for my uncle in a strange way. Here, I was thinking, this octogenarian has a lot to be grateful for. He has never spent a day in the hospital for any form of maladies, except for a dislocated right shoulder he suffered when he slipped and fell on black ice in the winter of 2005 en route to work. He has no congenital diseases most people his age suffer. I doubt he has any medication in his medicine cabinet. Therefore, if there was anybody who should give thanks for multiple blessings, it was him. I wondered whether or not my grandfather's words captivated any of his other progeny the way they did my uncle. My father, perhaps? My other uncles and aunts? If so, I will be on a quest to stamp it out once and for all, I silently vowed. Could the words, I love you be forever eluded wives, children, grandchildren, nephews, and friends in this family because of the seeds that were planted years ago? I wanted no part of that.

I reminded him of his upcoming 80th birthday, and he was quite happy for that auspicious occasion. He then changed the subject to his obituary. He wanted me to set up a time to interview him so that I could write a "nice obituary" for him. I told him that he shouldn't worry about that. "Somebody will be around to write you a glowing one when the time comes," I assured him.

I tried to fathom how he must have felt living without ever saying those words to anybody – especially to his spouse. What did he do when those moments arose; when he felt secured; when plenty food was in the cupboard and dry clothes on his back; when the bills were paid and he sensed a peace indescribable; when his wife was beside him; when they watched snowfalls transform barren playgrounds into winter wonderlands? How did he escape saying even one *I love you*? I then piggybacked on our earlier conversation about his father's three tenets to his sons.

"Not that I am getting into your business, Uncle, but are you telling me that of all the years you've been married, you have never told your wife you love her?" He said no.

"She knows that I love her dearly because of all the things I've done for her . . . By the way, I will be pushing her in the wheelchair later on this afternoon for her doctor's appointment," he offered.

He confessed that on several occasions she told him that she loved him, but he couldn't bring himself to say it. He felt that doing so would jinx his marriage to failure. I asked him what if his wife's healing were dependent on his telling her he loves her, and he said he didn't know.

But since he didn't hear "I love you" as a child from neither father nor mother (his mother died when he was four years old), I wondered how did he survive all those years. I said a prayer on behalf of his wife for the continued *I love you*'s she will tell him until her life is no more. And I strongly hope that he will begin to live at age 80 by saying those three simple words. Before we ended our conversation that day, I made sure to tell him I love him, and requested one simple yet major thing from him.

"Can you promise me one thing?" I asked him. "How about giving yourself the best 80th birthday gift ever? How about holding your wife close to you, look into her eyes, call her by name and say, "I love you, Honey?" He paused, and I could tell that he was choked up. He tried to switch the subject yet again.

"Well, I know you have advised me many times over the years – even in your twenties – and you have never steered me wrong," he said. "If it wasn't for you, I would still be frying bacon in a frying pan, but ever since you showed me how to do bacon in the microwave, I have not had crispier bacons."

I chuckled about his newfound discovery. Last May he fried bacon, poured out the grease into a mug while sipping coffee from another mug, and mistakenly took up the hot grease and sipped it for coffee. His lips were burnt for weeks, and I taught him a few safety tips around the kitchen and home in general. To date, no telephone call is ever complete without his mentioning microwaved bacon. Now, of all the advice he could remember my telling him, the most valuable one he could recall is pork belly? I mused.

"You know what? I am going to do what you say," he agreed. "You never steered me wrong so there must be a reason for you to tell me this."

He also spoke about the time in my mid-20s when I had to finally silence him for his constant telling me to stay away from bad companies when I didn't have a history of hanging out with the wrong crowd. He must have told me that line for the thousandth time. It grated on my last bad nerve and I had to put a stop to it. I did it respectfully but vehemently.

"Even you standing up for yourself, telling me, 'Don't you think that I'm old enough to take care of myself?' was a big lesson for me. You notice I never tell you that again?"

I asked to speak to his wife again, and I told her that indeed she was a blessing to her husband, and he was a blessing to her. I told her that before the week was over, she should write a short note to her husband, detailing a wife's blessing for her husband. She assured me that she would do it. Within minutes of our talking with each other, the most profound thing took place: My aunt's voice was without the usual grogginess or frailty. She was so upbeat — a voice that I had not heard in 15 years. I told her that many times healing is not found in the capsules or tablets but through the communication of unadulterated love and affection for each other. She agreed. I told them that I would call back in a few weeks' time to check up on their progress and to hear positive testimonies.

I called my uncle a few weeks later, as promised, to inquire how he was doing in the *I love you* department, and he was quite elated.

"Jimmy, I cannot thank you enough. You know when you're sweaty and dirty, and you go to the river for a long swim? That's how I feel. I am feeling so clean and new now," he said.

He went on to say that those three little words have revolutionized his life in a remarkable way. A day doesn't pass now when he hasn't said them to his dear Cordelia.

I am glad that my uncle was transformed with those few words.

My relatives will be richer for his obedience. Indeed, a love comes of age in Harlem, and I further hope that it will catch afire in the male lineage of the Palmer family beyond the periphery of New York City. Did somebody say life begins at 80? Well, in this case who could dispute that it does not?

CHAPTER NINE

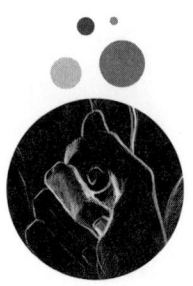

DIFFERENT ROUTES

I TAKE THIS PASSAGE IN THE BIBLE QUITE LITERALLY:
"The earth is the *Lord's* and the fullness thereof, and they that dwell
therein." Notwithstanding the acquisition of a passport or visa to enter
a *foreign* country, whenever I travel I've never felt alienated in any of
those countries. While I, like other tourists, crane my neck to look at
the Eiffel Tower in Paris, or the Petronas Twin Towers in Malaysia, I
feel as though I have the God-given right to experience all the good
things that emanate from those great sights. My policy is that if you
can smell it, taste it, touch it, hear it, or see it, then spiritually, you
can own it — it's yours. The Dunn's River Falls in Jamaica are for the
Jamaican people as much as they are for the tourists who are visiting
from New Zealand and Jordan. The Great Barrier Reef belongs to the
Australians just as much as it belongs to the visitor from Belgium or
Ireland. They were here thousands of years before we got here, and
they could be around for thousands of years after we're gone.

In many of those countries, millionaire tycoons abound. They
control large swaths of real estate holdings. Some cities could easily

be named for them because of the amount of clout they wield. But as unfortunate as it may be, reality will dawn. At 98 years old, if many of us live that long, the last thing that would be on our minds would be the day-to-day machination of piling on more money on our already burgeoning empires. We would be quite happy to get a little sunshine, TLC from loved ones, a comfortable place to lay our heads at night, and a no-frills meal to keep us alive.

Gone are the power lunches, the executive golf tournaments, and the nonstop promotion of ourselves in the mass media. We will have lived a full life – just waiting to be with our maker. The bottom line is that we own nothing!

I see China as my backyard; India as the big playground; Tanzania, where I visit my grandaunt; Brazil, where I plant my garden; St. Vincent, where the family picnics, as a break from the tedium of dining in our house. I view Japan as Uncle Charles' home where we're treated to exotic goodies. So all in all, if I can see it, taste it, touch it, hear it, and smell it, then I have the right to make it mine. It is mine as well as yours. I am joint heir with my family – the human race – spread out across the globe.

Friend, there are so many things that bind us together than what separate us. The same leaves your grandmother used to treat her malaria in the Ivory Coast are the same leaves your uncle used to heal his wound in South Korea. In the Caribbean, there is a plant called fever grass. This grass is only used, as its name implies, to cure fever. So while this plant is everywhere, it has no other use but to cure fever. I was completely shocked when I realized this same grass – called lemongrass in Southeast Asia – was an indispensable ingredient in Thai and Vietnamese dishes. On the floating markets in and around Bangkok, bunches of it are everywhere. I now make it a part of my broader use, not like years gone by when its use was solely relegated to sickness. Different routes can do that to you. I am not trying to brag here, but I have long come to the realization that I am a citizen of the world – not just to the country I've called home.

Why can't we mix things up and make a great medley? Try going on a different route today if you can. Next week. Next year. Some of you say, "Well, I am not going to that place because God is not there." You are wrong! God is everywhere. "I've lived on that block all my life and I can't move away from that $2.50 pork fried rice and chicken wings special from the Chinese restaurant around the corner," you say. But I am telling you today, find the courage to move. Better is waiting for you in a different city, state or country. I read this saying once, "Where the willingness is great, the difficulties cannot be great." Do it. It will bless your life richly.

Traveling to different routes will allow you to spend time looking at everyday things and coming up with grand ideas in the process. One friend once advised me to take up some fresh snow in the palm of my hand, watch it melt and be inspired. I promise to take him up on it one day soon. I sometimes draw a blade of grass and wonder at its uniqueness. Pick a rose and smell it; use your fingertips to fondle its most delicate parts. Take time out to know your neighbors: Jews, Arabs, blacks, whites, Asians. Extend a hand in friendship to them and then get to know each other as friend. Before long, the real enemy will be realized. Let us collectively trounce the spirit of divisiveness. We may come from different routes, but all of us have the potential to be a blessing to each other. Follow Paul's credo in Philippians 4:5: "Let your gentleness be evident to all."

The idea for this chapter came about because of a memorable assignment I had to do for a creative writing class in college many years ago. The professor asked students to go out of their way to find new ways to see and do everyday things. The project, entitled *Different Routes*, was a life-changing moment for me from that day onward. Even though it was convenient for me to take my regular bus and trains to school, I was forced to seek alternate routes to get to and from school and work. I started noticing flowers that were commonplace in my neighborhood. One being forsythia – the ubiquitous plant that bathed the neighborhood in bright yellow at the dawn of spring. I started to appreciate the creases in old men and women's faces. I truly came to appreciate the joy of laughter even among strangers. I found new beauty in God's creation.

I went out of my way to speak to all kinds of students from varying races and countries on campus. To put it mildly, I've learnt more about people and my surroundings in that one semester than I had ever experienced in my whole life prior to that class. The traveling bug set in, and before long, I was crisscrossing Asia and Africa like a true cosmopolitan citizen. And the strangest thing in all of my traveling experiences was that there was no fear at all. I felt kinship with the peoples of those faraway lands.

For example, my first trip to Africa was one of great excitement for me. I left New York City and made a two-day stopover in London, England, to visit relatives. On the second leg of the journey to Ghana, West Africa, I was sitting by myself at the British Airways terminal, waiting for my flight at Gatwick International Airport. A lady asked me where in Ghana I was going and I told her Accra. She proceeded to ask me if I had relatives or friends there, and I said no. More questions proved to her that I was a complete stranger going solo to Africa for the first time. Within minutes, a buzz went out and everybody started looking in my direction.

People were chattering in various dialects and I understood nothing – just the stares and the finger pointings. They started coming up to me in droves, asking, "Is it true that you are going to Ghana and don't know anybody?" I said yes. "So, which hotel are you staying?" I told them I did not know since I didn't make a reservation. "Ah! Ah!" was all I could hear, as Ghanaians are wont to utter in a state of surprise. The love that enfolded me that afternoon was indescribable. I was turning down lodging accommodations left, right and center. Finally, a lady said to me that her brother would be picking her up at the airport, and that if I were to change my mind about staying in a hotel, I could go home with them, but if I still insisted on going to a hotel, he would shuttle me to a few across Accra. I held fast to the latter arrangement.

As soon as I dropped my luggage inside that hotel room, I was back through the door as my hotel was a stone's throw away from Accra's teeming nightlife. Nighttime vendors hawked their wares from glass cases and open baskets to taxi drivers and pedestrians who crisscrossed that vast metropolis. Music echoed from lean-to joints to outdoor cafés. The pulse of the city seemed to take on a life of its own come 1 o'clock in the morning. And with the sights and sounds of West Africa, I felt very much at home. With quick handshakes, coupled with the clicking of fingers, everybody beamed the 1,000-watt smiles, and said, "*Akwaaba*" – welcome. I've never felt so genuinely welcomed anywhere with the word being tossed about so loosely.

Ironically, the only drawback of that trip for me was the overabundance of helpers. People only wanted to know that you were a *foreigner*, and they would go out of their way to accommodate you. "Did you see the Aburi Gardens yet?" someone might ask, and should you say no, there would be a 90 percent chance that individual would take time off from his/her job and chaperone you to wherever you want to go the following day or even for a full week. For awhile, I thought that they were doing it for financial gains, but after several attempts to tip them for their good deeds, they would look at me in a skewed way as if to say, "And what is this for?"

As I prepared to check out from my hotel that Sunday evening to return to the U.S., a gentleman tapped me on the shoulder and when I turned around, he had a $100 bill between his fingers.

"What is this for?" I asked.

"It fell out from your passport."

I had kept the $100 bill in my passport should there be an emergency or should I needed it for a taxi ride back home from JFK airport. I couldn't believe what I was witnessing. Here was a person giving me $100, unbeknownst to my missing it. I thought about how that money could have been that person's salary for say, a month, at the time, but he was willing to give it up. What a blessing, I thought.

As the plane taxied down the runway at Kotoko International Airport that night, I checked for my wallet and it was in place. My gold chain and rings were still on my body. My camcorder was intact. Foremost, I was alive and well. I thought about how many countries I could have gone and been robbed, but there I was with my limbs and possessions in place. I thought about the bravery on my part, how potentially I could have gotten cold feet and gone on a more "popular" destination like Paris or Rome. Flight attendants came with food and drinks, but I couldn't partake of them. I sobbed for more than two hours straight from sheer joy. Again, the love I received from complete strangers was mind boggling. I found a new appreciation for mankind. From that trip, I have met so many wonderful men and women. Some of them are my favorite friends today. Truly, I can say I found blessings at my fingertips because I refused to see the world through jaundiced eyes. I would not have found that love and trust had I not taken different routes.

Different routes can take you places you never dreamed of going. How do you explain a 19-year-old man leaving the comfort of his family and hometown in Romania with $40 in his pocket, and traveling to a strange land called America? Ten years later, he is a millionaire. What about the abused mother in Mississippi who packed up her four children and drove cross-country to California to escape the wretched hands of her husband? Even though she was a high school dropout, after spending less than eight years in Los Angeles, she is now a successful real estate broker, happily married, and her children are all enrolled in top universities, earning good grades. Changing up your routes is not always bad. The man credited for being the father of the world's three main religions – Judaism, Christianity, and Islam – was told to get away from his kindred to a new location. And as we're told, Abraham, through obedience, journeyed where he later found many successes.

In some factories today, you will find three generations of employees working. "Well, my momma used to pluck chickens so that's what I can do." Some say, "Daddy was a dishwasher and he hooked me up with a spot in the dishwashing department, and I am here for the last 22 years; I can't wait for my retirement." Folks, there is more to life. Think about it. Blaze some trails. Don't worry about what naysayers will say about you. In fact, they will want to do what you do but are too afraid to budge. Don't let them talk you out of your dream and blessings. The world is too big a place for us to create our little enclaves. Go on vacation to distant spots around the world. I am not advocating spending all of your money on overseas trips. All I am saying is that you should get connected to your broader surroundings. Take different routes in your mental and physical approaches.

Don't be like my former coworker, Andrew, who uses his 3-week vacation annually to sit under the boardwalk in Coney Island, Brooklyn, during summer. That dream idea you have long been praying about is on the horizon. You are now in Columbia, South Carolina, but you will have to travel to London, England, to get a glimpse of it in order for that dream to take shape. The rugged, tall, dark, and handsome man with the cleft in his chin you have long dreamed about as a husband perhaps is not in your church choir in Spokane, Washington, but sings in a quartet in Seville, Spain.

I am wondering how many unnecessary starvations we could have prevented if we had collectively pooled our resources together as they relate to medicinal plants and food? For example, while in Ghana, I saw multiple breadfruits fall from a tree and nobody ate them. I also picked a large pile of *ackees* – a very expensive and prized fruit/vegetable in Jamaica, and people just looked on in amazement. Again, nobody ate them. The world is fast becoming a global village, and it's about time we started sharing one to another. A man from Uganda knows more about his fellow brother in Kenya – not while living on the African continent they once shared – but in Boston, London, or Toronto. This ought to change.

FROM GALLOWS TO GLORY

PASTOR TONY Moore, a prominent Seattle businessman and former senate candidate, was supposed to head south to Portland, Oregon, to attend a scheduled conference. That morning, however, he could not budge to go, try as he might. As the morning progressed, more and more he found himself going off onto back roads and cul-de-sacs. Finally, he turned onto a road that meandered its way to a warehouse. He had no reason to be there. But as he was about to leave, he was dumbfounded. He was locking eyes with a former customer – a man who had credited thousands of dollars of goods from him for more than a year without paying a red cent. The man could not be located and Moore wrote off that credit as a loss.

As he made his way to the car, the man seemed disheveled and out of sorts. "You must be mad with me," he said to Moore, "but I can explain." He tried to tell him that he was struggling financially, but the businessman was quite matter of fact in his demeanor. The man begged Moore to come out of his car and walk back with him to his office.

"Not today; I will come back another time," Moore offered.

With a look in his eyes that seemed to say, "there'll be no other time," the man again beseeched his creditor to come and talk with him.

"I know you will never come back," he said.

While heading out to the main road, Moore heard a voice telling him to go back and talk to the man. He was obedient, and he went back to the warehouse and spoke with the man. Within minutes of their conversing, the man told the senate candidate that he was going through marital and financial struggles, and that he was at his wits' end.

What happened next would blow anybody's mind. The man took Moore to his office and showed him a gallows, hanging from the ceiling, which he had built to hang himself that very day. Had the businessman not returned to talk with him, the man would have become another statistic. The pastor prayed with him, forgave him, and felt one of the greatest joys ever that day. He missed his conference, but he gained a lifelong lesson, which he continues to share with audiences around the country.

It just goes to show that whenever you seem to be wandering aimlessly at times, you may never know whose lives you might impact. Going different routes can save lives and yield you a ton of blessings in the process. On the flipside, the businessman could have become belligerent on seeing this man. And instead of dispensing empathy, he could have fought him tooth and nail just to get even. But the ever-smiling Moore is one of the most caring individuals you would ever want to meet, and he continues to be prosperous in whatever his hand touches.

EBONY AND IVORY FIND COMMON BOND ABROAD

FOR THE last three years in Seattle, I've been friend with a blond-haired, blue-eyed man who was born and raised in Kingston, Jamaica. We did not know each other in Jamaica. As a matter of fact, it would take thousands of miles crossing two oceans for us to meet, through business contact, in the Pacific Northwest. We have spent hours at a time on the telephone talking about Jamaica. We are the same age, but the most interesting thing for me is the way how he would recall stories with stark contrasts from mine, even though we were brought up in the same society and the same time period. But I soon found out that different routes can do that to you.

At the onset of our friendship, I used to think that Bob was showing off, but the more I spoke with him, the more I realized that he was just talking about the life he knew. And by no means he should shy away from it or feel guilty about sharing his experience with others.

"Hey, do you remember when the prime minister used to read stories to children on the lawn of Jamaica House on Saturday mornings?" he once asked.

"Uh, um, uh?" I baffled. "When did that take place?"

"Remember as kids when you used to go downtown to the hotel and drink till you're full from the soda fountain in the lobby?"

"Are we talking about the same Jamaica I grew up in?" I would muse.

Bob told me about being picked up on weekends from boarding school in central Jamaica by his pilot uncle, who owned a fleet of small planes, and flown back to his home in Kingston. The closest I had gotten to a plane in those days was when it was doing some kind of mosquito eradication, spraying its white mist all around, blanketing the sky. Other times were when I would see people off at the airport, emigrating abroad. He also told me about his family picnicking on their large boat off Rockham Point near Port Royal, or their sailing down to the vacation home on another side of the island. Boyish pranks abound, too, like the time when he and his friend killed the family's prized bird and roasted it on an open fire. A good whipping followed. Now, that was something I could readily identify with!

Many times I wished I had stories like Bob's to talk about, but I hold true to my humble background. I am proud of the strides I've made despite my colorless story. I've come to realize that I, too, have a story to tell, and I don't need to be ashamed of doing so. I will never swap Bob's stories for mine as a way to look good in the eyes of my friends and associates. The geography buff is indeed a down-to-earth guy. His anecdotes are infused with helping others. The days when his mother would drive up to the old lady who sold beef patties on the roadside in Kingston, and buying off everything in her pan, with the intention of freeing her up to go home early for the day, is but one of them.

I am grateful that different routes have brought us together where we can fully live out the Jamaican motto: "Out of many, one people" even when we're thousands of miles away from our first home. I've told him several times that we should write a book together, detailing our diverse backgrounds growing up in Jamaica.

Many families are low in their finances but very high in love and stability. What some lack in education they make up in kindness. But if you rely on different routes, over time you will level the playing field.

CROSS-POLLINATION
AND DIFFERENT ROUTES

WHEN I stop to think about the power of pollination, it truly fascinates me. Through bees or the wind, one orange tree in Florida can pollinate another orange tree in Texas. Those trees need each other in order for oranges to come to fruition. Visiting the country as a child, I would often hear older folks referring to some of the most robust trees as "man apple tree" or "man mango tree." They looked just like all the other apple and mango trees – sometimes even more outstanding – but one thing they couldn't do year after year, was bear fruit. Their purpose, those old folks would say, was primarily to pollinate the "woman apple/mango tree." I guess I need a botanist to verify that claim.

So I am hard pressed to recall that relationship whenever I think about how much we're dependent on each other here on earth to complete one another or to be a blessing to one another. I strongly believe that for every prayer that goes out to God in a positive manner, the request often times is granted. For example, the college grad from North Carolina who has long been praying to be a teacher, God would have that person's request be honored through a principal in Pennsylvania. And out of the blue, that lifelong teaching job is granted. They are connected. Sometimes it could be by way of an advertisement on the internet or the weekly city paper, but no power could ever stop that contact from happening. Different routes take care of it.

JAMAICAN SOFT DRINKS
AND TOURIST WHO DISCOVERED THEM

SOMETIMES DIFFERENT routes will lead you thousands of miles away from your hometown. It could come about out of disillusionment or frustration. One of the best marketing profiles I have read to date was about a man in the United States who was going through some personal struggles, and decided to take a short vacation to Jamaica, perhaps for a weekend, to while away. While in Jamaica, one of his main observations was the way how Jamaicans and tourists alike were drinking the local bottled soft drinks, which came in various flavors. They were in hotels, supermarkets, roadside shacks, just but everywhere. They were a great match to temper the Jamaican sun and the spicy jerk chicken. They complemented the sapid coco bread and beef patties like nothing else. The visitor was really taken aback by the popularity of this product. He knew about the thousands of Jamaicans who emigrate yearly to the United States, and he thought what a bonanza that could be for him if he were to market those soft drinks in the U.S. Shortly before he left the island, however, he made contact with the powers that be. Before long, he bought the rights to bottle those soft drinks in the United States, and as they say, the rest is history. In large Caribbean enclaves like New York City, Hartford, Miami, Houston, Atlanta, Los Angeles, Chicago, among many more U.S. cities, no Caribbean restaurant or local market is ever complete without those popular, colorful soft drinks. And that was made possible by that man who spent a weekend in Jamaica. Who knows, perhaps he was praying or yearning for a long time to get his hands on a product that would yield him a bundle of money, but however convoluted it may have appeared, it happened. Through different routes. Perhaps he was praying for years and nothing happened, but God had an appointment made for him. It was not on Wall Street or Madison Avenue. It was not Downing Street or Pennsylvania Avenue. It was in Jamaica – a place where he would not have thought about to broker a business venture.

One thing you should always remember: be careful what you pray for. If you ask God to be in control, don't tell him how to handle the steering wheel. For many of us, it's just a habit. It's like trying to help a child assemble a toy, and midway through the process, the child grabs it from you, and is ready to make it operable. Maybe there was one or two steps left to be done, but all that child can see, is completion. Sometimes all it needs are batteries, but the anxiety to have that toy up and running, sometimes to show off on their little friends, can yield more heartache than blessing.

"Okay, Dad, give it to me now, I know what to do," that child would say. This line could be repeated up to five times, and inevitably he or she has to bring it back to Dad to fix it.

It is no different with God. Sometimes when you pray, Sasha and Kevin, your hanging buddies, will be dropped from your inner circle within weeks. You can't explain why, but don't go running after them when your 20th voicemail message you left a few weeks ago went unanswered. Don't wrestle God at the steering wheel on the bus of life to take over from Him. Some people will be dropped off from the bus, and new ones will be getting on. Don't be shocked to find Miss Darlene and Mr. Cleveland, those people whom you've looked down on in the past, getting on the bus. The bus is subject to take different routes as an alternative to a roadblock a mile away. Sometimes it will spend extra time just to wait for a special passenger. It could be the Vietnamese doctor, Michael Tran, who came to America and is now working as a busboy in your favorite restaurant.

It is the Southern grandmother with the "bad" English – yes, she has a lot to "learn" you and your daughters. Her quilting skills can open a million-dollar business for you. She is willing to pass on her strawberry preserves and peach cobbler recipes, too, to somebody since she has no offspring to bequeath those heirloom recipes to. All she needs right now is somebody to talk to – somebody to trust. Somebody who she feels will treasure this fifth-generation legacy. And you are that person. Thus, when you pray for a business idea, God is connecting you to her but you are so busy looking at what she's wearing, you hardly have time to discern that she's a walking bank. She is the lady on the bus with the empty seat beside her. She is waiting for you to strike up a conversation; her time is limited and she must pass it on. Seize the opportunity today. It's right there at your fingertips.

WHO IS SITTING IN YOUR BARBER CHAIR?

GOING OUT to different routes can truly take you places. Being the editor-in-chief of a small monthly newspaper in the Greater Seattle area, I'm always scouting out for new story ideas. One Friday afternoon as I showed up to this full-scale salon/barbershop, the barber said, "Here he is," a welcome line he uses to his customers as a way to say hello. The shop was packed with men and boys, women and girls – all trying to clean up to look good for the football game or the sorority party on Saturday. While patrons debated one topic after another, as most hair care joints are known for, the newspaper publisher, Ed Satterwhite, introduced me to a gentleman who donned a sweatsuit top, a pair of jeans, and a hat. "Oh, by the way, Nandell, meet Anthony – he's a writer – the same person I wanted you to meet," Satterwhite said.

"No way!" I shouted out.

"Why is that such a shock?" the man asked quizzically.

"Don't take this personal; I am not judging you, but it's just odd that I would run into two widely-published individuals in less than 20 minutes at a barbershop."

Less than 15 minutes before that writer entered the shop, I was talking with Julia Boyd, a noted psychotherapist and author, who has published several books over the years. She was under the dryer by then reading a book, and not hearing a word we had to say. I was meeting her for the first time as well. I had gone to that shop so many times but just never paused to see who was sitting in the chair. I know about a few attorneys and doctors and Microsoft executives who pass through weekly to get haircuts/shaves, but I simply treat everybody with the highest respect as I would to the garbage collector.

After talking with Anthony for awhile, we stepped outside to get away from the clashing dins of countless points-of-view. I learnt that he has authored several books about state-of-the art medical equipment, and that he was highly involved with the NFL. He gives speeches around the world, garnering coveted honorariums.

All three of us went to lunch that following Monday, and we chatted at length. Stories came up where he talked about being snubbed by other barbershop habitués, and how dramatic a change it was when they would see him alighting or entering his $95,000 Mercedes Benz. In a split second he would turn from "a nobody" into a nonpareil, sought after gentleman. He was feted and regaled to sumptuous dinners for free at some of the city's most august spots after being "discovered." But many times he turned down those offers. We toyed around searching for the most appropriate angle to write the story, but I could find nothing more fitting than, "Who is sitting in your barber chair?" for a headline.

Different Routes took that 18-year-old man from humble beginnings in Georgia where he rode the Greyhound bus to college in California. He hardly had enough money on that 4-day cross country trip to get by. But today he's better for that move. He was the first person in his family to enter and finish college. Right now he's basking in a whole *lotta* blessings because of his going out to different routes.

CHAPTER TEN

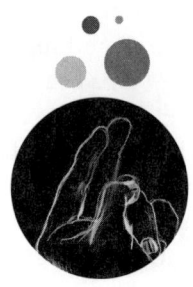

FROM BEDBUGS
TO BOSOM BUDDIES

WRITING ABOUT PEOPLE FROM DIFFERENT BACKGROUNDS gives me a comfort level second to none. I recall working in one of New York City's landmark hotels when I first moved to Manhattan, and what a special time that experience was for me. That epochal moment had me working as a house officer — a title that seemed to wield a considerable amount of power, now looking back at it. I was connected to every department in the hotel, which had me dashing to the 21st floor one minute talking with the general manager, and the next minute I would be three flights down in the basement talking with the engineering director or the housekeeping dispatcher.

What I liked most about being employed at that hotel, however, wasn't the perks of seeing a Naomi Campbell, Frank Sinatra, Barbara Streisand or Mohammed Ali up close and in your face when riding in an elevator or when joshing with them in the lobby. It was inside the employees' cafeteria, where at any given time, you would hear people of various tongues conversing. The Tower of Babel was no match to that place. In fact, at one time I counted employees representing 42 different countries. We had our own little United Nations going on in there. And I took advantage of that once-in-a-lifetime moment. When people were converging into ethnic or departmental cliques, I would purpose myself to sit with the German group or the greasy engineering group – in turn, forcing everybody to speak in English or non-engineering jargon.

I learnt so much from those sittings. Before long, it was not uncommon to find one table teeming with 10 people from 10 different countries. Wow! We talked about everything, from the Filipino exotic dish called *balut* to eyewitness accounts of the Nazi's occupation in Europe. That polyglotal environment allowed me to experiment with one of the strangest things that I have ever done to date, which over time came to engender trust, respect, tolerance, and gratitude.

I had my two days off and returned to work on Friday for another 3 to 11 shift that afternoon. Within minutes, I, along with a cadre of employees from housekeeping, front desk, security, and engineering, was summoned to go to an upper floor. Upon reaching the room, the place was in disarray. The people I met there were not saying anything to anybody. Finally, I probed as to what was going on, and in hushed tones, somebody confided that a family of three was taken to the hospital the night before after suffering multiple bites from bedbugs. I couldn't believe what I was hearing, and I blurted out, "Did you say bedbugs?"

As I looked down on the hundreds of yellow cabs rushing past busy tourists on some of New York City's tony avenues and streets, I couldn't help but think about the irony of the richest city in the world being plagued by bedbugs. Bedbugs on Broadway? When did those parasitic creatures become so bold as to share the spotlight with Times Square? When did they become so brazen as to get onto luxurious transcontinental jetliners and take up residency among the gentry stock of Gotham? My curiosity got the better of me because I wanted to find out if those bedbugs were the same bloodsuckers that made poor people's lives a living hell in my native Jamaica. I had not seen them for more than 10 years at the time.

Were they the same brown, smelly bugs I knew as chinks growing up? Could they be the same culprits for which many a mother and grandmother waged nightly battles, while keeping vigil over their sleeping children? I could not fathom that they were beyond the periphery of Jamaica. I held out hope that somebody would prove those victims wrong as there was no way possible *chinks* could have that amount of chutzpah to do such a thing. They've had a reputation to be bold, showing up on white shirt color in public places. But I didn't believe that they could be that bold.

I dismissed the incident as a hoax, and a few people nodded in assent. I searched the mattress from top to bottom and didn't spot any of those bugs. I soon got a hunch to look at the back of one of the huge picture frames hanging on the wall. Phew! I couldn't believe my eyes. I had discovered bedbug factory! I was the lone sleuth in search of those diabolic critters. As the nasty culprits lay dormant, huddled together on the bottom of the frame, which they're wont to do, I came up with a grand idea. I got one of the hotel's envelopes and another piece of paper and began collecting a few of them, stapling the envelope to keep them in place.

When the investigation was done, I went from one department to the next showing off my content to fellow employees. The first person I showed was Juan, a Puerto Rican porter who uttered, "Oh, *chinsay!*" Ali from Pakistan stammered, "*Katmol!*" Jeanette from Haiti, gushed, "*Pinez!*" Mohammed by way of Ghana and Nigeria shrieked, "*Kazuzubee!*" Margrit from Germany grunted, "*Die bet-wanzee!*" Judit from Hungary howled, "*Poloska!*" Many others would also give their respective country's names for bedbugs. And as mentioned earlier, it is called *chink* in Jamaica. With the exception of Margrit who wrote down the bug's name in German, I only spelled the names phonetically the way how those people said them to me. The scientific name is *Cimex lectularius.*

Contrary to what I had thought, nobody showed any disgust to the sight of bedbugs. It was as if a re-acquaintance of sorts was going on because long after I disposed of those blood-letting insects, people from other countries who didn't get a chance to see them, but were only told, came up to me to tell me their native names for the bugs. I learnt upward of 17 names for bedbugs in that short span of time.

What struck me most about that saga was to see how something as low and base as a chink getting prominence in the world's richest city, relishing in primetime exposure. After all, chinks were primarily consigned to areas where there were rampant bedwetting. In other words, in abject poverty-stricken areas. One of the quickest ways to start a fight among boys in Jamaica when I was growing up was to tell them about their mothers or call them *pissa bed* (bed wetters). Because where there was bedwetting, then there was bound to be chinks, and nobody wanted to be identified with chinks. I didn't know of chinks affecting the well-to-do. But I was wrong this time around in New York City. I could just see the headlines in *The New York Times*, *Post*, or *Daily News*: "Landmark Hotel Battles Lowly Bedbugs." Or, "Tourists Stung By Bedbugs in Posh Midtown Hotel." But thank goodness the media didn't get wind of it.

The main reason why I choose to highlight this circuitous anecdote is that people are people the world over. Again, we have more in common than differences. And if you are willing to get down to people's level, they will tell you things that they wouldn't even say to their dearest friend. The only thing was that example called for common bugs. I remember noted journalist, George Curry, giving pointers while addressing a group of journalism students on our campus. One of his foolproof techniques for a successful interview, he said, was to ask his subjects, "Tell me something that you have never told anybody else before?" This, he said, was quite a disarming method. I have used this line over the years, and it has never failed to deliver the prime goods. Sometimes it's through deep sobs or multiple sighs, but you have the potential to reach deep into people's souls when you ask this question.

I was asking that question to my fellow coworkers that Friday afternoon not in those same words but with the same outcome. To many of them, we did not exchange a word; I just showed them the insects. Prior to my showing those people bedbugs, I had never once heard the subject broached. I would often hear stories about the opulent lifestyles they left behind in their countries: the 10-bedroom house and the maids and gardeners who attended to the property, but never a story about their using a latrine (outhouse). I was regaled with stories about people sending money back home to lengthen the family's swimming pool, but never about their swimming in a creek when they were children. I have heard about lavish breakfasts each morning in some of those countries, but nothing from the people who drew a handful of lemon leaves from their neighbor's tree to make tea for their family.

Hence, what started out as a nebulous, seemingly embarrassing situation, turned out to be a ton of good for countless others. I began noticing the way how middle managers and room attendants alike would easily tell their stories unedited. It was as if the shame tree had given way to true dialogues straight from the heart. And some of those people who felt a little embarrassed admitting to knowing bedbugs in public would seek me out in private and tell me about their humble beginnings growing up with chinks. They would ask my advice on personal matters. Indeed, bedbugs had leveled the playing field.

Not in my wildest dreams did I set out to cause such a stir — well, albeit a positive one. I am surmising now that people saw an avenue where they could park their emotional vehicles and spill their guts. "Well, if he knows about chink, bedbug, katmol, chinsay, poloska, and kazuzubee, then he must know something about . . . ?" they seemed to say. I was inundated with requests to do this and that. I was in school at the time, and I would use precious break time to catch up on my assignments, but I could barely get a five-minute break by myself inside that cafeteria. I did not know that out of a brief, innocent show-and-tell with bedbugs, I would gain the enviable trust and respect of legions of my coworkers across the board. I credited that to my transparency. The biggest lesson I learnt from that experience was that it allowed me to understand people's body language, the elisions of the spoken word, and the concealment behind their verbiage. I didn't have to go off the deep end trying to use any extra pull to elicit their responses. They just volunteered information straight from the heart.

It allowed me to counsel the Harlem mother who kept a hot iron on hand to brand her disrespectful 16-year-old son should he follow through with his constant threats to beat her up. I was instrumental in stopping a Pentecostal worker from being overly unctuous. She would anoint every telephone and other office equipment daily with olive oil, and refused to stop doing so even after she was reprimanded many times by her superiors. I learnt one of the most beautiful poems about an abandoned, old house along the Eric Tracks of Suffrin, Ireland, from a waitress, with a master's degree in comparative literature. Again, I discovered that outhouses were not only found in Africa and the Caribbean but also in the United States and Europe.

I noticed that everybody was different in some ways, whether by religion, ethnicity, language, or age. But there were few commonalities that everybody shared: food and family. If you were ever at a loss for words to start a conversation around a table in the cafeteria, you would forever score touchdowns by broaching those two topics. They were instant icebreakers. They would take off like the bullet train in Japan. However, not everybody was Lenny Alvarez, the political science major studying at New York University at the time, while working fulltime as a bellhop. To date, Lenny has been one of the brightest and sharpest individuals I have ever met. He could tell people about what happened in their backyards 50 years ago in various countries, and they would look at him as if he was from another world. Whether it was arap Moi of Kenya, or Mussolini of Italy, he would go toe to toe with a Kenyan or an Italian, discussing political antecedents. He would single out rarely-discussed geography and draw a map of, say, Kalistan Valley in Asia.

Lenny aside, ask the Russian about *Blinis* or *Borcht* and you would have no break time left. Ask Claudette, the Haitian, who always brought her lunch to work about *griot* and *cremas* and you would have to take two vacation days to finish that conversation. A lot of them, unlike Lenny, could not tell you anything about their country's gross domestic product (GDP) or political hierarchy. They couldn't tell you the average inches of rainfall annually, but they could tell you about their grandmother's best pie.

Geneva from rural Virginia who would correct you in a nanosecond about her mother's illness not being Alzheimer's disease but *Old-timer's disease*, would tell you about the old lady's making the best collard greens in the state of Virginia in her heydays. The conversation would move from food to family with heightened passion.

Greetings of "How you feel?" would often be punctuated with, ". . . and how's the family?" And *family* was not necessarily those living in America. Olga from Poland would be readily asked by Lucy from Cuba about Anna – her ailing mother's progress – back home. Those employees would purpose themselves to remember people families' names that they were yet to meet. "Give this to your brother, Harold; you said he was studying engineering, right?" Barkley from Barbados would give to Sayed who was going home to Egypt to visit his loved ones. Yes, that's how it was.

I will forever be indebted to those people for my advanced state of food appreciation and a more closely-knitted family structure. Indeed that's what we were — family. The hotel was closed for a two-year massive renovation, and that's how our "family" was disintegrated. We had a few send-off parties leading up to its closure, and I've shed enough tears and got enough hugs to last a lifetime. Again, the most valuable lesson I have walked away with is that we have so much more in common than what sets us apart. And many times all it takes is for one person to make the first move, evincing that commonality in all of us.

While I would never advocate your searching for bedbugs in order to spawn a conversation with your coworkers, you should never hinder people from expressing themselves in whatever form they feel comfortable, if it is done so without malice or disrespect. Always keep an open mind. Don't shortchange somebody else's blessing. Engaging one's fellow coworkers to bring about understanding is never far afoot. You just never know, those pesky bedbugs might just turn into bosom buddies for life.

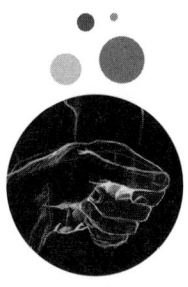

CHAPTER ELEVEN

THE WHISTLE BOY

AMONG MY FAMILY AND FRIENDS, I AM KNOWN as the recorder. Therefore, it's not uncommon for my own sisters to call me up, asking me what date their children were born, or a friend asking me the date she graduated from college. It's also commonplace for me to send 10-year, 20-year anniversary greeting cards to my friends around the world. I never missed birthdays. One cousin of mine said that he was shocked when he and his wife received a card from me for their 20th anniversary as both of them had not realized that they'd been married for so long. In fact, he said that neither his parents, his wife's parents and siblings, nor his siblings and friends, remembered anything about that date. I don't even want to know how he and his wife worked out that one when no flowers were given.

Thus, there have been merits and demerits for my elephant memory. One of the most enterprising and innovative memories I've ever had was at age 7. From a 16-ounce juice can, my uncle taught me how to make whistles. The two sides were not covered and one has to use his index finger and thumb at the sides and then blow in order to get the sound going.

My father operated a home-based picture-framing business, which had seen some very profitable days, while other times there were meager earnings. Many times, people would credit my dad's frames with the intention to pay, but those words to pay were merely empty promises. Whenever the lean days came around, I didn't do too well mood wise. But before long, the doldrums would give way to creativity. I would become the most creative of my siblings because my intention was never to repeat anymore of those days. I would think long and hard about how I could contribute to our household financially. I pledged, as the older boy, that I would not become a burden to my dad. Thus, every piece of clothes, shoes, etc., that I wore since the age of 14, I bought with my own money. Pretty much the only thing I got for free was room and board. So it was expedient on my part to find money. Fast!

I thought about some of the things I could do to earn money, but nothing suitable had come to mind. I was too proud to sell newspapers, wash cars or rake yards. And those were some of the menial tasks that most boys my age would readily gravitate toward for money. Night and day I would ponder, and finally, one night in bed, I got a breakthrough. It was like somebody asking me, "Why don't you perfect the whistle your uncle taught you to make and sell them?" I could not wait for the crack of dawn to implement that thought.

I was 14 years old, but I had recalled my uncle's teaching me years earlier how to make whistles. I could remember the intricate folds he made with the strips of metal over a cylindrical, hand-held piece of steel. But instead of using 16-ounce juice cans, I substituted them for empty oil cans from Shell®, Esso®, and Texaco®. Those cans were very attractive with resplendent colors of red, yellow, white, green, and blue. I would collect them at my nearby service stations, open them, get the grease out and sanitize them. They would be later marked out and cut into strips. Thank goodness, my father had every kind of tools around, so I was privileged to borrow his heavy-duty metal cutter, which gave a smooth finish to the metal's edge when cut.

I got to work making whistles, being creative enough to blend the colors: red, white and blue; white and yellow, etc. Wow, I was proud of myself. I was in search of some guinea pigs, and so I gave away that batch to neighborhood kids, and within minutes it was bedlam as children ran amok on the street blowing those ear-piercing toys, and adults, trying to no avail, to silence them. I felt as though I was a tangible, bona fide inventor ready for a ripe market. By the next day, kids were descending on my home in droves. Those who didn't get from the first batch, and those who wanted replacements were clamoring for the coveted toys. Again, I was proud as a peacock. And that's how my first business was born. I started that business without a red cent. All it cost me was a vision to think outside of the box.

The children began taking the whistles to their various schools, and the curiosity multiplied. I was now selling whistles to my neighborhood kids who in turn would sell them back to their friends at school for a profit. I decided to go straight to the source. I went to an elementary school and sold them for $.05 each. I made about $17 that first day. That trend continued, which resulted in very high sales peaks. But there was one caveat: the din was too much to bear for any one school; therefore, the honeymoon period was short lived as teachers, principals, and custodians tried to seek out the source of this madness, and had me moving.

Many of the school-gate vendors would see their sales dwindle, as kids were not interested in buying lunch or anything else. What got those kids' interest were whistles and more whistles. As a result, those vendors thought it best when they decided to buy those whistles from me wholesale and send me on my way. Actually, that move turned out to my advantage, as I was no longer the bad guy. That arrangement also freed me up to attend to more pressing demands, as nobody could seem to perfect the whistle, not even those people whom I had hired part-time. One colorful school fixture all school-children in Kingston would know back then, was a clown-like figure by the name of *Windy*. And he, too, couldn't solve the mystery of whistle making. He would come out with his version, but kids would flatly reject them upon contact.

My dad, along with three other individuals, would prepare the cans ahead of time for me, with my paying them a weekly stipend for their services. I opened my first bank account with $30 at the Bank of Nova Scotia in Kingston, and in no time, I had accumulated more than $1,000. With the time value of money, factoring inflation, that would amount to more than $65,000 Jamaican today. Many evenings, dinner was on me. And so we would have the choicest of steak, fish, chicken, you name it. Sometimes I would have to cook for upward of 25 people who gathered at my home at any given time. And what a joy that was for me to share the "wealth!" Old ladies would stop me for money to fill prescriptions. Kids who didn't have lunch money would come to me. Even my own daddy had to *borrow* money from me on several occasions. Aside from my entrepreneurial skills, others sought me out as advisor. Some wanted me to do everything, from writing need-based letters to their children's principals, right down to writing recommendations, and filling out legal documents. I felt like a small-town mayor of sorts.

When I first started writing those letters, there were no templates to pattern. I did the best I could by writing from the heart. Thank you Ammar's Department Store, Crimson Dawn, Bata Shoes, Sheraton Hotel, among other benevolent corporations that donated clothes, shoes, furniture and other valuables to poor mothers and children through my appeal for help to them. Thank you, too, for believing in me. It was just trials and errors on my part, but I am glad it worked. You responded. Many of you sought me out personally by making visits from your busy schedules and lofty offices to personally hand-deliver those boxes of goodies.

My cooking dinners, filling out forms, and writing letters for multiple people were a foreshadowing for the career choices I would make years later in America. They were so natural to me. Thus, it was no surprise to me or anyone else when I decided to attend journalism school, reaching thousands of readers at a time. I also founded a catering and events planning company, feeding and entertaining everybody from the jet-set to the poor.

I sold whistles to more than 200 schools in a 50-mile radius in Jamaica. I would sell them at fairs, or anywhere children gathered. About six months after my debut with whistle making, there was a large-sized feature article in one of our newspapers about the whistle craze. The reporter interviewed teachers, other school officials, and vendors, but I didn't make it into print for an interview as I was very elusive.

Summing up all of those whistle-making years, it just goes to show that you can search the dark recesses of your mind and come up with creative ways to reap those blessings at your fingertips. My own fingertips became so sore at times from shaping those pieces of sharp metal. But that's a period that I will never forget. It gave me hope. Courage. Chutzpah. Pizzazz. Resilience. Work ethic.

As an adult, whenever I reach a dead end in a business deal, or I feel like giving up on life, I just mentally roll back that big, heavy drapery, reach for the backup how-to kit, dust it off and read at length. After reading the manual, I am energized. Pumped up and confident again. I don't readily take no for an answer. I figure, if I could start my own business at such a tender age, becoming head honcho and bottle washer, with nobody to guide me, then I can do the same thing today. Sometimes in order to get to that kit, I will have to encounter roach droppings. Cobweb and mold. But that's alright because the instruction is still intact. Furthermore, the roach droppings don't faze me because they are not important to me. All I seek at that time are ways how to come up with some tangible solutions like the ones I've used before. Those which are drawn from the ultimate source of God.

Sometimes when the loan officer at the bank turned you down for that loan you've had your mind on for the last three months, just roll back the curtain and take out your manual. When you've invested so much money in marketing your business to position it to the next level, and sales remained stagnant, roll back the curtain. At 15 years, old I wore many hats without even realizing it. I was my own market-ing director. Accountant. Sales manager. Quality control manager, and product development manager. I had no formal training in any of those areas. Therefore, that collective knowledge had to come from somewhere. So, again, I draw from those years of experience whenever I am stumped. It's a time when I leverage all of my experi-ences to find my passion, making them work for me.

Remember also that starting something new is often the hardest part. Once you start the process, however, the next step is a little bit closer and may seem a little bit easier. So why not take the first step? And while you are ruminating on that thought, how about this other one?

"Many great achievements began as crazy ideas. Who could have imagined flying or putting a man on the moon? Where will your imagination take you?" – Anonymous.

SCRAP METALS SUSTAIN A FAMILY

WHENEVER I sit around and reflect on how some people make a living, I am just awed by the survival mode with which they will employ in order to get to the next level. Growing up, I saw men and women who raised their families on picking up and selling broken bottles, corrugated metal, and old pieces of iron. Some felled trees to burn charcoal and sell commercially. I know of a few families right now who have made big houses and bought multiple vehicles from the sale of refuse. Some of their children are top doctors, engineers and attorneys in many parts of the world today.

DO NOT GIVE UP ON YOUR DREAMS

BY NO means I would ever beat my chest and claim exclusive rights to what I have been through in my youth. Many of you were way ahead of your time. What happened to the great dreamers of yesteryear? Many of you were so vibrant, so full of life. Nothing could stop you. At 12 years old you were light years ahead of your peers. While they were jumping rope on the playgrounds, you had to man your lemonade stand. When others were going off to baseball practice, you were loading freight trucks or picking string beans under pelting sun. You were the parents at home to your nine siblings even though Mom and Dad were present. You rose early and retired to bed late. Now, it's reaping time. The harvest is ripe. You have put in too many hours in that field to now leave it for pests or stray animals to forage through it. All it needs now is a little weeding around the roots, and you can reap a great harvest. Resolve to do so today. Find the strength by looking at your God-perfected fingertips and let the change take place.

Perhaps a few words from Aesop could move you along: "It is no use fixing our minds on higher things if we ignore what is going on around us."

Picture yourself also as that big, towering tree in winter. You are stripped of your leaves, no blossom, no fruits – nothing. No birds grace your branches anymore to chirp songs of melody. But come warmer weather, the same tree that looked like it was dead, all of a sudden comes alive again. You are that tree. Springtime is right around the corner. Snap out of your winter doldrums. Suck up more of the sun. And start blossoming. Start bearing fruit again. Your season has come for change.

Perhaps you are that plant or flower where it got off to a good start and midway through its growth it took a turn for the worst. Well, before you toss out that plant, first you ought to make some diagnostic tests. You are not an agronomist, but by the way how that plant is looking you definitely know that something is awry. Could it be a lack of water? Too much water? Poor soil? Are parasites at its roots? These are some of the questions you would ponder before taking drastic actions. Nevertheless, if the plant meant anything to you, you will do your best to see it get back to its erstwhile state. If you stay with that plant, it could repay you immensely with beautiful fruits or flowers down the road.

Many of you are like that plant which started out well, but is now facing some hard times. Since you have the potential to weather the storms, why do you roll over so quickly, ready, waiting to die? You have a lot left inside of you. You have a lot of fruits inside of you to feed a community. There are flowers ready to bloom that will brighten someone's day. So persevere to your highest self.

Everybody knows somebody who is two or three classes away from getting his/her degree. The excuse for not completing was that he had to take care of his family, and after the kids are grown, he would return to school. But his youngest grandchild is now 18, and getting ready to go off to college, but he has not budged yet to go back. If you are that dropout mother, husband, or grandmother today, muster the courage to go back and finish what you've started years ago. I applaud you for taking the steps to enroll in college in the first place. Realize that the hardest part is already gone. A degree is waiting for you. Just finish those classes. Drop by the registrar, the admissions department or send for a transcript. Fill out the necessary paperwork and make things happen. Look at those fingertips and let them work for you. They've already gotten the approval from the main source – God himself – so step out in confidence and fulfill your dream.

What a stupendous picture to behold the sights and sounds of pint-sized children plying their wares at public markets, roadside stalls, or walking around on busy streets to make a living or helping to supplement their family's income. You'll find them in Nigeria, Brazil, Thailand, St. Lucia, just to name a few spots around the world. And the amazing thing about those children is that they are not waiting around to be given alms. They don't seek people's sympathy; they want their sale. They are as independent as they come.

PINKY, THE CHILD VENDOR

JULIET (PINKY) Hanse was about eight years old when she started earning a living for herself. Pinky's parents were separated, and she was brought to live with her grandmother, Curline Bryan. Since "Ms. Curlew" had some of her own children nearly Pinky's age, she hardly had the time to give Pinky the kind of grandmotherly attention she was looking for.

I could hear Pinky's high-pitched voice singing one of her trademark songs as she passed by our house on her way to collect items from purveyors to sell to her loyal customers. She sold everything from spinach and tomatoes to encyclopedias and jewelry. On Saturdays, she was in the marketplace selling her wares, trying to get money for lunch, books, and general upkeep. She would eventually enroll herself into private school, and again, she paid every red cent for her education. To see that young girl dress up on a Sunday was a sight to behold. And every piece of clothing was bought with her own hard-earned money.

Her mother, like mine, emigrated abroad when Pinky was about two years old. And I remember the time when as a teenager she received the first birthday card from her mother. She was very distraught when she got the card with a big green frog on the cover and a $U.S.1 bill inside it. What an example she was for many of us! The last thing I heard about this nonpareil young woman was that she was an RN in some major hospital.

Like Pinky, some of you were street vendors. No newspaper or candy boy could outsell you. You got your schooling from the streets of hard knocks. London School of Economics was no match to your business acumen, acquired on the street. With your success as a small business owner, you've garnered an MBA degree without even realizing it. At 11 years old, you were closing deals; you were lost prevention director, chief of protocol, and CEO. You were head of quality control and sales and marketing to the band of other vendors who looked to you for advice. With an eagle's eyes, you forecasted your market and became quite savvy with each sale. Your street smarts made you an indomitable force with which to be reckoned. Your mouth was so sweet with terms of endearment that you had everybody eating from your palms. Yes, I am talking to you – the feisty, no-nonsense tyke who would not go down without a fight.

But what radically took place over the last 10 years that have you become supine, just ready to keel over and die? Was it the nasty divorce? The tragic accident that killed your 3-year-old poodle? Seek help, and get back on track. Get back that wind in your sail. Start by writing the many successes you have made in the past and use those as planks to step into your future. Brush off the laidback you and find the once doggedly, determined person who blazed countless trails. You still have it going on. Just be inspired by those fingertips. All you need now is just a refresher. Get out a pen and a piece of paper and start brainstorming; write down about 10 things for your next project.

Take a few classes that will light your path to that cushy business or new job. Look forward to being promoted on the job. Look at your dusty high school diploma and use it toward your associate's degree. Look at your associate's degree and be encouraged to get ahead for your bachelor's degree; use that bachelor's degree to enter law school, medical school or toward that MBA. See each one as a stepping stone to the next level. It wasn't always easy to get good grades in order to graduate; some classes were downright struggling. When some of your friends were graduating *magna cum laude*, you were quite happy to say *Thank-you-Lawdie* for the joy of being in a cap and gown. Believe that your lifelong dreams will come true. Take a deep breath, say a prayer, and let God be your ultimate guide now.

Many of us are sitting on goldmines and don't even know it. Sometimes when situations come into our lives in the form of setbacks and chaos, they are a way to get us to pay attention to take alternate routes. Perhaps you've done everything you possibly can for that moribund business. But for some strange reason, there's no growth. You've done advertising. Many times you've even checked to see if there were still dial tones on your telephone as it had not rung for days. The bottom line is that the calls stop coming in. You've sent out cards and stayed in touch with some of your most valued clients, but even those things and people didn't seem to make the grade. You are singled out. You are spotted for greatness. Seize the opportunity. Look through the foggy horizon. Peer through the smoke screen and race to your destiny. There are bigger and better things awaiting you. Go for them! Just believe that God has a bigger plan and a purpose for your life. I wish to end with this lovely quote from Henry David Thoreau:

"I learned this, at least, by my experiment; that if one advances confidently in the direction of his dreams, and endeavors to live the life which he has imagined, he will meet with a success unexpected in common hours."

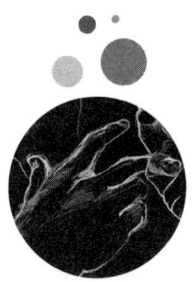

CHAPTER TWELVE

SNATCH BACK YOUR DIAMOND NUGGETS FROM THE PAST

ON JANUARY 6, 2007, I WENT TO SEE THE Dead Sea Scrolls exhibition at the Pacific Science Center in Seattle, Washington. It was the day before its culmination, and I pledged never to miss that opportunity to see it. What a monumental display! Hordes of visitors stared fixedly on 3,000-year-old artifacts as they gasped in amazement.

Since the past is oftentimes looked upon as a negative time period in our lives, we're constantly told to move on and give no thoughts about yesterday. But we should hardly be blamed for not liking the past. Who wants to revisit a time when he was dumped by his girlfriend inside the school cafeteria for all his friends to see? Who wants to go back in time to that community where her landlord put her out of her apartment in the dead of winter? Nobody wants to. But the past is not always bad.

Midway through touring the exhibit, I paused to think about the one simple action by two goatherds that brought about this mobile museum, which the world is now clamoring to see. The year was 1947, and the two young men were trying to capture one of their goats that escaped inside the nearby Qumran cave around the Dead Sea area. There goes that goat again. What is it with goat and discovering new things? Remember goat and coffee discovery in an earlier chapter? Are there correlations with goats discovering million-dollar projects through happenstance? Well, I need to find out.

In pursuit of the animal, the two young men began tossing stones inside the dark cave. Over time, they heard a thud. Their stones were not hitting a bulging goat belly but precious jars that had been hiding the Dead Sea Scrolls for millennia. Their curiosity drew them further into the cave. And with light to guard their path, they soon discovered the treasure trove awaiting them. That's more than 60 years ago, and as they say, the rest is history.

Archeologists from all across the world descended on Qumran when the news spread. And with ready cash being dispensed by those archeologists, many locals soon gave up their regular jobs to dedicate themselves to interminable diggings. Those men and women were not digging for the sake of digging, however. They were digging for a purpose. The thing about those diggings, though, was that archeologists didn't intend to hoard every clump of clay unearthed from that historical site. Their primary focus was to meticulously sift through the tons of dirt and rubble just so that they could find their treasure. Sometimes it was a broken piece of earthenware, other times it was a camel tooth. Still other times they would be satisfied with a piece of iron or a wrinkled, dried-out date or olive. For most of us, those things are trivial, but for the archeologist, he will have found a mother lode of precious items.

The Dead Sea Scrolls have shed new lights on some of the biblical renderings. But to read written texts during the lives of Moses, Isaiah, and other biblical who's who, it was quite a stupendous feeling. It then had me wondering again, if the past was so bad, why then did we still read three of the world's most holy books today: The Torah, Bible, and Koran? Every time the Jews gather for Passover, they are going back in the past. Every time Christians perform communion in church, they are going back in the past. And every time Moslems celebrate Ramadan, they are going back in the past.

David, a man who was likened unto God's own heart, waxed

heartily about God's hand in his life in the past: "I remember the days of long ago; I meditate on all your works and consider what your hands have done."

We go back in the past daily without even realizing it: eating with knife and fork – a habit shaped by the Greco-Roman aristocracy. Wearing stylish couture, another legacy from the Romans. Jurisprudence in our court system. If you look forward to having your credit score redeemed after seven years, you are drawing from the past. It's a Levitical obligation. Every time you repeat these words, ". . . To have and to hold . . ." as part of your marriage vow, you are revisiting the past. If you are the beneficiary of a bequest, then you are dabbling in the past.

Not everything in the past, however, is worth bringing back to the present. If you suffered from epilepsy in ancient Greece, you would be considered a demon-possessed person, and could be stoned to death by anyone so as to appease the gods. But we must give credit to Hippocrates – the father of modern medicine – who countered that claim and helped to shape public opinions in Western Civilization. Gone are the days in certain homesteads of Nigeria, when the birth of a twin or triplet would trigger instant death by village leaders to those infants. They claimed that multiple births were an abomination to the gods, which could interfere with crops and the overall environment. That country's government would later outlaw such a practice in 1959 throughout the land.

When you eat sweet strawberries, you are reaping the fruits from the seeds you planted in the past. The interest you're now earning from a matured CD or bond is as a result of a deposit you made years ago – a period in the past.

PICKING UP AFTER DISASTER

IT NEVER ceases to amaze me how television/cable news will show despondent victims of a disaster going back to pick through the rubble even months after that hurricane, tornado, or fire. Many people are not going back to find the $10,000 leather sofas or the china cabinet, pool table or Ferrari, as they know that those items are decimated by the flood or conflagration. Many go back simply for one reason: To reclaim a precious item which they have held dear over the years – their baby's picture, the anniversary album. The graduation ring. The precious bottle Grandma made in her class years ago, or some other notable mementos. You will see how their faces would light up, how they would hug that item, and so forth.

Sometimes those pictures are soaked through with mud and grime, but those things won't hurt or devalue their salvaged possessions. Most times the grief is so heartrending that they would prefer to move on and rebuild somewhere else. But before the mass excavation takes place, before the bulldozers start heaping up the rubbles to take to the dumps, those people just want to be afforded one last chance to go through those piles of junk and salvage their treasures. They know that it is not possible to retrieve the big-item products. What they go back for are the little things, which I call the diamond nuggets. And that one thing alone will cheer them up.

A few months ago we saw on the news how certain areas at Ground Zero from the demolished World Trade Center were cordoned off from the public. It was said that human remains were discovered after five years in some remote areas. It turned out that a finger joint was found, but that one joint gave some form of closure to the family. They are willing to walk away with this piece of treasure where they can continue to rebuild their lives.

THE PAST IS A BRIDGE
TO YOUR FUTURE

ONLY A few feelings can ever be compared to a clean and nice-smelling home. I also love to have space around the house. Clutter drives me crazy. But I will not dump my valuables for the sake of space or at the expense of quick work. One of the chores around the house we hardly ever give to our boys is general cleaning. It's good for them to clean up the kitchen, bathroom, and their room, but I would never, in a million years, allow them to clean up my desk. With their wanting to hurry up their work, everything in their sight over time becomes garbage. Be prepared to see valuable business cards, navigational gadgets, and even cell phone as part of their garbage to be dumped. We have to go through with a fine-toothed comb. We cannot count the amount of times gold watches, gift cards, and money made it to their garbage piles.

Our prized cutlery pieces have dwindled because of their casual treatment of them. It is not uncommon to look into the garbage after dinner and see a shiny object glistening, begging to be rescued to join its family. With further probing, you will realize that it's a fork, knife or spoon.

Whenever they clean their room, be sure to find a lonely foot of socks, the week-old underwear, their prized medal or certificate; valuable pens, etc. Now, I know why poor people flock to city dumps in some Third World nations. There are treasure troves of valuables tossed out with the junk.

I read over and over in the newspaper where prized rings and other prized jewelry escaped down the drain while a housewife washed dishes. Many owners found themselves tracking the garbage truck, all the way down to the dunghill. After carefully going through those stinking bags for hours, sometimes the prized objects would emerge. Many times they would take decades to be returned to their owners. And still other times they would be gone forever.

YOUR RESUME IS THE PAST

I AM yet to be interviewed for a job without somebody first wanting to know something about my antecedent. In order to get an interview, first one has to send in his resume – well, er, *curriculum vitae* (CV), for the big shots – to that corporation or organization. The President of the United States didn't get to that office overnight. Most likely he started out as a student council president from his high school. Some were small-town mayors or state governors. But they have to piggyback on their pasts to get a foot forward. The high school reporter used her writing clips to get access to her college papers. The college paper clips later land her a reporter spot with the New York Times, over time, paving the way for her to become a syndicated columnist.

Some neophyte line-order cooks who had to face the daily tirades of executive chefs are today world-class chefs in their own right at some swanky resorts. Many times they wanted to quit, but they knew that someday they would have to recall those dark days of the past in order to go forward. It was fuel for their tanks.

The pastor today at your church was perhaps a Sunday school teacher or a custodian years earlier. Gradually, after several promotions along the way, he became the head of his church.

How many doors have you had slammed in your face in order for you to build up your resume? How many pots of coffee you had to make each day for everybody inside the office instead of doing what you were employed to do just for the sake of your resume? A resume can tell a prospective employer a lot about you.

You have weathered the storms and now you are ready for harvest. Step out in confidence and fetch those blessings right there at your fingertips. Write the best resume ever – one that will leapfrog you closer to your destiny.

Before you take your suits to the cleaners, it would serve you well to search those breast pockets to find stray $100 bills or your Mont Blanc pen. Snatch back your diamond nuggets from the past. When you're dumping old letters and books, there is that one letter or book that will never be dumped. That's your diamond. If you dump it by mistake, you will go in search of it.

You're paralyzed whenever you recall your professor's encouraging you to drop his economics class because you couldn't keep up with the coursework. But you're energized each time your mother hugged you and told you, "Baby, you can be anything in life that you set your mind to." Your mother is no longer around today, but whenever you go back in time to snatch back your diamond nuggets, you still glisten with confidence.

Remove your diamond from the clutter of yesteryear and mount it for everybody to see. Don't linger in the past, just snatch whatever is valuable and leave everything else behind. There are lessons of perseverance Grandma taught you. There are words of wisdom from your Sunday school class. Find them.

A popular cliché goes, "Don't throw out the baby with the bath water," and often times a lot of us do just that. What have you got lurking inside your baby's murky, muddy, and roiled water today? Take one more look before you throw it away. I know that I am walking a lonely road on this subject from a spiritual standpoint because talking about the past in certain spheres is tantamount to spiritual declension.

EVEN JESUS WENT BACK INTO THE PAST

BUT EVEN Jesus himself often went back into the past in order to flesh out practical illustrations to his hordes of followers or when he wanted to put Satan in place: The parable of the Prodigal's son; the Centurion; the Talents, among others. In Matthew 4:1-11 when the devil tried to tempt Jesus in the desert and on the mountaintop, all Jesus had to say to him was, "It is written" on three separate occasions. He was drawing from one of the Mosaic five books. He was snatching back diamond nuggets from the past.

Some of you have testimonies that are laced with not-so-sterling attributes, but you know what? Those testimonies, when told, have the power to transform lives in a more positive way. Don't worry about rocking the social-circle boat. Don't hemorrhage about whether or not your friends will fail to set the 10-piece chinaware whenever you are over at their house for dinner again once they found out about your surly past. If you were to lose them, then you will gain 10 more. And to boot, your conscience will be much freer for having blessed someone else.

There is no fun wallowing in the mire and grime of yesteryear. When your house is cleaned up from top to bottom and perfumed with the latest air freshener, the last thing you want to see and smell is the rank, discolored 2-week-old sweaty gym shorts stashed away under your son's bed. You don't want to see the ring around the toilet. But occasionally you are forced to search through the garbage and snatch back your precious pearls and diamond nuggets. Sometimes you have to get a little funk in order to forge ahead. We owe it to ourselves to occasionally sniff out the malodorous scent from our lives and isolate it; either we wash it out or dump it. But it must not stay around. We don't want it around to smell up our clean laundry. Left unchecked, it will do just that.

For those who have complained year after year that they were singled out for a life of despair, just perish that thought. You look at your friends, colleagues, and other relatives, and see the strides they've made in life, and you feel as though you are just barely getting by. You cannot wait for the time to come for you to check out of here once and for all. There is hope. I can assure you that is not the life God wants you to live. He wants you to enjoy life – not endure life. One of the principles I have prided myself on over the years is not to be jealous of other people's accomplishments. Why do some of you keep comparing yourselves with others?

Visiting the past is not always negative. As a child, you've heard your mother singing the praises of Henry Ford, Walt Disney, Frederick Douglass, President Abraham Lincoln, Nelson Mandela, Thomas Edison, and Harriet Tubman. You are able to repeat word for word what she said about those people, but that meant nothing to you. After all, it's the past. Most of those people have long been dead, but their stories are as current as a crisp $100 note today. Mama was calling out those people's names for a reason. She thought that their stories would be the right antidote for your flagging confidence in life. Today, go to your library and read up on those people's lives. Search them out on the internet and peruse until your heart's content.

Some of them were barely schooled, and some were not schooled at all. Others had formal education, but by and large, they all had to go through struggles in order to blaze their trails. They were criticized for being too ambitious; some were imprisoned, while others were castigated publicly. They, too, could have blamed their lot in life and curse God for placing them in the wrong family, the wrong body, and the wrong city. But instead of cursing the darkness, they lit a candle.

Your chore of taking out the trash twice weekly was no match to theirs. You had no cows to milk or chicken coop to clean, or water to fetch before walking five miles to and from school everyday. Sometimes they did so in inclement weather. You didn't have to chop piles of woods for heating and cooking or had to crush stones by hand at the quarry. So keep hope alive. Draw inspiration from them. It's all there at your fingertips.

Even better, do you still have that family Bible Mama left with you? Its passages are chock full of inspirational stories. Read about the lives and times of Moses, Joseph, Esther, Ruth, Paul, and Priscilla. They faced insurmountable struggles, but they never gave up. Like our contemporary counterparts, some were taken into captivity. Others spent time behind prison bars, while some suffered abject poverty. Nevertheless, their eyes were constantly fixed on the prize. They never lost sight of it. They didn't lose hope. They didn't compromise their future with quick fixes. They knew that they had to go through a process. Therefore, they were willing to stay in it for the long haul. They sensed their destinies, but they also knew that they had to go back to the garbage heap now and then. Yes, their stories are old. They are thrown way back in the past, but you know what? Their stories can enrich your life for years to come. Leaf through those pages today and find healing right at your fingertips.

Some of you complain about not having any positive role models in your lives. Everybody you knew is either dead or in jail. But here's your chance to get beyond your comfort zone. Look through the looking glass of hope and see your future. Start out by using those people's lives you've just read about as role models. Great things will happen, by God's grace, for you.

Sometimes when the demons of your past cloud your mind with junk, use those junk as punching bags. Crush them down and use them as fuel for your journey en route to your God-given destiny. For every "You are no good" quote the devil has ever told you, or what your stepfather or even a former classmate told you, convert that into 100 steps to your dream castle. Pop in one of those CDs in your car as you drive to and from work. Remember the one you bought three years ago at the spur-of-the-moment sale? The one you bought at the week-long conference? Play it over and over again. You need to hear that message again. Look around at your CD collection. Bathe your house with music that delivers your mind from fear. They are all at your fingertips. Recall the days when you couldn't come up with the mortgage payment when other bills were due, and how God made a way for you. Yes, I am daring you to go the same route. The same God is at work today. He did it then, and He'll do it again.

THE TRUFFLES OF YOUR PAST

Truffles are some of the most expensive food items found anywhere in the world today. If you were to visit France or Italy, it would amaze you to see where those prized items are cultivated. Hogs and dogs are used to sniff out large soggy plots of ground, most of the times former vegetable fields, to unearth these delicacies. Farmers would gingerly follow behind these animals, and meticulously dig and clean up those truffles to get them ready for sale. At the market, those same truffles that were buried in soggy soil and dug up by swine less than 24 hours earlier, were now fetching upward of $400 per pound from eager shoppers. Picture this, fungi, which were left over from a field, and rummaged through by hogs and dogs, were now commanding an attractive price in the open market.

There are truffles in your seemingly barren wasteland today. Don't mind the hogs and dogs that run about your field, uprooting every square foot in sight. They are there for a purpose. There are truffles of new beginnings; there are truffles of hope and future; there are truffles of prosperity, and there are truffles of happiness. Yes, they are in that same soggy, smelly field that you left two years ago; the same one that caused you so much grief and pain. Start digging selectively today for those truffles. Leave the occasional carrot, turnip, beet, or potato you may stumble upon during your digging. This should be a purpose-directed digging. Snatch them, clean them up, and delicately place them at the right market where they belong. Willing shoppers are ready to pay top dollars for them.

A nurse turned radio personality did just that – converting somebody's put down remarks into success. One of my good friends, Desrene, whom I love and respect dearly, used to tell me about a story at least three times a year. I doubted she was even conscious about the amount of times she was retelling it. I've come to realize that it had profoundly affected her in many ways. Her sharing it with me has prevented me from ever making her mistake in this regard.

She told me that while she was in the sixth grade, the teacher was drilling the class one afternoon shortly after lunch, asking each student what he/she wanted to be when he/she grew up. Everybody had his turn, and when it was time for one particular girl to announce her future avocation, all eyes were focused on that little girl. The smirks were everywhere, and you could hear a pin drop.

I understand why that child was singled out, based on Desrene's description of her. She came from a large family, and funds were sparse. She was often times unkempt. She didn't wear shoes to school and her uniform had a thousand holes and patches in it. Her hair didn't sport the colorful bow ribbons or bubbles like the other girls', and to top it off, she had a perennial sore on her shank. Finally, everyone waited breathlessly for the bomb to drop. I was told the young lady's name, but for privacy sake, I will call her *Karen*.

"So what would you like to become, Karen, when you grow up?" the teacher asked.

Without missing a beat, Karen answered, "When I grow up, Miss, I would like to become a nurse."

The class went into an uproar, spurred on by the popular Desrene. As if that was not enough, Desrene dashed to the black-board, and in bold letters, wrote: "WHAT A SHAME; THE NURSING PROFESSION HAS GONE TO THE DOGS!"

The laughter intensified, with some of the students drumming on the desks with their hands for greater effect. It was out of control, as Desrene told it. The poor teacher could barely control the class for that period. All Karen could do, Desrene said, was to put her head on her desk and sobbed uncontrollably.

With graduation where students moved on to different schools in various locations, Desrene and Karen's paths were never crossed again until about 15 years later.

Being the mother of five children, Desrene was forced to visit the hospital a lot of times with one child or the other for some relief from numerous illnesses. One day her eldest son was sick and she took him to the emergency unit. She was referred to another wing of the hospital, and as she waited, a svelte nurse, armed with a stethoscope around her neck, and clad in pearly whites, introduced herself to Desrene. The woman whose future Desrene had wrong-fully predicted and derided was standing up close and in her face. Desrene thought that she was seeing a ghost. She said that she felt as though she was the patient rather than her son. She felt queasy in the stomach. And if she was standing, she was certain that her legs would have given way, with her falling to the floor. All she was look-ing around for now was the nearest exit, and she couldn't wait for the nurse to be gone for even a minute. She got that opportunity when the nurse had to attend to something else for a short time. Desrene bolted from that hospital with her sick child, and did not walk down those hospital corridors again for years.

Yes, she came face to face with Karen! And while Karen was living her dream, Desrene's dream was somewhat deferred or aborted along the way. With her quest to find out more about the nurse, Desrene would later learn about Karen's every move. Karen left nursing and became a radio personality – over time becom-ing a household name. She was happily married with children, according to Desrene. I, too, used to listen to Karen on and off via her radio program, and many times Desrene and I would listen together. Perhaps that was her reason for rehearsing that story so many times. Did she gain some sort of catharsis from retelling that story? We perhaps will never know.

No power can tell Desrene that Karen didn't become a nurse just to spite her or prove her point that indeed Desrene was flat out wrong. She argued that most little girls' dream then was to become a nurse or teacher, where they would later grow out of it, but it was as if Karen was determined to prove her wrong. I am convinced, too, that Desrene has learnt a big lesson from this. She has become a more humane and personable individual. She is one of the most devoted mothers you could ever find. She's kind, caring, and industrious. By her ongoing benevolence, it's as though she has a lifetime of pen-ance to do for her youthful error in judgment and indiscretions.

Well, as the world can see now, the nursing profession is still in the hands of capable women and men – and it is light years away from being turned over to Rover, Frisky or Bringle – the dogs.

DON'T TRAVAIL IN THE DARK, TRIUMPH!

"WEEPING MAY remain for a night, but rejoicing comes in the morning." – Psalm 30:3.

As a child, I loved going to the country to spend time, but come night, I was scared to death: I couldn't stand to see the pitch-black night, with fireflies dancing their way over the vast expanse of hills and valleys. No, I was never able to get used to it. I could not appreciate the cacophony of croaking frogs, owls, and crickets. It wasn't until I grew up that I could truly enjoy those things. I couldn't wait for morning to hear the roosters crowing. The sun would later bathe the dew-bedecked leaves with its warmth. And we as children would run about with abandon throughout the entire day.

Night was the setting to tell stories of every kind — especially the spooky ones. And oftentimes, the "miracle" bed would hold up to five children huddled together as nobody wanted to go to his assigned bed. Nevertheless, despite the fear of darkness, we became so creative during those periods. Many a song lyric was changed to suit our own. Many of the folklore stories were adapted with starring roles going to our siblings, cousins and friends. Some of those nights had us placed in our dream jobs: majestic estates with maids and gardeners to boot. We would giggle on and on, sometimes drawing the ire of our grandparents, aunts or uncles. Warnings of "go to your bed or else . . .," would not deter us. They were like fodder to us, a way to keep the creative juice flowing. But alas, come morning, those dreams and aspirations would long be forgotten.

Sometimes many of us need to refrain from cursing the darkness and embrace it. Don't be afraid of it; stand up to it. In our times of darkness, we become most creative. When you get fired from that dream job, don't go questioning yourself for months, asking, "Why me?" Ask, "Why not me?" There is a big lesson in the darkness of lost careers. There are larger lessons in the darkness of destitution, despair, drudgery. Find them.

How else then do you explain a single mother of eight who regularly bakes batches of cookies with commonplace pantry items like flour, sugar, and shortening, turning these cookies into a million-dollar fortune? Many times perhaps that mother couldn't pay the light bill; other times her children had to miss the class outing at school, even when the cost was a paltry $2 per student. But a light bulb went off inside her head, and she saw where she could use those readily available ingredients as stepping stones to greatness. She has perfected the many trays of burnt cookies of the past, and is now smiling all the way to the bank.

A HOMELESS MAN
SNATCHED BACK HIS DIAMONDS

Is IT the sign of the times or what? Once upon a time I used to look forward to traveling on airplanes because I was always certain to meet somebody in line or who was seated beside me to make me have a stronger belief in faith or mankind. I had some of the most riveted, real-life conversations in the air. But for the last few years, most of the people who became my seating mates wanted to be left alone, preferring the company of the latest music gadget attached to their ears busy working away on their laptops. Some go off into deep slumber.

I will never forget a gentleman from the Caribbean who struck up a conversation with me while I was waiting for a cross-country flight at New York's JFK Airport. He told me how he was homeless, where each night he didn't know where he would sleep. He slept under open cellars; on public benches, for months — just but anywhere he could find to rest his head. With no money coming his way, he turned to panhandling.

Roasting three corns from the roadside one evening for his dinner, a tourist asked him if he was selling them. He sold him two of the corns and he ate one. Before long, he had a grand idea of buying more fresh corns, and the thoughts of starting a business selling corns infused his mind. Within days, the man who first patronized him went in search of him, asking for more roasted corns. Five more new customers turned into 20; 20 turned into a hundred, and within months, that number exponentially increased to hundreds more. And voila! The dream intensified. He could not keep up with the demand. Therefore, he had to get hired help. He set up a shed where he also included boiled corns; corn soup, mussels and clam soups, roasted fish, among other items. Over time, he added four more joints. All of them raked in thousands of dollars in profit weekly.

In less than two years, this self-made businessman became a force with which to be reckoned, he said. He went on to buy a beachfront home in a tony section of the island, with state-of-the-art gadgets and furnishings. He bought fancy cars. While he perhaps enjoys the luxury of a comfortable home, no doubt his mind every now and then goes back to the dark days of his sleeping from pillow to post. He learnt his lesson from his dark days, and he was able to switch on his light, through God's grace, and keep it burning. Seize those blessings at your fingertips today. What fortune is lurking around your darkness that you can spot? Take advantage of those blessings. He didn't go back in the past to wallow in his hurt; he didn't go back to camp there; he went back to snatch his diamond nuggets of perseverance, resilience, and faith. And they all worked out well for him.

THE BIG HOUSE IN YOUR COMMUNITY

EVERYBODY CAN recall that one family who stood out in the community when he or she was growing up. Remember the family who had the biggest house, the breathtaking landscape, those who made sure to get the first big-screen television, satellite dish or 8-cylinder motorcycle? This family would go on cruises like how people travel on public buses; their children went to the best schools, and so forth. They welcomed Christmas Day by singing carols, the grand piano keeping tune, while they sipped warm apple cider. Their compounds are highly fenced at times, merely affording you a glimpse of "paradise" whenever the gate was swung open.

Many times you were that child who had to walk more than a mile across the train tracks to get to your house. You did so rain or shine since there was no transportation to take you to and fro. You often wondered why God couldn't place you into that family who had everything good going for them. Every time you passed by that house you couldn't help but stare on it — even when you had willed your mind not to do so again, because doing so only made you get madder. You had an alternate route to get home, but you couldn't resist passing by that big house. You didn't know what to think anymore as the object of your admiration sometimes turned to despair.

One glint of hope emerged every now and then, though. That house was the template you would use for your own dream house when you grew up, you said to yourself. You even found ways to change around the majestic columns. You wanted to add a moat instead of the fountain it boasted. You became an architect, engineer, carpenter, mason, electrician, and interior decorator, all wrapped in one by just daydreaming about this house. You grew more detail oriented over time from thinking about this house. You wanted to make sure to plant every detail in your mind so that when the time was right, you could build with ease.

At your house, your mom could barely pay the utility bills. You went for up to three months without the luxury of electricity, and so many nights you had to eat dinner or study by candlelight or lamp. Mama would scrape a few dollars together and pay the light bill, but like clockwork, as soon as the power was on, it would be off again. In the shower, you performed and perfected Diana Ross' *Stop, in the name of love* even when you were not conscious of it, by blocking the cold water from raining down on your body. But over time, your body had gotten so inured to the cold water that it didn't matter any longer. Roaches and mice had become permanent residents in your quarters. But one day you got a chance. A chance that changed your life forever.

That chance of a lifetime came about through a friend's prodding. In fact, you didn't know that he had submitted your resume to HR at his Fortune 500 company. And here you are, you have gotten the job of a lifetime. You don't realize it, but all along that friend saw in you the hallmark of a true survivor. He smelled a winner. Your backwoods days have given way to power lunches and overseas trips. The ragged, hand-me-down clothes have long been traded for designer suits. In fact, you are now rubbing shoulders with some of the occupants of that big house you once admired.

On one of those overseas trips, you felt very much at home, unlike some of your colleagues. But know that during your childhood-suffering days, you were being groomed to weather the harshness of life later on in life. When they were squirming from seeing the sights of mice and roaches, you grew stronger. And while others shivered from the cold wind piercing their bodies, you were saying, "Bring it on!" You have come prepared.

The contract promised a 6-figure salary, and you were not bothered by those temporary inconveniences the least. After all, you had a *big house* to build; you had student loans to pay back, and you had to leaf off a number of those crisp hundred dollar bills for a down-payment on Mama's house, too, to get her out of that roach-infested house across the train tracks. You didn't fuss about the grub of undercooked beans and fish. It was like eating from one of those *"whole pot o' nutten"* Mama made nightly, anyway. The darkness didn't faze you, based on your many nights without light.

Friend, I know that analogy could come across as exaggeration, but never give up hope. You might feel as though you were from the wrong family, school, side of town, or whatever, but know that your *crutches* could bring you *credits* and credentials. The same Creator who gave wealth to the family who stood out in your community way back when, is the same Creator who can turn your midnight into day. What you think is a curse in your life now could very well be a blessing right at your fingertips. Find it today. Don't delay. You've often heard people talk about the good ol' days, but you could never trace back your good ol' days to 20 or 30 years ago. Your good ol' days are now.

All those days of passing by that big house, that boy was storing up treasures; he was educating himself without even knowing it. He became determined, shrewd, and successful. It afforded him the ability to blaze trails his young mind could barely comprehend at the time.

Today, I am challenging you to free up some faith. There are millions of dollars left in the treasury where millionaires get theirs from. Find the source today. God will make a difference. He will allow you to gain influence, favor and acclaim. Search for those blessings at your fingertips. But first, think about some of the things it will take for great things to happen in your life? Will it take a loan or a grant for you to kick start that new business? Remember, many successful companies today like Amazon and eBay started out with a grant. If you have to beg, buy or borrow, make it happen this year. Snatch back those diamond nuggets from your past. They cannot wait to sparkle for you again. In the meantime, be encouraged by what Paul has to say in Romans 15:4.

"For everything that was written in the past was written to teach us so that through endurance and encouragement of the Scriptures we might have hope."

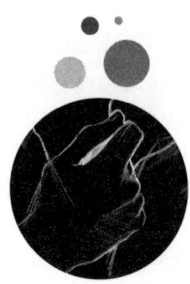

CHAPTER THIRTEEN

DARE TO BE INCONVENIENCED

"*EVERY ADVERSITY, EVERY FAILURE AND* every heartache carries with it the seed of an equivalent or greater benefit." – Napoleon Hill.

I read with fascination the story of Michael Lee Chin, a Jamaican of Chinese descent. As a cash-strapped foreign student studying in Toronto, Canada, in the late 1960s, he faced a daunting dilemma: All he had to his name was $600 Canadian. His tuition was $2,000. He didn't have any relatives or friends in Canada to either give or lend him the money to continue his education.

Nevertheless, he thought up a wonderful plan. Chin wrote to the then Jamaican Prime Minister, Hugh Shearer, telling him that he noticed that every year the prime minister would send an emissary to recruit fourth-year graduates from the Canadian university. Shearer responded by inviting the student to see him the next time Chin was in Jamaica. Using $400 of his $600 to purchase a plane ticket to Jamaica, he convinced Shearer to fund his way through university. He promised to help Jamaica bountifully in the future.

Well, it would appear that Chin had the gift of persuasion or that Shearer was prescient, because in less than no time, Chin was back in Canada, armed with a 3-year scholarship for him to complete his degree.

"That is the beginning of my indebtedness to Jamaica, because without that scholarship I would not have completed university," the billionaire said.

He supplemented his earnings by working as a bouncer at a night club. It would take some years for Chin's aspiration to come to fruition, but today, this self-made Jamaican-Canadian billionaire made true to his promise after amassing great wealth in the real estate and financial markets. He was instrumental in purchasing the moribund 400-branch National Commercial Bank. He further plunked down hundreds of millions of dollars more on office buildings, hotels, and other prime real estates. He built a state-of-the-art, 350-bed nursing school/hospital in central Jamaica with his own money. He is such an asset to Jamaica today. What a blessing!

But think back. Suppose Shearer had not given him that money for his tuition, where would the spate of Jamaica's economy be today without a Chin? Every time you look around, Chin is purchasing, building something or giving away something to a worthy cause in Jamaica. That gift comes back full circle, as my sister-in-law holds a very prestigious position in one of this big-hearted mogul's corporations.

I don't know whether or not that money, in the form of a scholarship, Shearer gave him was taken from the country's exchequer or Shearer's personal account. I couldn't say how many people were temporarily inconvenienced by that sacrifice. But today all I can say is that Jamaica is a thousand times better for that one selfless act of generosity.

TEMPORARY INCONVENIENCE, PERMANENT GOOD

IT WAS the day before Christmas and David Connelly called to ask what my family would be doing for Christmas. I told him that after turning down a few invitations from friends, we decided to just hunker down at our humble pad and do dinner for the five of us. After listening to David's story, I had a change of plans. Fast. This young man has been living in Seattle for a few years now, having left his dad and siblings in Ohio for military work here. His mother died some years ago, which has created a void for David. He has not been home for any of the major holidays, his spending them sometimes alone here in Seattle.

"Man, I'm forcing myself to go to work tomorrow, not that I want to, but because I don't have anything better to do on Christmas Day," the 27-year-old man said midway through our conversation.

"Come over tomorrow," I said. "We would be most honored to host you for dinner."

"What time should I show up?" he asked, not missing a beat. "By the way, what should I bring?"

"Around 5 o'clock is good," I said. ". . . Come as you are."

"Don't you want some Squirt?" he teased.

"Bring some if you wish," I said.

He knew how much I love that grapefruit-flavored drink since he first introduced it to me some two years ago.

You could readily hear the change in his voice – a change of hope – that somebody cared.

Jevaughn and I had been running a few errands dropping off dinners and gifts to a few friends, and 5 o'clock was fast approaching. I called David to tell him that I was running late, and he said that he was about three minutes away from my home. He said he would wait at my house until I made it back. Yvonne and the rest of the boys hosted him until I got home.

Upon reaching home, we embraced each other and we set to work getting dinner ready. We had quite a cornucopia of foods to choose from: Cornish hens, rib eye steak, ham, pork tenderloin, among other things. David only nibbled away at his cornish hen, with a spoonful here and there of rice and vegetables.

It then dawned on me that he was not merely hungry for food but friendship. A two-year old child could eat what he ate at the table and still begged for more. As we engaged each other with diverse conversations, he became alive. He later pushed his cornish hen aside, preferring a "doggie" bag to take home.

"So where is the Squirt you said you were going to bring?" I asked jokingly. He made a sheepish smile, and pretty much ignored me for the next 15 minutes. The young man later got up for a moment and started fumbling for something in his coat pocket.

"Here, you guys can replenish some of that food you've always been giving me," his bass voice boomed, while he handed me a gift card from one of the supermarkets in our area. I couldn't believe what I was seeing or hearing.

"Oh, that means I can buy myself a few extra bottles of the Squirts you didn't bring," I ribbed him.

Before the night was over, he told us that the card valued $50. I am still in shock, not by the value, but by the way how we could let blessings pass through our hands like that had we been reticent to invite him over. My mind drifted to a scenario where three more zeros could have been attached to that amount from another source. It helped me to realize that many times things/situations get in our way as tests, and it's how you deal with those situations that will pass you or fail you. I am glad that my family and I were willing to inconvenience ourselves to share our blessings with a young man who in turn, blessed us, not only monetarily but with love and grace.

As the evening progressed, our youngest son, Jason – the geography buff in the family – started to show off on David by asking him the name of states/capitals/countries. Little did he know that David competed in the Junior National Geography Bee as a teenager. David agreed to tutor him in geography over the next few months. This I considered another blessing right at my fingertips. I now know that temporary inconvenience can bring about permanent good.

I cannot begin to tell you the ton of good that David has brought to our lives. When I wanted to meet somebody who had knowledge about Forex trading, it was David who came to my rescue, introducing me to his friend, Joe. I wasn't feeling well one day while I was driving home from a meeting, and one telephone call did it: David came and drove behind me all the way home, and made certain that I was safe. How can I ever repay such kindness? But, again, if you dare to be inconvenienced for the sake of others, then it will come back to you. David is a living proof of that.

NO PAIN, NO GAIN

WHENEVER I go to the gym and have to lift those weights, a thousand and one excuses would cross my mind why today would not be the right day. I would say tomorrow or next week, but those days sometimes never come. But when I dare to go in, sweat profusely, sustaining some aches and pains temporarily, in the long run I will have started seeing a markedly changed man. Plain and simple, "no pain, no gain." Thus in order to get to the next level spiritually and physically, inconvenience is imminent. There's no getting around it. It's a must.

POWER OUTAGE STRENGTHENS THE BOND

IT WAS late Saturday evening, and we had just returned from feeding and giving out gifts to a group of homeless families, when we decided to face a third night of darkness at home. A windstorm had swept the Pacific Northwest, wreaking havoc for more than a million residents in its swath. Gargantuan trees toppled power lines and homes, while people found shelters hither and yon among relatives and friends. Some went to hotels. But we decided to stay the course, settling in our dark, dank space.

Earlier that morning, we stopped by to check up on a few friends, and one of them in particular was dressed in about eight layers of clothing. She invited us in for breakfast, made on her interminable fire in her fireplace. She made scrambled eggs and toast, with the skillful hands of a pro. We laughed, chatted for awhile, and then we went on to meet up with the multiple volunteers at a local church to host homeless families. I was completely flabbergasted to see so many volunteers, displaced by the windstorm, show up to help the homeless. They were without power and heat, but the smiles on their faces seemingly could have lit the world.

When I pondered how the homeless had lived without the basic hot showers/baths, heated homes, microwave ovens, etc., throughout the year, what many of us take for granted, there was no power that could stop me from showing up that Saturday afternoon.

So it was in that spirit we came home to make do with what we had, and be joyful in the meantime. We draped the living room in African prints, festooned with candles and ethnic artifacts. The fireplace was going full blast as the two younger boys stoked the fire. The rest of us sat around as if we were in an African village with a *griot* telling stories. We started regaling each other with fire stories, which branched off into anecdotes of all sorts; suddenly, we heard a knock on the door. When I inquired, it was one of Jevoy's classmates who said his grandmother was outside, beckoning for us to come to her house since their power had been restored.

"It's okay; we're fine. Tell your grandmother that we are fine," I said. Within minutes, the grandmother stormed her way into our living room, not taking no for an answer. "Come, come, come, you have to leave now. This is not safe," she implored.

When we told her how our friend made breakfast for us over the fireplace, she said that may be good 200 years ago, but it was not cool in this day and age. I was still adamant in our not leaving, and after she persisted, I decided to send the boys along with her. Yvonne and I continued telling stories and reflected on God's many blessings in our lives. We were happy to be inconvenienced temporarily, to evince the joy of thanksgiving even though Christmas was nine days away. About two hours after the boys had left, the power came back, and Yvonne somewhat felt disappointed for its coming back on so soon.

The Friday night Yvonne and I were out, and when we got back, the boys were huddled on our bed. Nobody had begged to go to his room, so we all crashed on that king-sized bed until in the wee hours of the morning.

"I would like to see the light come back, but seeing you guys come home safely means a lot more to me than having power again," voiced Jevaughn. To say the least, I was truly touched hearing his comment. It took our being inconvenienced to unearth some of our deepest sentiments to share among each other. Make the best of those inconvenient moments, and reap those blessings right at your fingertips.

I was discussing the power outage with a lady a few weeks after the storms, and she told me of her story some 10 years ago. She said that on Thanksgiving Day that year, as soon as the turkey got out of the oven, the power went out. Since no candied yams, mashed potatoes and other feast-time goodies were prepared, they had no choice but to eat the turkey, along with some cold rolls, in front of a lit fireplace. They played a multiple of games and bantered one another until the light came back on about 10 o'clock that night. But she said that her children still consider that Thanksgiving Day the best one ever.

INCONVENIENCE GIVING
BIRTH TO DREAMS

As FAR back as I can recall growing up, my home was never without transient people. Whether it was a cousin coming in from the country to finish his studies in Kingston or an aunt who had to do doctor's appointments at the regional hospital. It was the occasional itinerant pastor or the middle-aged woman seeking refuge from her abusive common law husband. Our house was never without sojourners. Sometimes my dad would rent out a room to families who were down on their luck, and that would inconvenience our family yet again. He wasn't renting that room for financial gains, as many times months would pass without those "tenants" paying him a red cent. In hindsight, I am surmising that he wanted permanent babysitters for us in the form of tenants.

A week would pass after somebody moved out, and I would finally be happy to get more room at home, but my hope would come crashing down with yet another hard-luck story. And my dad would be quick to oblige. I am not ashamed to say that I did not sleep by myself until I was in my mid teenage years. Sleeping by myself was a luxury. Even going to bed alone didn't guarantee my waking up alone.

Here is a classic example: I had summered in the country with my great-grandmother, and those country folks seemingly looked forward to going to funerals. They put on their Sunday best and took time off to be with the family. A few months shy of my eleventh birthday, my great-grandmother took me to my second funeral – the first one being Mr. Tabb less than two months earlier.

The dead woman was laid out in final repose behind the back of the house. Large chunks of ice covered the top of the galvanized zinc, which housed her body. I was commanded to sleep in the bed where she had died in just days earlier. I tried to rebel, but I was no match for the grownups. On funeral day, I was warned not to stare too much on the dead, but I had enough viewing to serve 10 more people. I ignored that rule.

After I had been away from my great-grandmother's home for about four days, she and I returned home at last in the thick of darkness. I hurriedly went to bed, and all I could see in my mind's eye was that dead woman lying in her coffin. I might have tried to turn around on my bed, and lo and behold, I felt somebody beside me. I yelled so hard that other neighbors were forced to get up. I was running around in the darkness, thinking that the dead woman was beside me.

"It's me; it's me, Wilfred," a voice said in hushed tones. But I was not comforted the least. The chamber pot was all spilled, the floor now awash in urine. I found out in the morning that Wilfred, a community hobo of sorts, was doing one of his stopovers. He had a heart of gold, but I did not know of Wilfred owning a place to lay his head at night. He would take turn sleeping with families and friends until somebody got tired of him and sent him moving. I didn't mind being inconvenienced by Wilfred as he was one of the kindest people I have ever met. He taught me how to fish, swim and climb towering waterfalls.

Back in Kingston, our erstwhile transient people seemed to pass on a sixth sense to their progeny, prevalent in salmon and penguins. These so-called extended cousins would find back their way home to us just like what their mothers or fathers had done 15 years earlier. And they would have no problem adjusting to our environment. It's no wonder that whenever I watch migratory salmon going upstream to spawn, I get a chuckle in remembrance of our ever spawning home of my childhood.

From our being temporarily inconvenienced, our humble homestead had been the launching pad for many of our transient relatives and friends. Today some of them are teachers, business-men, police officials, just to name a few. My uncle who taught me how to make whistle was one of those transient people who lived with us for more than a year. As I have detailed earlier, his teaching me how to make whistles had yielded a ton of blessings for me and countless other people.

Inconvenience has taught me to make the best of an otherwise unpleasant situation. Hence, my being peeved when those boys had to leave while the power was out. I felt that they could have learnt some invaluable lessons about survival and gratitude in that darkness that could later blaze trails for bigger and better things down the road. If I come across as being stoical in despair, it's just my defense mechanism kicking in to weather the storms. I am not easily tossed by any and every wind. My years of being inconvenienced have anchored me sound and deep to face and withstand any situation. If it's not a *Katrinaesque* disaster, then I will not be moved.

At our home, it's very hard for us to cook a meal for one sitting. And that has been a legacy from as far back as I can remember. At any given time, four people could show up without prior notice and they would not leave without eating from the family pot. If there was not enough, parents would see to it that there was enough.

If you are a pastor mulling over the rapid departure of your organist, don't lose hope with this temporary inconvenience. You could be simply freeing up a spot for the talented Geena or Nigel who will be a great asset to your congregation.

Perhaps you are that mother who wants to go back to school to make yourself more marketable, don't despair while you are being inconvenienced to carve out something more meaningful for you and your family.

You are that young woman who gave your all to the dashing man you called your soulmate. You have invested a lot of time in that relationship, thinking after five years, it could only get better. Now, out of nowhere he dropped the bombshell, telling you it's over. You begged. You beseeched. But he will not budge. Yes, your heart is broken. You now cry without ceasing, but know that weeping may last for a night but joy will come in the morning. Probably you have been crying for more than a hundred mornings, but don't lose hope. That joy is on its way. Your temporary inconvenience with matters of the heart is about to give way to legions of blessings. Believe it. Make way for the real deal – for that man who will love you unconditionally – your faults and all.

If you are that young man who finds it hard to connect intimately with that special someone because of your extreme niceness, don't lose hope. You have brought flowers and sent cards to that girl, who over time, has taken your love for granted. Actually, every woman you have dated since high school has resulted in the same way. You're about to throw in the towel and say, "enough is enough!" But remember God has that perfect woman waiting for you out there. Don't fight any longer. Don't beat up on yourself. You will be happy. You will be loved. Your temporary inconvenience will yield great dividends.

FLYING THE CONCORDE WITH STANDBY TICKETS

I USED to hear old people saying this line, "What is for you cannot be un-for you." And if you stop to think about it, there is definitely some credence to that maxim. Many times, though, be prepared to go through several periods of inconveniences, but if you are patient enough, being inconvenienced will pay off for you. I recall a story one Mr. Williams told me some years ago. He bought roundtrip standby tickets from JFK Airport in New York to Heathrow in London via British Airways. Because of the limited nature of his ticket, he decided to go to the airport early so that he would stand a good chance of getting on a flight, and not returning home. He doggedly watched the departure screen to see which flight would be out next. A surge of excitement enveloped his body every time a flight was due to leave. That anxiety would push him up to the ticket counter several times where an irate woman constantly shooed him back to his seat. She talked down to him a few times, but he couldn't control his urge to go back to her again and again.

"Sir, if I have to tell you again, then. . . !" she chastised him. He felt as though the woman had it out for him or that she was having a bad day. Nevertheless, he kept his ground by exercising patience.

A Concorde landed and he whiled away by daydreaming about flying on that regal iron bird. He stared on it nonstop, wondering what was the inside like. He entertained grand thoughts of flying on it someday. Perhaps soon, when at least he could get some respect, and not get put into his place by a miserable agent. At that time, he consoled himself, he wouldn't have to suffer the disdain of flying on standby tickets again.

As he tried to refresh his thoughts, trying to see which other flight was due to leave out, the cranky woman beckoned for him to come to her. She cordially gave him his boarding pass, and wished him well on his transatlantic flight to London. He couldn't believe what she was saying to him. In fact, he went back to her to verify whether or not he was boarding the right flight, and the irate side of her was coming out again. She assured him that, indeed, he was going on that flight.

As Williams walked to the plane, his dream less than an hour before became a reality. His knees were buckling, he said, but he made it safely to his seat. He was stupefied. He was flying the Concorde – the world's most prestigious airlines – for less than $300! He talked about the gold-embossed menu they handed out; the chinaware; the gift bags with expensive colognes, champagne, the pampered treatment, and so forth. It was a joy to watch him and hear him tell that story. His eyes were ablaze with excitement as his voice crescendoed to a bliss that could only be matched by the apostle John who so colorfully described the New Jerusalem in the Book of Acts.

On his way back to New York, while checking in at Heathrow, a ticket agent took his ticket, and her fingers danced frantically on the computer keyboard. She had a strange look on her face, but he didn't take it for anything much. He was smelling the Concorde.

"Mr. Williams, you are telling me that you flew the Concorde on a standby ticket? And I have been working with British Airways for more than 16 years and not setting foot on that plane?" She went on to tell him that somebody's job somewhere was on the line, mumbling off into something else. He was put on a regular flight back to JFK, doing coach. What a bummer!

The Concorde has now been permanently grounded, and Williams said that he would spend $10,000 of his own money tomorrow to fly on it if it were ever to fly again. One of the Concordes is on display at the Museum of Flights in Seattle at Boeing Field. I took a tour onboard with my boys last year, and truly I could get a semblance of what Williams told me. What is for you, will come to you. And whenever you are inconvenienced, look out for a great reward.

THE SUBWAY HERO

IN EARLY January 2007, television and cable news broadcast around the world featured a New York man who rescued a student after that student fell onto the subway tracks. I was hardly surprised to see such selfless demonstration of love and kindness. New York has had its share of racial tensions over the years, but that was a classic example of New Yorkers reaching out to each other despite racial and socio-economic differences. The Good Samaritan was black and the student white. But giving aid to a helpless person sees no color.

For those 20 minutes of being inconvenienced under tons of iron and metal, the Good Samaritan and his family were rewarded with a lifetime of goodies. Within days, he was cited by Mayor Michael Bloomberg at City Hall, and Donald Trump presented him with a check for $10,000. The New York Transit System gave him a year's worth of free rides on its trains and buses. And the gifts kept rolling in from all corners of the earth. Hence, it's a good reminder to all of us that doing good and being inconvenienced for a worthy cause will not go unnoticed. There are a lot of blessings abound from such deeds.

There is a benefit at hand when you've being inconvenienced. Look at the widowed woman who had to sacrifice her food, inconveniencing herself and that of her son, to give Elijah the prophet some food from her meager portion. And as the story goes, because of her obedience, she could not find enough containers to store oil and flour. Bob Marley sang, "A hungry man is an angry man," and for most of us, isn't that the truth? Only a few other forms of emotions can bring about anger and frustration like hunger. So, for that woman to be calm and cool in preparing a meal for the prophet, her character spoke volumes about her. She didn't roll her eyes or make the Z formation with her head by telling Elijah, "Who-do-you-think-you-are, old man? My son and I have been starving and you have the audacity to come out here and ask us for food! Where are your scruples?" But because of her inconvenience and obedience, she passed the test. A lot of times, obedience is directly linked with those acts of kindness.

It pains my heart just to relegate her to being a friend because Sybil is even much closer to me than some of my own relatives. I would give a kidney to her tomorrow if such a need ever arises with no question asked. That's how much I adore that woman. She has been a tower of strength to me and my family, and I trust that many people will come to have a Sybil in their lives like the one we know.

Indeed, it was no surprise when she told me about her new neighbors in a Toronto suburb who needed extra space to store some of their furniture until their basement was fully complete. She gave up her two-car garage in lieu of their using it for temporary storage. She refused any kind of financial remunerations. But as the saying goes, one hand washes the other. The new neighbors are so grateful for Sybil's gesture that they are beside themselves. It was established from that point on that Sybil should not be seen shoveling snow, a decree from her neighbor's husband. And who wouldn't welcome such a respite from the Toronto snow?

Out of her temporary inconvenience, Sybil has found one of the most priceless relationships with that family. She considers the family's moving into the neighborhood as nothing short of a blessing.

Go out of your way to bless others. Bill Gates gave millions of dollars to the poor worldwide; Oprah Winfrey and the Angel Network also funded million-dollar projects in the U.S. and abroad. Jimmy Carter and Habitat for Humanity made thousands of people own their own homes because of their tireless contributions to better lives.

Some of you say, "I don't have Bill Gates and Oprah Winfrey's money to change lives." Others say that they don't have the foresight of a Jimmy Carter. But you know what? You can make a difference. Your teenagers can give two hours a week at neighboring hospitals, bringing water or flowers to patients. You can help out the single mother who is overrun by five active kids. Help cook dinner for her and take some of the children to the park for picnic and fun. Don't underestimate the role you will play. God sees your heart, and He will reward you most handsomely.

In the lives of David and Joseph, we see how much they suffered at the hands of jealous and spiteful people. Some of you are feeling that your punishment is that dead-end job at the juvenile home for the last five years. Your schedules are constantly chang-ing, and you feel as though the supervisor has it out for you. You want to advance your studies but you feel trapped. Don't despair. You are in that job for a reason. Before you embark on those new courses, there are a few books you need to read, and with your constant sitting down at your desk, with hardly anything more to do, you have all the time on your hand to get through those books. Reading valuable lessons from those books, you will be poised to rise to greatness. Don't be dismayed.

You have a few miscreants to talk out of murder and theft. Abandonment. Low self-esteem. And only your words will be able to reach them. They are disrespectful to everybody, but for some strange reason, they cling to every word you have to say. So while you are mewling about being singled out for something bad you did in the past, God is building up within you character, devotion, love and trust. You are being groomed to be somebody. Don't worry about the mixed-up schedules and the low pay. Today's inconvenience will be tomorrow's blessings.

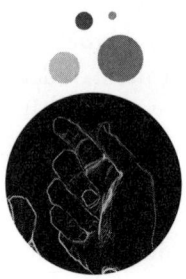

CHAPTER FOURTEEN

THERE IS SOMETHING IN A NAME

I COULDN'T WAIT TO MEET HER. THE LADY, I was told, who makes things happen. I had made some cold calls to her office a few days earlier, and was elated when I got the chance to come and showcase my goods and services to some of that company's movers and shakers. The executive assistant scheduled a time and date for me to meet the vice-president of the prestigious company. And I was determined to nail that account.

I seem to beat every red light in sight for my 10-mile journey. I am trying to avoid the downtown lunch-hour traffic. I must not be late. A sizeable account is in the offing. I am nattily attired in my business suit, well-starched shirt, and my favorite tie. The one I tend to get favorable compliments with. The same one I bought for $3 at the corner of 46th Street and Third Avenue in New York City 11 years earlier. I am depending on it today again to work some charm for me. Phew! I am about a minute shy of my appointment. Things are looking good. Good product. Good company. Good, sunny day. Good tie.

"Hello, Nandell, I am Joella Collins," says the genteel woman, extending her hand for a handshake. I am detecting a patrician economy of gesture from her. She radiates the room with her 100-watt, pearly-white smile, while a coterie of assistants looks on happily in the background. She beckons for me to come to the boardroom. But there seems to be a few things that need to be straightened out before we proceed.

I should know better, but since I only have limited time for the meeting, I am yearning to cut through the chase; throw formality overboard, and get down to business. I am not always like this, but today I have a lot of things to cover. And I need to do them fast.

"It's a pleasure meeting you, jo-ELLA," I mumble, ensuring that I call out the part I am familiar with — *Ella*. In a nanosecond, this woman grabs me by the shoulders with her two hands, looks straight into my eyes, and says loudly but slowly for everybody to hear.

"The name is Jo-el-la Col-lins, sir!"

She makes sure to break down her name in syllables. The 100-watt smile wipes off her face like a solar eclipse, which I am surmising will spell doom for me or any business prospect I have been entertaining. I am feeling like dirty laundry, ready for the wastebasket. My good tie and all. She is not letting go of me until I pronounce her name correctly. It is a spectacle for everyone looking on. I don't think I am doing any better the second time around, pronouncing her name. But I am still trying. A sheepish smile is slowly creeping back to her face; I am surmising it is to lighten the moment.

Well, to say the least, after displaying my product to Ms. Collins and her staff, her promise to follow up was never materialized. And while there could be other factors involved as to why that company did not offer me a contract, I still believe that my less-than-flattering attitude, improperly pronouncing Ms. Collins' name, cost me that deal. I called her office a few more times, making sure each time to rehearse the name before calling. But alas, it was too late. That bungling will go down in the annals of life as one of my most embarrassing moments.

The day was March 13, 2004, a day I will never soon forget. It has been more than three years now, but it is not possible for me to ever mispronounce that name again as long as I live. I also walked away learning a very big, big lesson that day, at the expense, I would say, of a coveted account: Make sure you go out of your way to call people's names properly. Show the utmost respect when calling their names. If you do, many times you will have them eating from the palm of your hands. And if you don't, it could spell doom and gloom for you.

According to William Shakespeare, "Good name in a man and woman is the immediate jewels of their souls." It is also said that a name can make you or break you. Furthermore, we've heard it said that when life gives you lemon, then make lemonade. In other words, if your name is one of those hard-to-pronounce names, then go out of your way to make sure that people call it correctly. And Joella did just that.

Finding the perfect name for a baby is a nerve-wracking experience on its own. Parents face societal pressures to stay politically correct. Some want to hold on to familial allegiance, naming their son or daughter after a beloved grandmother, grandfather, aunt, uncle, etc. Some parents want to stay classic, while others want to feel that they have come of age; therefore, their baby's name should reflect this newfound independence.

Nowhere this independence is more prominent than within North America. For the last 30 years or so, the world has welcomed enough *Sheniquas, Shequondas, Nilquon, Derowgees,* and *DaShawns* to fill the state of Texas side by side, and the names are getting more colorful as I write. But do we blame these parents or do we commiserate with them? Some argue that they have to get back to their roots – Africa – the motherland, as a way for them to feel connected. But the reality is that coasting from Nairobi, Kenya to Dakar, Senegal or from Alexandria, Egypt to Johannesburg, South Africa, most likely you will not hear the aforementioned names in any of those countries.

Since these innocent boys and girls are given these names by well-intentioned parents, will these children's names become liabilities instead of assets? Do these names spell out a clear future for these children or do they foretell stagnation? What a lot of people fail to understand is that for the most part, Africans painstakingly think about names long and hard before giving them to their progeny. In fact, many of their cultures have naming ceremonies days after the birth of a child. The name has to mean something to the family, community, and tribe. One of my friends from Nigeria named all of his children after money. For example, one child's name means "money is in the house." Another is, "Money is on its way to the house." You will never find them at a loss for words explaining what the meaning of their names is. We see that commonality in the country of India, in the Jewish community, the North American Indian communities, and among royalty. Is it any wonder then why names like Charles, Elizabeth, Henry, James, Victoria, etc., are around for centuries? There is something in a name.

JEWISH TRADITIONS AND NAMES

EVER SINCE the Abrahamic Covenant by way of circumcision, names have always played an important role in Jewish lives. In a ceremony called *bris*, literally meaning covenant, 8-day-old baby boys are circumcised and given a name, borrowing from the principles found in Genesis 17:10. Jesus himself, being a Jew, had to undergo this process as well. Naming your child was not something you took out from the Baby Book, which sounded cute. The name had to mean something. Your name was significant.

Even God changed people's names to make them reflect the true purpose of those individuals: *Abram* to Abraham; *Sarai* to Sarah, *Jacob* to Israel, and so forth. Good names are blessings. All of these names over time have taken on characteristics of their own. These truisms that are reflected in these names are like wind in those people's sails. Many of them go through life feeling confident.

Among one of the major highlights of the birth of a Hebrew child, was getting a name. The primary reason for giving that child the right name was pretty much as a foreshadowing of his or her future. The name was to denote the child's personality. As a result, proud moms and pops would go out of their way to choose the right nomenclature that they deem bode well for their children's future. A lot of responsibilities came with that name. And often times it was incumbent on that child to live up to his name, whether for the earlier part of her life or the latter part of his life. For example, Joseph's name means, "May he add." And what an addition he was to his family – even for generations to come. He *added* prestige. He *added* favors. He *added* calm where there was chaos. He *added* forgiveness instead of bitterness. While others veered away from the responsibilities of their names, as we can see, the name Joseph was definitely not a misnomer.

What is your name saying about you today? Have you lived up to it? Has it opened doors or closed doors for you? Well, if there is no etymology on your name, write one denoting an expectant future, teeming with all the great blessings from God. If you are having difficulty accepting your name even in adulthood, write yourself a blessing today with the meaning of your name. Some of you are gifted, you are outgoing, brilliant, but the world wouldn't know that. Begin to shine today. Start feeling good about yourself. It starts by doing something about your name. If there's no record or etymology of your name, write a glowing one: "My name is Justirena and it means a blessed woman of God, who has been gifted with . . . Justirena means tower of strength, savvy and articulate. And I am all that and more." Practice it on yourself until you believe it. It works.

Find a quiet place today. Sit down with a piece of paper, and with a marker, pen or pencil, begin to write your name on your heart. Imprint it on your brain. Consciously write every letter with the feeling of a blessed person, because indeed you are blessed. When you do so, you are positioning yourself for greatness. Draw from the reservoir of blessings. Incorporate your name in your daily devotion. Start converting pronouns like you, I, and me into your tangible name. For example, in Psalm 91:4, "He will cover you with his feathers, and under his wings you will find refuge." The converted version would be: "He will cover *Charmaine* with His feathers, and under His wings *Charmaine* will find refuge." How about this one? "Though *Herman Warren* walks through the valley of the shadow of death, *Herman Warren* will fear no evil."

Align your name with greatness. You may be without a vocation, but be audacious enough to write your name as Michael Brown, Esq. It will be a foreshadowing to being that attorney you've long aspired to be.

You currently work as a home health aide, but this is just a job you do to pay the bills. God has a lot more in store for you. Go ahead now and write out Desrene Morgan, RN. Jay Chang, future millionaire. Just don't have it bottled up somewhere in your mind, make sure you manifest it on paper. Write it down. It helps also to say it out loud every now and then. Don't lose sight of it. Visualize it. Feel it. Taste it. Touch it.

I am not encouraging fraud – people going about writing *esq.* and *RN* on job applications or formal letters when in fact they have not held those positions. Doing so is fraudulent. What I am advocating is the essence of living to your fullest potential. And I strongly believe that if many of us start associating ourselves with our future endeavors, before long we'll start seeing positive changes in all arenas of our lives.

One popular song bellows, "I've got the power!" Start believing that you, too, have the power via God's divine power. "His divine power has given us everything we need." Draw from that source today. Get plugged in. With God, all things are possible. Do what you can do and let God do what you cannot do. God will provide the means to buy you a pair of shoes, but certainly He will not put them on for you. He has allowed your parents to give you a name, but He cannot make you feel good about your name until you fully accept it. That job belongs to you.

Just picture a brilliant student in a science class who wants to be challenged beyond her classroom assigned work. To do so, most likely she would have to do further research during her spare time. One Monday morning, out of nowhere, she presents a paper on the pros and cons of *in vitro* fertilization to her teacher. Since her teacher didn't give her that assignment, what a surprise for that teacher when he's presented with a 10-page paper on this scholarly work from his 14-year-old prized student. All of her sources are fully referenced, backed up with proper spelling for those scientific jargons. I strongly doubt that her teacher would ever frown and berate her for going ahead of the class to do something that was not assigned. I could see a proud teacher congratulating his student and showing off her work to every colleague in the lunchroom. That girl would have no problem getting recommendations from that teacher even after 20 years later. She will have carved a way out for her future because she was proactive. Because of her extra work, too, that could open many doors to an MIT, Harvard, Yale or Princeton, with a full scholarship to boot. Recruiters would seek her out instead of her seeking them out. Why? Because she was proactive about her future.

That is how I liken our existence on earth. I alluded to this in an earlier chapter, and it's worth repeating here, too. God is not going to hold your hand to do every minor task. But He will allow you to do things on your own. He will not tell you how short you should wear your hair or which social club you should join. He will not tell you whether you should plant begonias in your garden or daffodils. He will not care if *Rene* is also spelled *Renny*. If you want to drive a Mercedes Benz for five years, that will be okay with Him or if you want to ride a bicycle or a rickshaw for the rest of your life, that's fine with Him, too.

Nevertheless, if you want to raise the bar in your physical or spiritual life, he will sanction your decision. Like the proud teacher who sanctions his student's unassigned work, God is ready and waiting to sanction your unassigned work. He's ready to give you thumbs up for thinking outside of the box and being proactive. If it's something that He feels is in your best interest, He'll give you the go-ahead, but if it's to your detriment, He will veto it.

Hence, he will honor your request when you take it upon yourself to be empowered by your name. He will see to it that every good thing that you request for your name to denote will be fully evinced before long. Don't tarry; start that extra assignment today. Not because you have personally heard about or known of many examples where name actualization is documented, doesn't mean it is not effective. Your name, when you decide to examine it and make the necessary changes, will become a tenfold blessing for you. Try it today.

JEZEBEL, TRYPHENA AND TRYPHOSA

WE ALL want the best lives for our children, based on the names we choose for them. That's why no meaningful parents would name their beloved daughter *Jezebel*, which is translated to mean daughter of garbage in Hebrew. They would never name their son *Hitler*, albeit a last name. And although *Tryphena* means delicate and *Tryphosa* means dainty, I doubt any ambitious mother would be eager to name her twin daughters these names found in Romans 16:12. Your name should mean something just like how it is documented for the following people: Zöe – life; Peter – rock; Hilary – cheerful; Ethel – noble; Clement – merciful; Barack – blessing; Amos – burden bearer. Why don't you add Sheniqua as regal; Nilquon as resilient, and Tawana as caring?

Some cultures, like the Ashanti tribe in Ghana, West Africa, have elaborate naming structures in place for both men and women. For example, if a boy/man were to tell you the day of the week in which he was born, that country's people could readily determine his generic first name: *Kwabena*, Sunday; *Kojo*, Monday; *Kwesi*, Tuesday, and so forth. In fact, former UN Secretary Kofi Annan, by just hearing his name, a native could tell you that he was born on a Friday, and that he is from the Ashanti tribe.

DIASPORAN BLACKS AND NAMES

SOME DIASPORAN blacks throughout the Americas and Europe have argued that they can hardly feel good about their names because every time their forefathers were on the auction block, inevitably there would be a name change. Hence, in one slave's lifetime, he would have gone through five name changes, depending on how stable he was to one family or the other. He could go from Taylor to Clarke to Gayen to Brown to Campbell and to Knight without feeling any allegiance to any of those names. After all, he was viewed as chattel possession, not human. And so, his name became a lesser part of his persona. We see how Kunta Kente in the *Roots* saga rebelled against being called Toby, to the point of near death.

Well, apart from Kunte Kente and Alex Haley, only a few diasporan blacks can ever trace their lineage back to their homeland. Thanks in part to scientific studies, with DNA analysis more and more families are trying to make some connection to their past. But in most cases, all that remains in those regions is just oral history, and no concrete name to build from. Nevertheless, there is hope in feeling good about the name you currently carry. Make it yours. It all starts with being proactive. Allow that name to work for you despite its less than sterling past.

Some of you perhaps are saying, "He has the nerves to be criti-cizing other people's names when his own is no better." And I would agree with you – to a certain degree. For a number of years, I had the hardest time accepting my given name, *Nandell*. I had made several attempts to legally change it, but could not bring myself to do it. As far back as I can remember, I have always felt duplicitous because at school I was known as Nandell, but at home or among my neighbor-hood friends, everybody called me Jimmy. That would get even more complicated when others started to call me James. "Isn't Jimmy short for James?" they would ask.

Many times I felt like a scam artist by the way how people would look at me when they heard me answer to a different name from the one I had told them 20 minutes earlier. I can just see those eyebrows arching and lips puckering for a verbal contretemps. "Didn't you just tell me that . . . ?"

My dad said that he named me Nandell in honor of his brilliant friend in elementary school, and my mom said that she named me Jimmy from a little boy she had adored. They couldn't decide on one name; thus, I was stuck with the two names.

The biggest problem, though, wasn't the fact that I was known by two names; it's that my registered name was a "strange" name. All my siblings have double names: Maxine – Gwendolyn; Barry – Donovan; Dimsey – Rosemarie, but none had any out-of-the-way names like I had. The double-name phenomenon is also a practice among many families in Jamaica and throughout the Caribbean. They treat names like how they treat their clothes: the clothes you wear at home are not the same clothes you would wear to church or school.

That double-name thing crippled my emotional growth immensely. And I pledged that the two names shall never cross paths. Even today, if I'm on the street and somebody shouts, "Nandell," through the process of elimination, I can tell whether the caller knows me through business dealings, college days, and so forth. On the other hand, hearing Jimmy, I can tell that the person is a family member or very close friend.

Some years ago, I had a joint birthday party at my home with a college mate, M'Shell. I invited coworkers, relatives, friends, professors, advisors, and fellow classmates. Being the main host, throughout the night, my coworkers tried to get my attention by calling out, "Palmer" – my last name (everybody was called by last name at work). Some people were calling out for "Jimmy" and others were shouting out "Nandell."

"Who is Nandell?" my Jimmy-calling friends would ask, and the Nandell-calling friends were asking, "Who is Jimmy?" I had never felt so disjointed in my life. The funny thing is that I would have had no problem being called by either name – Nandell or Jimmy. But I was most uncomfortable when the people who knew me as Nandell started calling me Jimmy, and vice versa. No, again, the two should not meet!

I've heard of Vandell, Handel, Mandell, but never Nandell. I felt alone for a long time swimming through the ocean of one One-Named Nandell. I dreaded going to places where my name would be called out publicly. Nurses and examiners would soothe their tongue with free-flowing names like Andrea Brown, Peaches Hill, Tyrone Bennett, Mark Smith, Chris Joseph. But I would watch or listen for that punctuated pause. That time when eyes are squinted, brows are knitted and paper drawn close to face. Most times I would get up, walk over to them and save them the agony. Others were brave and confident when they called out: *Naydell, Mandale, Landale*. The latest one I heard was *Lionden*. I would cringe! Thus, my name was more of a curse than a blessing to me for a long time.

Thank goodness for the Internet. I would search for my name to see if anybody else in this world was named Nandell, and surprisingly I found a few. But unlike your James, Anthony and David, there was no etymology attached to mine. I contacted a man via email to see if I could learn something about the name, but he said that his parents named him after his two grandfathers by combining letters from the two names: Norman and Wendell, respectively. Talk about a dashed hope. Phew!

I am grateful for funny-named people like Oprah Winfrey. I've gained a lot of courage from her by the way how she had weathered the storm with her name and became successful. She told the story of how her bosses wanted her to change her name to Suzie, but she stood her grounds. Today, it's chic to name your baby girl Oprah. Some other names that gave me courage were Barack Obama, Condoleezza Rice, and Meadowlark Lemon. Wow! I'm just wondering what junior high school was like for them. Thank God they were all smart, which perhaps lessened the blows. Many of you would not dare go back to a class reunion, dreading the pain those nasty nicknames will evoke. What about those garbage nicknames, which replaced your real names? Are you truly *Dutty Mug*? *Jackass Face*? *Easy Edith*? I didn't think so.

Another form of solace I would harbor was: If God had apportioned wealth for people based on names, then while 10 million Michaels, Harrys, and Johns have to divide their fortune among themselves, then there wouldn't be a crowd waiting around the pile of goodies reserved for funny-named people like me. Ergo, Oprah didn't have anybody to compete with her allotted wealth.

The biggest breakthrough for me to date was when I sat down that afternoon around my dining table in September 2006 and wrote the most glowing tribute about my name. I also made bulleted points, singling out the characteristics of what Nandell means. Since I would never see an etymology about my name in books or on the internet any time soon, I thought, who else is better to write one but me? For all the Georges and Roberts and Karens and Gretas and Hyacinths who have been recorded as to what their names mean, somebody wrote those down, perhaps even a thousand years ago. So I said, if you cannot find one about yourself, write yourself one. I listed 10 things to describe the essence of what Nandell means:

- Nandell is unstoppable.
- Nandell is a pioneer.
- Nandell is enterprising.
- Nandell is innovative.
- Nandell is a blessing to others.
- Nandell is wealthy.
- Nandell is happy.
- Nandell is wise.
- Nandell is empathetic.
- Nandell loves people.

That was a life-changing moment for me. I recited those sentiments that day beside my name until I was truly sold on making my name work for me. I imprinted them in my psyche. In my heart. In my soul. That day, I felt a peace that I had never felt before. I felt much calmer. It didn't matter anymore whether or not if somebody calls me Nandell or Jimmy at the same time because I had made peace with that dilemma. I sealed the culmination of that recitation with a short prayer, asking God to hold me accountable to live up to what I say my name should mean. I can only hope for those things to be made manifest in my life for the remainder of my time on earth, and by the look of things, it would appear as though they have already begun working.

If you are one of those people who have ever struggled with your name, struggle no more; you can change how you feel about yourself. Find the tools right there at your fingertips. Don't blame yourself. Don't blame your parents for giving you that name. They meant well. Don't suffer any longer. You didn't have a say in their choices but you do now. If you are a Beatrice struggling to be a Tiffany or a Zedekiah wanting to be a Kevin, come to terms with your name. Not doing so could potentially squeeze out the emotional life of your being. Get out of the hall of shame closet today and brag about your name. You know that when you abbreviate the names, C.K. Walker, V.G. Russell, and D.P. Mullings, you aren't just doing it to show corporate status. You shudder daily with the thought of being found out what the abbreviated letters would mean to others. Family members are sworn to secrecy never to divulge your real name to anybody.

For years, most people – even among some of his most devout adherents – didn't know what the first two letters of their beloved pastor's initial, V.T., stood for. The charismatic preacher, who is named for an apostle, did not readily warm up to anybody calling him outside of his name. Therefore, unless you were privy to the inner circle of this man's life, or there was a public citation where his full name was declared, you would not have known that V.T. Williams stood for *Vincent Theophilus*.

WINETGA ANN REYNOLDS AND CUNY

FORMER CITY University of New York chancellor, W. Ann Reynolds, is another one of those people. I recall as a student journalist meeting the chancellor for the first time at a press conference where she was introducing herself to the many editors and reporters from the various campuses of the City University. We were all eager to match a face with the glossy picture sent out in the press kits of the incoming chancellor weeks earlier. Before long, the beaming Reynolds walked to the podium to field students' questions as the klieg lights beamed on her and cameras clicked away. As reporters asked her everything from A to Z, one obvious thing kept boggling my mind. I couldn't resist it.

"Madam Chancellor, what the *W* in your name means?" I asked. By now, you could hear a pin drop. She gulped, sighed, and stared at me in a way that seemed to say, "Why did you have to go there?" A few more gulps later, and she offered, ". . . It stands for *Winetga*."

She said that she grew up on an Indian reservation, and her parents named her in honor of that group. She also said that some people over the years have had difficulty pronouncing her name properly; hence its abbreviation.

I know a very prominent nurse's practitioner in New York City whose elderly mother called the hospital one day asking for her daughter (Icilyn) – a pet name or home-use-only name – instead of the woman's preferred name. It took a long time to find *Icilyn* at the hospital, and that caused her much grief after it was brought to light among her coworkers. She was also very hard on her mother for naming her that "despicable, old-fashioned name" in the first place.

Have you noticed most of the times people treat you based on how you carry yourself? If you command respect, most often than not, you will get it. If a stranger shows up at your house and he sees two pairs of shoes at your main entrance, he will not think twice to take off his shoes before he enters and walk on your plush beige carpet. Well, unless you tell him that it's okay.

In contrast, if a lady visits your home and everywhere is filthy, she will not make any effort to clean up behind her as the tone is already set in place.

It is no different from the way how you comport yourself. When you declare who you are, people will be able to sniff this out from afar. Your spirit will take on a newness that you've never experienced before. The same Sheniqua that once blocked doors for you will now open countless doors for you because of how you feel about yourself.

On the other hand, a person with the "right" name but still doesn't feel as though his name is significant will be stalled.

My former boss' name is Sheba. And she epitomizes the sheer essence befitting a *Queen of Sheba*. By the way how she carries herself, you would believe that King Solomon was alive and well today, and she was the apple of his eyes. She is knowledgeable, confident, articulate, chic, and strong.

Get out a blank sheet of paper and begin receiving blessings right there at your fingertips. Start writing! Mothers and fathers, you can write them for your young children. Don't lose hope. Write it; confess it, and you will begin to see positive changes in your life. Picture it as planting a seed or taking medicine, the result doesn't happen in a snap minute, but will take effect over time.

When you accept your name, people will have no choice but to fall in line and accept it, whether they like it or not. And the more you accept you for you, the more they will give you the respect due. Those who hear it for the first time perhaps will giggle, but over time, it will be accepted.

Confidence. I am sensing that JoElla Collins wasn't always that forceful in saying her name to people. But over time, she perhaps got sick and tired of people calling her everything except the way it was supposed to sound. She perhaps got to a place where she said, "Enough is enough; folks need to start calling my name correctly!" She would not accept mumbled tones to pass as her name as I did. And so, with acceptance, she was able to move on to the next tier – confidence. Confidence perhaps allowed her to hold the coveted positions she has held throughout her career. Surges of confidence buoyed her along where she could tell some naysaying Marys, "Well, I am JoElla and you are not!" With such confidence, I could see no problem in her telling somebody that her name is Gertruda Zipporah Lattibudiere.

How many of you have decided to change your hairstyle, only to hear family members and friends say things like, "Finally, you have entered the 21st century." Or, "This new style doesn't do anything for you; why not get back your old style?" "It should be longer." "It should be shorter." Woe be unto that individual who makes decisions based on the whims of others in the court of popular opinions. You better accept your change and take the compliments and criticisms in strides. The bottom line is that one way or the other, they will not change how you feel about yourself. Begin accepting your name today.

FRENCH-SOUNDING NAMES

I'M OFTEN mesmerized by how we English speakers, especially in America — are captivated by French-sounding names — when items are packaged. We see it in the culinary world, fashion, and other fields.

The same 2-year-old chicken you refused to eat from your grandmother's kitchen table is the same chicken you paid $35 for at a French restaurant all because this old fowl has a nice-sounding name — *Poulet de . . . .* Every-day eggplant dishes are dressed up and called *Le Marie Aubergine.* Regular cornmeal commands a hefty price when it is put on the table at a 5-star Italian restaurant as *polenta*. Thus, any struggling restaurant which serves commonplace food items, if they're ready to create a marketing blitz, all that owner needs to do is just jazz up the menus with a few French-sounding names. And voila! See the result.

All a typical shopper needs to know is that a bottle of perfume came from Paris: *eau de toilette.* Did somebody say toilet water? Now, mention the words "toilet water" to an English speaker, and you will have stocked shelves at your stores from January to December with nary a buyer.

We see the same trend in clothes. In fact, not too long ago, scores of American designers had to get the nod from Paris before they could get an inroad in New York City with their careers. A frumpy frock, with a French-sounding name to its label, could fetch upward of thousands of dollars.

Wouldn't it be nice if we could use the same renewed sentiments as they relate to our names? Talk about a name makeover. I could see lives changing for the better. Greater relationships among spouses. More production on the job because people will have felt good about themselves.

THE NAME WHICH DOESN'T DELIVER

SOME OF you were named after your fathers who didn't spend a day in your lives. Still others were named after dads who are spending a life sentence in prison. Some were named after great-grandmothers or grandaunts who suffered from all kinds of ailments under the sun. Some of these people had no claim to fame; some of them, you, argue struggled badly in life. And now you think your fate will be just like theirs or worse. Therefore, a lot of you feel as though you are fighting a losing battle. "There is no escape for me," you say. "My fate was set in stone, so it's inevitable for me to go further in life." You take anything life throws at you, often times even welcoming the crumbs, as you don't feel deserving of better things coming your way.

Many of you have parents who are divorced or separated. And the constant comparison of your mother saying "You're just like your good-for-nothing father," has reached its breaking point. Hearing that drummed home everyday to your young ears is unfathomable. After all, Daddy is always drunk. Daddy has never held a job beyond one week. Daddy has 22 children by 10 baby mothers and still counting. Thus, your name is soiled long before you even had a chance to become a man. You feel then that the only option left is to walk in Daddy's footsteps, and you can't wait to grow up to the ripe age of 21 when you can buy liquor and get drunk like Daddy. Daddy had 22 kids but you want 32 – telling yourself that a son has to outrun his daddy in every aspect of life: drinking more. Gambling more. Womanizing more. Cursing more, and the list goes on. You feel like you are the man! After all you are Pascal, Jr., a spitting image of Pascal, Sr.

If you are that boy or man today, don't believe the lie. Hope abounds for you to get out of this evil network of confusion. You deserve more than that. You are bought with a price. Reach out for those blessings at your fingertips. Call on God to change your life. Allow Him to infuse your thoughts with renewed hope. Rehearse your name yet again. Say it aloud yet again letter by letter. Write something glowing about Larry today. About Darryl. About Martin. About Granville.

If you are that girl or woman, you, too, write something glowing about Sonia. About Freda. About Josephine. Those are some of the most rewarding blessings that could ever enter your life. Reach for them. Start feeling good about yourself once and for all. Start feeling good from the inside out. And if you are crippled by a name you are ashamed of, then do something about it. Either you change it for a name that you will feel comfortable with or polish and burnish the one you've already had. God is willing and able to oversee this transformation. He wants to see you whole again. There is hope. Find it. There is more joy somewhere. But not where you are currently.

THINK POSITIVELY ABOUT YOUR NAME

SOME NAMES can make you think positively or negatively about people. Think of a Stan, who or what comes to mind? Is it a best friend who meant the world to you in high school? Does Stan remind you of anger, hate and bitterness? What about Marie? Who is Marie to you? Does she conjure up the girl who is always helping everyone around her, or is she the woman who backstabs people in order to get ahead?

Many times when we recall a name, we are imprinting our past experiences on the people we are meeting for the first time sharing those names without realizing that we're doing so. Hence, if the Stan we knew 20 years ago was nice, the Stan that we meet today would benefit from the niceness of the Stan we have in mind and vice versa. For all we know the Stan we just met could be a felon, but by virtue of his being a Stan transcends great thoughts from the "good" Stan. Similarly, if the Marie we know today turns out to be an unpleasant person, all future Maries will bear the brunt of our ire for the one so-called bad Marie.

Names from a secondary or collectively source can yield you a lot of benefits as well. I cannot think of a person named Denzel right now in America who would not be readily accorded VIP treatment, by virtue of his sharing the name of the beloved Denzel Washington. Well, unless Denzel Washington failed to sign his autograph on the soccer mom's piece of napkin a week ago.

My sister-in-law, Janet Jackson, a few years older than the Janet

Jackson of Hollywood fame, came upon multiple good fortunes because of her namesake. She's now married. (Mr. Sloley, you are a blessed man.) But she got all the perks befitting a Janet Jackson. Every time she boarded an airline, she automatically got royal treatment. Her name has earned her enough extra peanuts and pretzels to fill a silo. Upgrades from coach to first class were commonplace, I was told. She was always engaged in conversations where somebody was asking about her celebrity namesake.

I read an article some time ago about a contingent of Jamaicans who traveled to some country in the Middle East. The immigration officer had a hard time processing their paperwork. He later summoned other officers, but there seemed to be no breakthrough. After asking for about what seemed like the hundredth time where the group was from, a member of the contingent had the grand idea of mentioning Bob Marley. That was all those officers needed to hear. "Ah, Bob Marley?!? Jamaica!" They made the association with Bob Marley and Jamaica, and that one thoughtful insight shone the light for the group's clearance. The immigration officers started to sing almost every recording from Marley's huge repertoire of music, and the group was given a warm welcome from that point on.

Yvonne sang with the Brooklyn Tabernacle Choir for eight years, and you would be shocked to see the treatment accorded her whenever she tells people that she was a member of the 6-time Grammy-award-winning group. For that reason, she hardly ever says it to people, not wanting to be singled out unnecessarily. Mention Carol Cymbala's name – the choir director – and people want to touch her vicariously through Yvonne. The power of a name.

Be empowered by your name. Think back on a baby elephant. When it was born, the handler would tether it with chains on its feet to a tree. Over time that baby elephant would grow up believing it cannot go past 15 feet from its surroundings. This could continue until it becomes a full-grown elephant weighing several tons. But because somebody put it in its place and showed it that it couldn't go any further, it remained in its place. With a body mass of great proportion, that grown elephant could tear the tree down, damaging everybody and every object in sight. But it doesn't know it has that potential power until it is set free mentally. It has been conditioned so long to believe that it cannot move beyond 15 feet.

It is no different with our names. Somebody gave you a name, and told you that all Patsys are dumb, and all Marks are drunks, and you believed that lie. But have you ever tried to prove them wrong? What are you exhibiting now to change their mindset? You have that potential, with God's help, to change that negative perception about you because of your name. Start believing the opposite is true. Your life depends on it. Like that elephant who found freedom and started living more powerfully because of his sheer size, find the courage today to get out of that mold. Your name also carries a big size, too. You are endowed with robust zest and vigor to make change happen by feeling good about your name and who you are as a total human being.

WHEN YOUR NAME IS OFFENSIVE TO OTHERS

MASAHIKO F., who had just emigrated to the U.S. from Japan, didn't know anything about America's social politics. His name was quite a mouthful for most Americans to call, and so he decided to shorten it, *Massa*. One day he was shopping in a store in Harlem, New York, when one of his African-American friends shouted, "Massa, Massa," to get his attention. All eyes turned in his direction and a few people took it upon themselves to go over to him. "What's up with this Massa?" one disgruntled gentleman asked. By now the poor Japanese man with limited English became frightened and wondered what was all the fuss about. He soon found out that the term Massa was offensive to a select group of people. A term only reserved for the antebellum South. A horde of people gathered and was getting riled up now on the African-American man who called the name. They castigated him for using such a word from his lips. Masahiko told me that when he found out that his name was offensive to some people, he decided to use his last name, but it, too, turned out to be offensive to others because phonetically, it sounded like an expletive. So what a man to do without his name? He toyed with a few American-friendly names, but none of them made him feel whole. I still get a good laugh out of it every time I remember that incident.

Masahiko, after spending more than 10 years in the United States, went back to Japan about two years ago.

FROM THE WRONG SIDE OF TOWN

EVEN JESUS himself had a hard time shaking off labels – the stigma of his hometown. Remember when someone asked, "Can anything good come out of Nazareth?" The next town over with the right name, and he would have been celebrated.

I was doing feature articles on a few landmark buildings and neighborhoods in Harlem in the early 1990s for the *New York Amsterdam News*, when a gentleman took me to task. During the interview, I asked him how long had he been living in Harlem. It was as if I had blasphemed. "Young man, get it straight; get it straight; this is not Harlem. This is Sugar Hill! Don't ever make that mistake again. And put me on the record for saying so." While most New Yorkers considered the blocks between 138th Street through 145th Street on the Upper West Side of Manhattan as Harlem, the residents there considered it exclusively Sugar Hill. From that small enclave you also have Hamilton Heights – named for Alexander Hamilton, and which boasts his home, now converted into a museum. It just goes to show how people can get very territorial or incensed about a name.

Based on the various examples fleshed out from the many applications of name, we see how labels can make us or break us. They can engender relationships or sunder them. A name is one of the primary reasons why people go out of their way to either think less of themselves or treat others less than human beings. But it doesn't always have to be so.

THE RIGHT SOUNDING NAMES

SOME PEOPLE choose onomatopoetic names to work for them. For example, I am told of a diminutive man who was always pestered by his given name, changing it to the testosterone-heavy, Bruno, as a

way to command more respect from his bigger peers and coworkers. The sole reason for him to do so was that even conversing on
the telephone, once people hear the name Bruno, he said, they will
envision somebody fearless. Bold. Powerful.

Maybe he has a point. Nobody could walk away from hearing
the word *draconian* and not conjure up the wicked, tyrannical Greek
lawgiver, Draco. You don't have to be punished before sensing the
severity of the adjective, draconian, which stemmed from his name.
Draco sounds evil; rigid, and suffocating.

How about those whose nicknames followed them through
life, their correct names playing second fiddle to them? I
recall a roommate in Jamaica who had a girl visiting him from
America. She knocked at the gate and asked, "Is Fluffy home?" I
said, "Who?" and again she said Fluffy. We went back and forth
with neither of us coming to any agreement. I invited her inside
and she sat down. She double-checked her address. "Is this 14
Artemis ___?" I said yes. "Does he play soccer for _____ ?" I
said yes. She went on to tell me that the man's girlfriend in New
Jersey gave her some items of value to give to him. Suddenly,
it dawned on me to ask her, "Could it be Shaggy you are asking
about?" I surely made her day because she jumped from the sofa,
thrusting her fist in the air, while yelling, "Yes! Yes! I remember
my friend telling me Shaggy, but all I could remember was that
his name was a dog's name, and that's why I kept saying Fluffy."

Shaggy, being about 6ft. 3 and 190 pounds, definitely did not
look anything like our furry friend. To this day, I doubt that more
than 20 percent of people know Shaggy's correct name.

People who are afraid or ashamed of telling their "right"
names to others need to know one thing: Doing something about
your name can make you feel better about yourself. Take, for
example, an old house, which has not had any repairs in its 80-
year-old existence. The wear and tear over time can make this
erstwhile grandeur look like something from Shanty Town. But
with adequate renovations, this sore eye, abandoned dwelling
can be transformed into a prime piece of real estate. Prospective
buyers who turned up their noses and walked on by a year ago,
would be too happy now to buy it above market value. Remember,
nothing will have changed. The house is situated at the same spot.

But the new paint has brought it back to life. The new windows and lighting have given it a new lease on life.

What about the 1955 antique car that has been sitting idly under a shade tree? Give it a few touchups, and it will be transformed to its glory days. That car would get admirers and takers in a New York minute. But how about your name? What are you doing to spruce it up? You can do the same thing to your name just like what was done to that old house and car. Do a spiritual renovation. Some major cleanup needs to take place. Elevate your name to prime-time status. The good thing is that you don't always have to change your name in order to feel like somebody. Let it turn heads and command respect. Find those blessing at your fingertips.

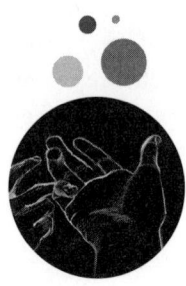

CHAPTER FIFTEEN

YES, OUR THREE BOYS
WERE ADOPTED

WE WALKED THROUGH THE KING COUNTY Courthouse in Kent, Washington, on the afternoon of Wednesday, August 31, 2005, for the finalization of our boys' adoption. We were privately ushered in by the court's officer to face the judge's ruling. That was my third time facing a judge — all times being positive. But this time was exceptional! The judge was extremely nice. He exhorted us to be a closely-knitted family. He told the boys how blessed they were to have us as parents, and in turn, told Yvonne and me how blessed we were to have the boys in our lives.

The judge asked us if we would like to take some photographs, but since we knew the difficulties in toting around cameras and cell phones in government buildings, we tried our best to stay clear of any bureaucratic impediments. But the judge, with much alacrity, handed us a disposable camera, and called a court officer to take some pictures with us posing beside him. We were most delighted to click away as he and the boys mugged for the camera. That day truly made me feel complete. It was a very difficult and tedious process for us to reach the glory days of final adoption. By the ending of October the boys had received their American passports, after their becoming full American citizens.

MOVING FROM NEW YORK CITY

ON SEPTEMBER 6, 2001, I decided to move from New York City to Seattle, Washington. But in less than a week of my being in the Emerald City, I was reeling from survivor's guilt: The Twin Towers were no more! I knew of people who died in the rubble and just couldn't bring myself to lick the effect of that tragedy. For all intent and purposes, I was coming here for a more laid-back lifestyle – whale watching and Mount Rainier with all her majestic appeal under azure sky. I wanted more king salmon and more iced coffee. More Dungeness crabs and crispy apples. But that was short lived. All those things were interrupted when I got a call from my sister, Rosemarie, in New York, sometime in mid-January 2002, telling me of my niece being admitted to hospital with meningitis. Being more than 3,000 miles away, I was making plans to go and visit her. But on Sunday, January 27, it was too late. My sister called again to say that Lorraine Campbell – my eldest niece – was dead. I missed her dearly. She was the child who had the audacity to interrupt my childhood, making me an uncle when I was just 10 years old.

The World Trade Center tragedy resurfaced again, and I said a prayer for the surviving family members who would never see the remains of their loved ones interred in a grave or put away in an urn. I took solace in the fact that at least there would be a funeral service, with her actual remains lying in state, for Lorraine. My heart went out immediately to the orphaned boys. Who would assume their responsibility? The telephone calls poured in. Family members cajoled me into taking them, but that hard, icy spot in my heart had a difficult time chipping away.

When I went to Jamaica to make funeral arrangements, as usual, everything came down on me. Thank goodness for the financial contributions from my father and Rosemarie. I asked out loud why me? Where is everybody else? I had to contact funeral home, church, hospital, among multiple places. I had to pick out dress, makeup — even the underwear for the dead. I didn't know that shoes were part of burial. And so I went to a store in Kingston, which specialized in selling apparels for the dead, I breathed a sigh of relief! The store manager showed me a pair of white bed slippers that would cost no more than $10 in the United States. When she quoted a price that would be equivalent to about U.S.$50, I flatly turned down her offer and began to walk out.

"Well, that is the only shoes of choice for the dead, sir," she said.

Without missing a beat, I retorted, "Well, in that case, my loved one will have to walk on the Streets of Gold barefooted."

I later bought a thick pair of white socks to complement Lorraine's silky white dress.

At the funeral service, the boys looked on wide-eyed as people went up to pay tribute to their mother. I was able to spread my arms around the two younger ones, while Rosemarie consoled the eldest. Before the service could come to a close, the frozen tundra of my heart had somewhat drifted away or melted. And I was again ready to do exploit for the boys. I vowed then and there that as long as I was alive, they would not become wards of the state.

I took them back to my hotel room that evening, put them into the Jacuzzi, and we all huddled in the king-sized bed until daylight. By the next day, I could feel that a bond had been formed. I have loved them ever since.

Two days after Lorraine's funeral and a day before I left Jamaica, I petitioned the Jamaica Adoption Board, filling out multiple forms to start the adoption process to get the boys to America. Separate forms were later filed with various other government agencies in the U.S. It was quite an ordeal, to say the least. Nevertheless, I had met some wonderful people who guided me through to the end. I also had to deal with Homeland Security, the King County Court in Seattle, an adoption agency in Seattle to conduct a home study, a complete physical medical checkup for us and the boys, and a comprehensive background check on Yvonne and me, among other things.

On July 4, 2004, while everybody was chomping down on barbecued chicken and ribs in the park, I was spread out on the grass from about 10 a.m. to 8 p.m., filling out reams of biographical data, and other legal documents for three boys. I did it all by myself without the aid of an attorney. I felt so naked after filling out those many forms. What more possibly could they ask of us?

There was such a favorable atmosphere at the Homeland Security office, attached to the American Embassy in Kingston and just about every bureaucracy I had to deal with. At no other times had I recalled such a favorable period in my life. People seemingly went out of their way to do good in the most legal sense. No money traded hands, no bribery – just sheer, unadulterated niceness. Doctors and consulars bantered with the boys, which by that time, they were being treated like celebrities. That didn't stop there. On booking our economy-class flights to come to America, when we showed up at the airport in Kingston, the ticket agent said, "So you're all flying first class?" I was speechless. How did that happen? That seemed to augur well for the greatness they're destined for, I mused. We had favor left, right, and center.

Thank God for our adoption agency, and our caseworker, Marge. She is one of the nicest persons I've met this side of the Pacific Ocean. I cannot say enough thanks to Desrene Davis and her daughter, Sherine (Apple) Johnson, who dedicated their time to take care of the boys at their home for a year. They were my eyes and ears in my absence. They ferried them to and from medical, court, passport, and other appointments.

Thanks to Jamaica's Honorary Consul to Seattle, Enid Dwyer, and the members of the Friends of Jamaica-Seattle, who put on a reception for the boys at Carmeta Francis' home – the group's treasurer. Thanks, too, to my friends, Neville Williams and Ermena Vinluan of New York, who sent a ton of wonderful books; Sybil Thompson of Toronto, Canada, who sent a nice check; Kennedy and Doris Akinlosotu, who, along with their four children in tow, descended on our home with sacks of rice, pasta, chocolate, etc. Brenda Burke, who suited them out in designer schoolbags and sweaters. Tywan and Khush Gonzalez, who met us at the airport, and helped to transport us home. They also turned over their Xbox to the boys that same evening.

Yvonne's former coworker, Susanne, along with her husband, Doug, also hosted a reception at their Issaquah, Washington, home in tribute to the boys. That's where we fell in love with the lawn game, croquet, as we played all day that Saturday afternoon in their backyard. Oscar Stephenson, Lorna Coke, and Saday Barrett-Hudy, who all wrote glowing references for the adoption process. The many friends who prayed for us, sent cards, emails, and made innumerable telephone calls to keep abreast of what was happening.

Every month we used to wire money down to them for their upkeep. They also had the support of a very selfless human being, Charmaine Smith, an attorney in Kingston. She supported them in every which way. The boys attended private school in Jamaica, and every quarter she paid the exorbitant school fees for them, with some assistance from her church, she told me. And she had never faltered once in doing so. Now, talk about doling out blessings at the fingertips.

The teachers and other staff members thought the world of the boys. They encouraged them to excel to the zenith. That was one of the reasons why Jevoy, in less than two years at the school, was able to become Head Boy (Student Government President), the highest student-held office at the school. He chalked up multiple awards, which yielded handsome cash prizes. He was interviewed live on primetime TV, and spoke glibly about his aspirations in life.

People talked about them with water in their eyes, always echoing that they were blessed. They had great rapport with street vendors, their peers, the school security, and the man in the street.

Frankly, I am very happy that I have made a 360 degree in my decision to adopt those boys. At the time of their mother's passing, I was spent. I didn't want to be bothered. I had felt that enough was enough. People needed to give me a break. I was tired of being the one who was always bailing out some family member. "Why can't others pick up from where I left off?" I murmured. I went back to the time when Jevoy was born, and how my sister was trying to wheedle Yvonne and me into adopting him. We pondered over the matter long and hard, and decided against adopting him. The big factor in all of this was that I didn't want him to struggle with the allegiance to his birth mother. We didn't have to worry about a father because he was not in the boy's life.

Coupled with that haunting thought, was the crippling effect some adoptees have harbored: I had heard enough horror stories about children who were given to an aunt, grandmother, or stranger out of hardship from a mother who had an over-abundance of children to care for. Many times, those stories did not have happy endings. Those children who were "given away" have a harder time coming to terms as to why their parents would give them away instead of another brother or sister. Sometimes they felt unloved. To add insult to injury, their guardian aunt/grandparent would physically and verbally abuse them, and the child had no recourse but to accept his or her fate in life. Some of them have contended that if their own parents – the primary people in their lives – could give them away, then whatever came their way negatively in life was justified.

They often felt a silent solace in the abuse they suffer, saying that they deserve it. Those children and their birth parents seemed to always be at loggerheads with each other. Children were furious and parents felt guilty for having done the unthinkable. Hence, those were some of the factors why I turned down my sister's request.

Two more boys would subsequently be born, and again, the subject was broached. We refused to give it a thought for the simple reason that I loved my niece, and didn't want to see her children get taken away from her. After all, she wasn't a hen whose baby chicks were snatched away by voracious mongooses or hawks. She wasn't a cow that gives birth periodically with her calves being weaned before their time then taken away. I've seen that forlorn look on the faces of animals when their young are taken away. And that feeling in human is even more intensified. I wasn't prepared to be plagued by that look in my mind's eye. Despite her struggles in raising her sons, I knew that she loved them to no end. She wanted the best for them, but she didn't have the financial wherewithal to make a lot of things come to fruition. She was a very proud woman so she suffered silently.

In the summer of 1998, my sister – Lorraine's mom – emigrated to New York City, and that's when Lorraine's world crumbled. Elaine was the fulcrum of Lorraine and her progeny. Even though she was 26 years old, Lorraine had never lived on her own until Elaine's departure. This posed an insurmountable problem for her. She ended up in a neighborhood that was many notches below her earlier lifestyle. Meanwhile, Elaine agonized night and day over her only daughter and her beloved grandsons. What a travesty! Ten months after Lorraine's death, her mother died, leaving the boys without a mother and grandmother.

MY FATHER'S COMING TO AMERICA

I LOVE my family dearly, and would give them the last shirt on my back. In fact, on a cold morning in January 1991 after I was sworn in as an American citizen in Brooklyn, New York, two hours later I was at Federal Plaza in downtown Manhattan filing paperwork for my father's emigrating to the U.S. By October of that same year, he came to live with us. I remember meeting him at JFK Airport in Queens, New York, and the pride and joy I felt seeing him on American soil. I had always told him that one of my dreams was to see him come to America. And if I was privileged enough to see such a day, then my purpose in life would have somewhat been fulfilled. Hence, I would not mind dying the next day because my mission was accomplished. Every October 16 my dad would call me to tell me thanks for being so selfless in allowing him to come to America. He never fails to rib me with that martyrdom line, about my dying after he landed in the U.S.

By 1999, Yvonne and I had hosted 11 family members from Jamaica – father, sisters, nieces, and nephews – who I had filed petitions for directly or indirectly. Our home was their launching pad. I would later rent apartments for them where I paid their rent for six months, furniture and appliances to boot. Things changed for me when some family members refused to honor their end of the bargain after they refused to pay the rent where I had left off. I grew cold and rueful. What more could I have given? I questioned myself. I personally knew people who had to sleep on the subways for weeks after been put out by a mother, husband or uncle. And here I was trying to spare my relatives of this distasteful treatment. Some people said it was my fault for "spoiling" them, and that I should have allowed them to experience some modicum of hardships. But I couldn't do it. If I could lighten somebody's burden, why make them suffer first? I didn't get it.

Over time, the bile had found its way into our marriage, and I felt overwhelmed. I wanted to be free. I longed to buy a pair of shoes at the spur of the moment without feeling as though I was shortchanging somebody's rent money or grocery money. Since the age of 14, I have always played a strong supporting role to my family members. I knew no other life. But it was getting tired. I wanted to be gone. Far, far away from every family issue. I vowed never again to fill out another immigration form. I also pledged never again to question the motives as to why some people with American citizenship failed to file papers for their relatives to emigrate to the U.S. I silently begged their pardon for my criticizing them. I'd had enough, and I wanted out. I didn't want to move to Philadelphia or Charlotte. As I mentioned earlier, I wanted to go far. Far. Far.

With four prior failed attempts to visit Seattle, I finally found the courage to come alone on April 26, 2001. I stayed at a hotel downtown, not knowing anybody prior to my coming. I spent five days, but it was more like spending five weeks in five days. I went everywhere up and down the Pacific Northwest, and Vancouver, Canada. I immediately fell in love with the terrain's verdancy. I love the cleanliness of the cities and the quality of life. I saw the beauty of the Washington landscape in every waking hour. So, by September 6, 2001, I said goodbye to New York City. Living in the Big Apple for 16 years, it was hard to say goodbye to a lot of my friends, coworkers, and acquaintances. But it was time for a change. That drastic change was changing from a family of two to a family of five.

People sometimes ask me whether or not it was easier to love the boys since they were already blood relatives, and my response is always no. If those boys had come from a crack den in Newark, New Jersey – unrelated to me, I still believe that I would love them the same. Unconditionally. Yvonne and I actually looked into the possibility of adoption in the United States after we had spurned Elaine's request. Had there been three girls, it still wouldn't change anything. Kids from Russia, China, Korea, Costa Rica or Ethiopia, we would welcome them just the same. I also try to search my heart now and then to see if there are any gaps that need to be closed. Would I love my birth children better than adopted children? No such gaps abound.

One of the amazing things I've grown to realize is that our moving to Seattle was divinely planned. All that time when I thought that I was finally going to live for me and me alone, God had other plans. He was just sending me to scout out the landscape, to make preparation for Yvonne and the boys. My seemingly moribund marriage would benefit greatly from this arrangement. In New York City, Yvonne and I had different schedules. I worked nights, while she worked days. Many times when she was sleeping I was up and vice versa. And that helped to drift us apart, too. We barely had dinner together unless we purposed ourselves to go out on the town because of our schedules.

I was chauffeur-driven to work nightly, and together we earned a decent salary. We went on exotic vacations. We had exquisite furniture in a beautiful space we called home, but over time, I was still empty. That void needed to be filled. I longed to find my true purpose in life. It came in the form of our three angels. They put back the pep in our steps. They brought healing to our marriage. Every time we sit around the dining table now as a family, I thank God for that privilege. I never once take it for granted. I wonder how would I still work night and try to bond with three active boys when I needed my sleep time. I had seen the ruins of many promising boys who got into selling drugs because of their not having adequate supervision from parents who had to do multiple jobs to make ends meet for their families.

Would my heart still be hardened had I not moved away from New York City? In hindsight, with my hardened heart, would Lorraine's boys have a chance to come to America? I am still asking those questions. But all I can say is that God is truly amazing!

They are enjoying their new lives in Seattle. They love their schools, libraries, parks, and church. They adore the people who go gaga over them.

Looking back on how things have unfolded, I found out that the same spot where death took place, new births began. When I recall Lorraine's suffering and how her boys' lives could have taken a turn in the wrong direction, I'm amazed. She died physically, and for them, they died emotionally. But with our adopting them, there was rebirth. I liken it to a field that was slashed and burned. The hewn-down trees and bushes, later burned by fire, would, to the naked eye, seem barren and good for nothing. But given a few months, coupled with a few showers of rain, that plot of ground will have teemed with all kinds of foliage. Life ceased for one thing, but gives birth to other things. When I look at a single bean or corn, the crops all died, leaving that dried bean or corn, but those seeds have life within their seemingly dead state. And they could start life anew, given the right climate or environment. That's how I feel about what happened in our case. The seeds were planted. They burst forth from the ground, and one leaf at a time, they eventually turned into branches. Wow!

One thing we're happy about is that we had the time to make a decision on our own regarding the final word on taking the boys. We didn't do it because others said we should. Yvonne and I did so of our own volitions. Thus, we knew all along that those boys were destined to be with us. Many similarities abound: All of their names begin with the letter J, and my pet name begins with J – Jimmy. I see a little of myself in all of them.

Every now and again somebody would ask me whether it was true that our boys were adopted, and when I tell them that it was true, they are shocked beyond description. The youth pastor, who is fairly new to our church, said that when he found out that the boys were adopted, he had a harder time being convinced that we were not their birth parents because of our interaction with them. The hardest question to answer is, "Why didn't you adopt one or two instead of the three of them?"

By no means would we consider ourselves super heroes because we adopted our boys. Some people consider that deed a Herculean task, as I have mentioned earlier. But if there's a feeling that I am supposed to feel in order to get maximum ecstasy, then it is a long way coming. The main reason why I made the decision to adopt was that I would have wanted somebody to care for me if I were down and out. It's that simple.

We don't have the capacity to adopt more children, but it would be my greatest desire to see other orphans get settled with caring and loving families. I was at an adoption forum two years ago where Washington State's attorney general, Rob McKenna, gave the keynote address. He talked about a woman who was walking on a beach at low tide where hundreds of jellyfish were stranded. She tried her best to toss a few of them back into the water when a man walked up to her, telling her that what she was doing was futile. His contention was that it was impossible for her to save all of those jellyfish. "Well, I can save this one. And this one. And this one," the woman said, throwing one fish at a time back into the water. Her point was that while she was not able to save the hundreds of stranded fish, she was able to save a few. I believe that many of us could take a leaf from that woman's example.

OTHER UNSUNG HEROES OF ADOPTION

MANY UNSUNG heroes who adopt are floating about in your church, gym or college campus. I discovered one such couple in November 2006. Yvonne and I were complimenting them about their children when the conversation shifted to adoption. We told them that we adopted our boys, and they were in shock. When they, too, said that four of their six children were adopted, I almost collapse to the floor. Sorry for being stereotypical, but they did not fit the profile. The husband appeared to be about 30 years old and the wife looked somewhere around 27. They wear "trendy" Generation X clothes at times, which can belie their parental roles to six charges. The 3-girl, 3-boy brood looked the picture of health and profound happiness.

The husband said that most people didn't even know that some of the children were adopted because he didn't want any distinction among them. They adopted three boys and one girl, and a prouder father and sons you'll never meet.

In July 2006, because of a paternity snafu, the youngest boy was temporarily returned to his birth father, according to the couple. But they prayed and trusted God for the boy's safe return. One week before Christmas, the proud mother was in church giving praises for the return of her son. She later said that was the best Christmas gift a mother could have ever received. I have the utmost respect for that selfless couple and their children. They truly give us deeper appreciation and respect for our boys with their big hearts.

JEVOY'S PERSPECTIVE ON ADOPTION

I WILL never forget the night on Lorraine's birthday last year, we commemorated her life by having the boys reflect on how they were feeling. We wanted them to talk freely, and Jevoy delved into one of his matured insights.

"I know that my mother's passing was all a divine plan. God saw that Mommy couldn't take care of us physically, emotionally, and spiritually, and so, He saw it fit to call her home."

He went on to say that instead of her "messing" up four people's lives, she stepped aside so that a family who could handle his brothers and him would get into the picture to make them a part of their family. He said that he hoped to see her in heaven someday where they'll live as one big, happy family eternally.

At home, we contribute work collectively as a family. We made it clear that they would not be paid for doing chores around the house. Instead, we let them know that their contribution acts more like a communal setting: Dad and Mom provide the money, cook, help with homework, etc., and they wash dishes, take care of the garbage and fold clothes. Each one contributing toward the common good of the family. Thus, everybody has a stake in the unit. They do get cash on and off, but no payment for helping a family member.

BOY OF THE WEEK

WE HAVE a system in place where we choose a boy of the week over dinner on Friday evening. They look forward to Friday evenings. The boy of the week sits in a special decorated chair. His plate and flatware are singled out and different from all of us. We personally serve his dinner like a waiter at a 5-star restaurant. We tell him thanks for being a wonderful boy for the week. He's rewarded with perks and certain privileges from Friday evening until the next Friday comes around. You literally can hear them planning, talking among themselves from midweek, asking each other who would be boy of the week.

REAPING FROM AN EARLY HARVEST

I AM often amazed at seeing miniature fruit trees bearing oranges, mangoes, peaches, etc. A 2-year-old toddler can pick a fruit from those trees at her beck and call. I tend to question the authenticity of those trees, wondering whether or not if they were so advanced by way of the latest chemical engineering.

As a child, seeing a tree come to fruition usually took years. Many of its planters never lived to taste a fruit from their trees. Having the boys around has brought back the miniature fruit trees to mind. Many times while driving together as a family, one of them would utter, "Love you, Dad/Mom." My quickest reaction would be to look around to see if we were driving past their favorite store, or whether or not a birthday was coming up, with their pushing for some kind of bribes. They said it while we drove through the boondocks. They would say it upward of 10 times a day. Ashamedly, it took me a long time to overcome this awkward feeling, searching for the subtle trick that was not there. The boys were merely giving fruits from their trees. I didn't realize that harvest time had come. Well, not so early.

What I was looking for were those erstwhile trees that took years to bear fruits, but instead, I got some miniature trees, ready to yield an early harvest. Why did all of this shock me? After looking back, I realized that indeed we were the planters. When they couldn't utter the *L* word, night and day we would tell them nonstop "I love you." When the role was reciprocated, I couldn't believe it. I couldn't stand it.

Plant that tree today. Water it. Fertilize it. Mulch it. Prune it. You may never know, before long, you will reap an early harvest. Blossom will start to appear, and fruit will start bearing.

Yes, it is still possible for your children to say "I love you, Mommy/Daddy" with no ulterior motives. They will say it at home in private, at public gatherings, driving through the boondocks — just but anywhere. If you planted the seed and took care of it, start believing your children when they surprise you with one of those day-brighteners. What is happening is that you are realizing an early harvest. Forget about who will keep you or who will place you in the nursing home when you reach 90. Just live for the moment, and enjoy those fruits of unadulterated love.

If you were never to get a cup of coffee from their earnings, but they are able to say, "I love you . . . ," then bask in it. Look no further, those are plain blessings right at your fingertips.

One of the most moving gestures to date that has had my full appreciation for Jason was on New Year's Day 2007. We were up late the previous night, arriving home at 7 in the morning. The family was exhausted, and everybody slept past 2 p.m. Actually, when I looked at the time, it was 2:47. I heard pots and pans clanging in the kitchen, and Yvonne went from our bedroom to inquire as to what was happening. When she returned, she said that Jason wanted to make "breakfast." She told him that it was close to dinnertime, and that he should wait until dinner was served. I told her to allow him to do whatever he wished.

In about half an hour later he knocked on our door, heralding his grand entrance. In walked Jason gingerly as he tried to balance his well-decorated tray with hot chocolate, scrambled eggs, toasts, among other goodies. As he presented me with my full breakfast, my eyes welled up with tears. I quickly dashed to the bathroom to flush my teary eyes with water. My thoughts soon drifted back to that Monday morning when his mother and I had a long conversation on the verandah in Jamaica. It was alleged that Lorraine was pregnant again for the third time, and her mother was quite furious. Elaine asked me to give some counsel to Lorraine in relation to responsibility, accountability, and sex, along with the ramifications that stemmed from sex. The sharp Lorraine was way ahead of the game. We had a hearty conversation going – everything from STDs, abortion issues, relationships, etc. Every time I look at Jason, I feel guilty for having broached some of those topics with her that day because at the time, Jason was *in utero*. It has dogged me terribly. Not that I had advised her to do anything untoward.

To put it in a nutshell, Jason has been a blessing to our family in many ways than one. For every moment spent filling out those adoption papers for him and his brothers, I had found blessings at my fingertips. Lorraine and Elaine are no longer with us, but I am truly grateful for their contributions in giving us these three wonderful young men.

YOU WERE CALLED TO ADOPT A CHILD

I ONCE heard a man say, "Never underestimate the power of your presence," and more and more I understand what he was really saying. One of the areas where the power of your presence can be magnified is through adoption. Adoption can result from your mere visit to a foster home or a little league baseball game. Sometimes your friends dragged you kicking and screaming to play basketball, but don't underestimate the power of your presence. The little boy who stared at you in the bleachers is without a daddy, and he sees the perfect father figure in you. Find out more about him. All along, that boy was looking at his future daddy – you!

You just decided to drop by the orphanage on your way from work one evening when the little girl with the curly hair started giggling with you from her crib. She hasn't laughed with anybody else for over three months, but she cannot resist you. You picked her up, and she immediately buried her head in your bosom. You tried to put her down 10 minutes later, but she refused to budge. She saw the mother she didn't have in you. You are now haunted by her laughter; you now go back and forth with your decision to adopt her. Understand that your presence was needed to bring hope to this little girl. Help to complete her life. God will do the rest. Become a mother to that child.

How about that boy who has changed eight homes in the last 10 months? He's waiting for you to be the rightful dad to him. You can reach him where nobody else can. His acting up is deliberately done as a way to bide time for you – for the kink in the adoption process to be ironed out. Silently, he's been praying for the "perfect" dad like the one his friend Raymond has. And you are praying for the "perfect" son. You have had five great, upstanding daughters, but you yearn for a son. Subtly, it is gnawing away at your marriage. Those girls, too, long for a brother to spoil.

You and your wife want to try one more time for a son, but that son will not be fertilized any time soon by you two. That son is already here. Perhaps you are in Houston, Texas, and he's in Lima, Peru. He is destined to be somebody of great standing in society. He will be a force with which to be reckoned in his professional life. Wouldn't you want to be the proud father of such a young man someday? Stop those sleepless nights by contacting that adoption agency. Today. Dial that telephone number. Shoot off that email. They are right there at your fingertips. And they are called blessings. Be prepared, however, for a double bonus as many women become pregnant months after adopting a child, after years of trying to conceive. Adoption can open doors to more blessings.

ADOPTION COMPLETES
MY FAMILIAL SYMMETRY

MY FATHER'S mother died when he was two years old, and his father died long before I was born. Based on what I was told, my mother was raised by her grandmother long before her 13th birthday. She became a mother a month shy of her 14th birthday. I laid eyes on my maternal grandfather for the first and only time on Saturday, April 10, 1981. To date, I am the only grandchild from my mother's children who knew him. He died about eight years ago. The only grandparent I ever spent any period of time with was my maternal grandmother. As kids my siblings and I would sporadically visit her for a few hours at a time. The only times I spent more than four hours at her house were when I stayed overnight in August 1970 and December 1975. Thus, the luxury of kids being spoiled or pampered by their grand-parents were way off left field for me. I longed to be hugged by doting grandmothers, and grandaunts, but I had none of that growing up. I tried to ferret out siblings from the east, west, north and south. I was fortunate to unearth two brothers – one in 1978 and another in 1980, respectively – by then two grown men.

My adopting these boys came full circle to what I have always longed for. By no means I am trying to be a super dad because I am still learning new things everyday. Nevertheless, I wanted to do the opposite of what my mom did. She left her children, but I wanted to nurture children. Ironic, uh? Once and for all, I want to send the spirit of abandonment in this family packing. Thus, I find this arrangement creates a nice symmetry. I hope that the family dynamics can be ameliorated in a very big way over time because of Yvonne and me adopting our boys.

Some of you are perhaps saying that I am romanticizing adoption. But truth be told, it is not a cakewalk in the park. After I brought home those boys from the airport on June 23, 2005, reality dawned. I sat in my home office pretty much paralyzed for about three days, with all kinds of emotion running through my head. I don't recall taking a shower that night. Everything was so overwhelming. I stared fixedly into the ceiling for what seemed like hours, questioning myself. "Do you really know what you've gotten yourself into?" Well, if new mothers battle post-partum depression, then what do adopted fathers of three big boys suffer? I again asked myself. Indeed, it was a bittersweet moment for me. I was happy that the voluminous paperwork was finally drawing to a close. I was also happy that we were given a chance to love those orphaned boys unconditionally and to groom them into great men for the future. But the flipside of that coin had me racking my brains trying to come up with the best method to train them. Yvonne and I turned over our bedroom to them and we slept on the sofas and floor for eight months.

I felt guilty for bringing them into our 2-bedroom space, where each boy didn't have his own room. Granted there was an Olympic-sized swimming pool, a family-sized Jacuzzi, a tennis court, a play area with swings and other kids-friendly apparatuses, a full state-of-the-art gym, fireplace in our living room, just to name a few basic necessities. They readily took advantage of those little perks, but I was still feeling guilty. That's one of the few times when I missed New York City. I longed for the days when our home was nicely decorated, with much larger space. But that was the past. We sold or gave away everything from a pin to an anchor before moving to Seattle. As a result, we had to start from scratch here.

Things only got worse when Jason's constant prayers were going unanswered. He wasn't praying for the latest videogame gadgets or other fanciful things, which boys use to pass their time. He was praying for a 5-bedroom house. At family devotion, grace for breakfast, lunch, or dinner, Jason's prayers were revolved around that house. Brown-stewed chicken became the boys' meal of choice for no other reason but for them to get the wishbone from the meaty breast. Somebody told them about wishbone and what it could do, and again, those wishes were not for fanciful boy toys or a trip to Disneyworld. It was for that 5-bedroom house. Soon all the boys were on that campaign. Sometimes that house was drawn with a picket fence. Other times it was a Tudor mansion home with the swimming pool off to the side of it. Many times I wanted to tell them to ease up on that prayer, but how could I stop them from doing so when we were the ones who told them to pray specific prayers whenever they pray? All I could do at times was just chuckle and dream with them.

Sales for my business plummeted because of the lack of time I had to do marketing for new clients. I used that precious time instead toward getting them settled in their new domicile. Our 401Ks, CDs, IRAs were soon cashed in, incurring massive penalties over time. Our finances trickled down to nothing, but silently, I believed that we were doing the right thing. We moved from New York with a large sum of money to keep us floating for even two years, but over time, those funds were gobbled up, too.

Staying up late at night gave me invaluable perspectives on life. I reflected on the many fathers who left home, thinking that they were a failure to their families when their finances dwindled. I felt like them, too. Useless. I will be rebuked for saying this, but it actually crossed my mind about leaving for a moment. I am ashamed of myself now for ever entertaining such thoughts. I told Yvonne, and as the consummate wife, she totally understood how I was feeling. We prayed about it together. And I purposed myself to pray for those fathers who felt that they had to leave because they didn't have the willpower to stay and fight for their families' survival. I was no longer judgmental, pointing the finger at them.

Because my credit score was always in the highest range, I didn't know what it was like to have outstanding debts, but that period had some of my credit cards singing a different tune. I said a prayer, too, for those families who were battling financial dilemmas. Indeed, I was getting a taste of their medicine.

We got the greatest compliments from family, friends, and even strangers for raising our boys, but one meddlesome grandmother, who couldn't seem to get her nose out of our business, told us in no uncertain terms that we had no business adopting, since adoption was set aside for rich people. We tolerated her for awhile, even when she suggested that we were not quite "real" parents because of our adopted status. I had to sever that relationship when she crossed the line. "Real parents don't allow their children to ride public buses," she castigated me. I had dropped off Jevoy, more than 14 years old, earlier that day at his new after-school program, and had to shuttle his other brothers somewhere else. Time was of the essence, so I told him to catch the bus home that Friday afternoon. She spotted him on his way to get the bus, and offered him a ride home. That's when she let it all out.

In hindsight, with all the dark days and sleepless nights I have been through, I would adopt those boys again at the blink of an eye. As long as a pound of flour and some sugar can still be converted into a breakfast, I should harbor no fear about tomorrow. As long as a pound of beans and some rice can be converted into a night's dinner, then I should not rack my brains worrying about T-bone steak. When I look back over the years on how I grew up, there was hardly a comprehensive medical coverage in place for me or countless other families. Thank God that is not the case with them today.

As long as love can be given to activate ambitions and dreams, then I will give it freely and without reservation. As long as I have people praying for me and emotionally supporting me, then I can face tomorrow. As long as God promises to supply all my needs according to His riches in glory, then any financial setbacks were only temporary. As long as a shelter was over my head, and I have a warm place to lay my head, I can say with certainty that those boys will be there also. As long as laughter will remain free, I promise I will ensure to make joy my best friend.

One of the things that propels me to do even more for our boys is their deep sense of gratitude. If you were to share an apple among them, they would never walk away without saying "thank you Dad/ Mom for the apple." Sometimes the thank-you comes out one at a time, and at other times, it comes in unison. Something as simple as an ice cream cone would make their day.

Truly God is amazing. He has been faithful throughout all this process. He has favored us in so many ways. I walked into church not too long ago, and a brother presented me with a check for $500, telling me to do whatever I wanted to do with it. Yvonne was talking to a family friend in Georgia recently on her way to work, and the woman asked her if she needed some money to borrow. Yvonne told her no.

She insisted on sending $2,000 for her, telling her it was a gift. We hardly ever borrow money from people. So for her to volunteer to lend us money, it is nothing short of divine intervention.

As student government president of his school, Jevoy was nominated in March 2007 to serve as a page in the Washington State Senate. He spent a week there learning the day to day operation of American government. That's where he also received his first paycheck. He hopes to one day hold public office, he said. He's poised to excel in that arena by the way how he can glibly deliver himself out of any argument. He is currently enrolled in the rigorous and coveted Cambridge Program at his school. Jevaughn was one of a few students culled from his school in a district-wide young writers symposium to read his work publicly a few months ago.

He was also the first-place winner in a citywide essay competition, celebrating Dr. Martin Luther King, Jr.'s legacy, in the middle school category. Jevoy, as a high school freshman, beat out many seniors to take second place in the high school category for the same citywide essay competition. Both awards came with financial rewards and certificates. It was truly an honor to see two brothers onstage receiving their awards at a civic function with public officials. The emcee had the audience chuckling when he said that "something is definitely going on inside the Palmer household." Jason is holding his own by being a Leopard Leader for his class. He just got back from a leadership conference in Portland, Oregon, with his school. All of them are holding their own scholastically.

We are truly blessed for having our boys around, backed up by the wonderful people who support us with their love and prayers. That judge's words are definitely coming to pass.

CHAPTER SIXTEEN

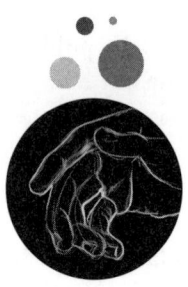

THE JOYS OF
HONORING OUR CHILDREN

EVERY CHANCE YVONNE AND I GET, WE GO OUT of our way to honor our children. We tell them that we love them, and what a payback it yields! It's not uncommon for them to be watching TV and one of them grab a pillow, put it in our laps and lie down undisturbed. I thought that the pride factor would have kicked in once strangers were around, but quite the contrary. A family friend was over for dinner the Sunday after Thanksgiving, and Jevoy, the eldest boy, didn't have any qualms about tossing a pillow and lying on my lap. Jason was all over Yvonne, while Jevaughn pulled on some soft fabric on another sofa, awaiting his turn to switch place with one of his brothers.

I dubbed our sofas the miracle sofas because not in a million years I would have ever thought that those seats could hold so many people at one time. I would liken the scenario to that of a litter of pups or seals sprawled out on a beach sunning. The warmth has brought us so much closer together. There's no TV in our bedrooms.

Thus, family time is very valuable. I am not trying to kid myself as I already know the answer, but lately I'm starting to wonder if this setup was divinely planned all along. Everybody has become more touching and caring over the past months.

KIDS AND TECHNOLOGY

"WHAT WAS hidden from the wise and prudent, is now revealed to the babe and suckling," goes a popular song lyrics, gleaned from Luke 10:21.

With technology so advancing, many older folks are at breakneck speed trying to catch up with the latest gadget. I often wonder about the possibility of people who died 30 years ago coming back to life now, and how they would cope with the new additions since they said the big goodbye: cell phone, emails, Fax, DVD, CD, Tivo, videogames, just to name a few.

I have a few LPs around the house just as souvenirs, and the boys are mesmerized by them. I often wonder what would they say about 8-Tracks. As soon as I turn around, one of them is there to change the configuration on the computer, cell phone or car gadget. While I would read a manual to navigate my way around setting up an appliance or instrument, they readily set to work finding a solution, and by the time you can clear your throat, they will have already assembled that thing. My cell phone ring tones and configuration have rarely remained the same for long as they are always meddling with something. For me, my children are, hands down, blessings at my fingertips. What a blessing it is to have them around.

Things that I have discovered about my own car and van in one month with their help and without the use of a manual, I could not have done so in three years. They are always on the prowl to search out new discoveries. I get so scared at times to undo some of the things which I've enjoyed over the years, that it's hard letting go. Many times I have to kick and scream in order to be let out of my cocoon, but the boys have nothing to lose. They flesh out the best in me. Their attitudes in going about things have helped me to relax more and trust them more. It all makes for a harmonious existence – the young teaching the older ones and vice versa.

Their dexterity on videogames is bar none. Playing with them on their games is not for the faint at heart. While you run off the road in confusion, they handle their controls with such equanimity. It's like second nature to them. They would give me some pointers and what a blessing it is to learn from them.

THE BIG TELEPHONE

SOME YEARS ago, a friend of mine told me of an incident where a man died, leaving a lot of possessions. Within hours after his passing, a group of people descended on his house and raided his belongings. The person who walked away with a "big telephone" went home and set up the telephone in place. Not very long afterward, the telephone began to ring, and when nobody answered, a funny sound ensued. The paper in the big telephone started to move and words began to appear on it. The family gathered and bolted from their home as they had never seen or heard a telephone making such crazy noises and action.

Before long, people began talking among themselves saying that it was an omen. Word got out that the deceased man was trying to punish them because they had stolen his possession. Over time, they came to the realization that the "big telephone" was actually a Fax machine. I am certain that had a technology-savvy child been present, the family would not have run from their home unnecessarily that fateful day.

Again, while many grown folks cower over new technologies, children are gladly welcoming them. It's as though they have the built-in receptor, which makes everything foolproof upon contact. The Bible says that children are a blessing. "Sons are a heritage from the Lord . . . Blessed is the man whose quiver is full of them." Children are never out of season. What would immigrant parents do hadn't it been for their children born in their new country? I've always watched with awe how a little 9-year-old child would translate for her mother at a doctor's office or fill out vital information on complicated application forms. You see them inside pharmacies. Ticket counters at airports. Many children are the eyes and ears for their non-English-speaking parents or non-French. Non-Spanish. Depending on their country of domicile.

They balance checkbooks. They oversee pertinent financial matters. They read out dosage on their parents' medications. And the list goes on. Every now and then, you see on the evening news where a 3-year-old dialed 911, seeking assistance for his mother who had fainted or suffered some kind of seizures. Children are indispensable.

Children can be providers. Not too long ago, I watched an interview with Tiffany, the songbird who has sparked a sensation in the music industry. She talked about how her parents, along with multiple siblings, were homeless, living out of their van. While driving through Atlantic City, New Jersey, the family stopped at one of the casinos to use the restroom. As she passed by a ballroom, she heard music, and before long, she was onstage doing what she did best – singing. In that split second, she was on her way to being a star. She later won several competitions, which amassed large financial gains. With that money, she was able to buy her family a home. Think about it, a child saving her family from homelessness and a life of despair!

A CHILD CREATED HEALING PROPERTIES FOR HIS MOTHER

CHILDREN CAN come through for you when you least expect them to. Ask 16-year-old Spencer Brooks. About a year ago, Spencer's mom, Floretta, was driving in Seattle when her car was hit by a drunk driver. She suffered severe injuries and was in quite a lot of pain. She underwent several sessions of chiropractic evaluations and multiple physical therapy sessions, but the pain seemed to get worse. She refused to take some of the medications prescribed to her, calling them habit forming. The more she writhed in pain, the more downcast her teenage son became. He was tired of seeing his mother in agony.

Being the only child left at home, young Spencer considered it his responsibility to see his mom get well. He started coming up with ideas to see healing come to the fore. So one morning, unbeknownst to his mother, he made a bath for her, which comprised of various salts. He later escorted his mom to the salts bath, and she soaked herself for awhile. When she reported marked changes in her level of pains, he continued making the bath. Over time, he began to add more salts to the bath, along with other aromatic flavorings.

Out of that incident, Spencer started his own company – Spencer's Healing Bath Salts – marketing his product all over Seattle. The commodities are packaged into multihued bags, and the salts themselves are colored in an aquatic tint. The scent is most pleasant. In fact, it was at one of those marketing seminars I first met Spencer and his mom. The symposium, put on by the Seattle Association of Black Journalists (NABJ) in January 2007, had his ebullient mom beaming with pride. She said that she attributed a big part of her healing foremost to God, enabled by the work of her son's hands.

Spencer went on to tell me that everything about his product was designed with his mother in mind. Even his mother's favorite color – blue – found its way into the packaging. What a blessing to have a son this great. He definitely found those blessings at his fingertips and utilized them the way God intended them to be.

CHILDREN CAN TEACH US
A THING OR TWO ABOUT LIFE

A VERY WELL-RESPECTED and influential lady told me that she has learnt a big lesson from her small children. She spoke about being invited to a social gathering with other well-heeled couples, but that evening her husband didn't feel like attending the function, and he opted to stay home. On returning home, she grumbled about being the only person present at the party without a spouse by her side. Finally, her two young sons turned around and began to scold her.

"Mom, you should be grateful that you have a husband who you could come back home to, and not somebody running the streets," they pummeled.

That evening they went on to tell her about the good qualities their father and her husband possessed, minus his less than gregarious bent. From that day onward, she said that she has never made the mistake of feeling less than a wife whenever her husband would refuse to join her at other grand affairs. The lesson is, never discount the counsel of a child.

A lot of parents also get trapped in complaining about what their children are doing wrong instead of being grateful for what they are doing right. They aren't disrespectful to parents, teachers, and other adults. They don't hang out late without calling home. But they don't clean up their rooms the way they should. Be thankful for the fact that they are not in jail or being unproductive. There is hope after a messy bathroom and frowsy blankets.

YOUTHS IN SOUTH AFRICA

THE YOUTH were the ones who had been most instrumental in tearing down the evil walls of apartheid in South Africa. They were the ones who faced police bullets, truncheons, and armored tanks. While their parents, uncles, aunts, and community leaders were in exile or imprisoned, they were the ones who took to the streets of South Africa to demand change. And with one voice. Then two. Then five. Then 50, then a million. Then many more millions, change finally dawned on the South African landscape. The world would witness the triumphant release of Nelson Rolihlahla Mandela on February 11, 1990, after his serving more than 27 years in prison on Robben Island. Mandela went on to become president of that nation. But the point of the matter is that the youth were a big reason why the process was sped up to usher in the monumental office for that nation's first black president. Thanks in part to the National Union of South African Students.

THE PURITY OF A CHILD'S BLESSING

SOME PEOPLE collect precious stones, rare coins and seashells. Some collect historical stamps and figurines, but I collect babies' smiles. Nothing brightens my day faster than a baby's smile. I go out in search of them, and whenever I get one even in passing, my world just simply comes alive. I collect them. I deposit them and cash them in whenever I am having a hard day. I take on their innocence and refuse to see people with jaundiced eyes. I assume their indiscriminate ways. A baby will smile with a homeless bag lady just as quickly as he/she will smile with a princess. I look for babies' smiles in church, at the checkout counters, at the banks, at the doctor's office. And those smiles never fail to do the job. They have the power to inject sunshine into dark clouds; they can tower over deep valleys of burdens and lost hopes.

I've often joked that if somebody were to smell a baby's breath, that baby would be definitely in need of urgent medical care. Frankly, in all my time being around babies, I'm yet to meet one with halitosis. Never! You see, there's just something special and supernatural about this arrangement with nature. The same baby who slurps down many helpings of her mother's breast milk or other milk-based formulas daily, does not need to maintain oral hygiene for months. Nature takes care of their dental care with that reservoir of hydrogen-filled spittle constantly drooling from their mouths. It doesn't get purer than that.

In like manner, if a child were to move to Japan from the U.S., in no time that child would be so fluent in Japanese, that it would boggle the mind. Again, purity within the mind of a child. What that child could learn in a month, some parents couldn't learn in a lifetime. A big reason why that is so is because children harbor no hang-ups like most of us adults do:

"What sayonara has to do with goodbye in English?" you asked. "It doesn't sound like it, it doesn't feel like it? So it doesn't make any sense for me – a grown man – to substitute my good English word for goodbye in lieu of a strange word called *Sayonara*, which means nothing to me."

Children don't question diphthong and cadence, they just learn them as is. And that's what makes it so remarkable for them to excel in record time.

Using the preceding examples of the purity of a baby/child, I cannot help but to apply those baby-like characteristics into our blessing pool. I remember studying for a rigorous exam, which had me up until in the wee hours of the morning. Jason went to use his bathroom and saw the light in the living room. "Dad, you're still studying?" he asked. I said yes. My brains were fried — so saturated with a ton load of facts and legalese. All I could do at that time was to ask my 9-year-old son to pray for me. He laid his two hands on my head, and pray he did! After coming home from that four-hour exam, Jason met me at the door with a big grin all over his face.

"So where is your result?" he asked confidently.

"Which result?" I teased. "Do you expect me to pass?"

"Sure," he said, "I prayed for you this morning, and I know that God heard my prayer."

I wanted to tease him some more, but I couldn't contain my joy. I hugged him tightly and blurted out, "Yes, yes, yes, Son, I passed!" I showed him my temporary documents, which recorded my passing score. He and his brothers all celebrated with me. As a matter of fact, 90 percent of the words my eldest son said for prayer over grace that evening were utilized in thanking God for my passing the exam with flying colors. I considered myself a blessed man, indeed, that evening, to have sons who care so much for me.

Now, don't ever shy away from bringing your child to the forefront of family matters. Sometimes children can bring about changes so effectively that would render you speechless. For a child who has never heard those magic words, "I love you" from Daddy or Mommy, that child can shift the family dynamics in a most positive way by being proactive and start saying "I love you, Mommy/Daddy."

Get them involved in the planning of family reunions. Have Tamara and Justin write a blessing for their 95-year-old great-grandmother on her birthday. For those of you who teach Sunday school or are working with juvenile delinquents, you can start them off with this — whether or not they are writing a blessing for a daddy/mommy in jail and so forth. This, I foresee, will be very emotional at first, but work with them because healing will not be very far afoot. Remember, the blessings of the Lord maketh rich and addeth no sorrows.

Forgiveness of self and others is very paramount for you to write this blessing. Even though Jacob was blessed, he could not fully reap his full blessing, as he was hard on himself. Esau had to forgive him before he could move on and live out the fullness of his blessing. Jacob also needed to forgive himself.

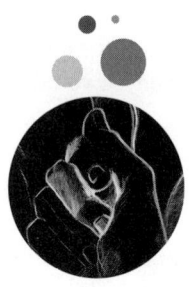

CHAPTER SEVENTEEN

WHAT DOES FORGIVENESS HAVE TO DO WITH BREAST MILK?

NOT TOO LONG AGO, A FRIEND OF MINE SENT OUT an email, reporting the tragic passing of his beloved aunt. The incident made front-page news in a major newspaper. He sent a link to connect to the online newspaper reporting the horrible death. I pondered long and hard what to say to him. I finally braved the courage and called him. To my disbelief, I soon found out that he was the one encouraging me. I have witnessed this thing talked about on talk shows when people come face to face with the people who have hurt them. I have also heard pastors and other religious people preach it from the pulpit, but many times when they or a loved one is hurt; when their mettle is tested, then it takes on a life of its own. By the time forgiveness was to be put into practice, many of them will have marched down the halls of justice playing hangmen, judges, and jury. People are so grief stricken at times that for many, it would take years to heal their broken hearts.

But here I was on the telephone with a human being – not via television – but somebody whom I've known personally. It brought redemption to my flagging distrust in that area. Frankly, I doubt I would be that readily forgiving as my friend, Paul C. This man loved his aunt to the hilt. In fact, she helped to raise him as a child. So it must have been utter shock when he learnt that the sprightly 74-year-old woman, weighing less than 100 pounds, was strangled by her deranged female tenant.

As Paul C weaved his way in and out of the tragedy, he balanced both sides as deftly as a tightrope walker at the circus. He would grieve for his aunt, but within split seconds, he was grieving for the accused and her family as well. The defendant was engaged to be married, and she has a teenage daughter who will now grow up without a mother. Even though it was established that the woman was mentally unstable, she was one of the kindest individuals on the planet, Paul C said. She always chipped in to assist his aunt whenever those needs arose. But just thinking about the kindness of the past, many of us would toss out all that "good deed" stuff overboard for the swiftest penalty.

Listening to Paul C that day, I was very touched by his empathy toward that woman. He has grown a 100 feet taller in my eyes as truly a great human being. What a blessing he is! Where did he find understanding when many of us would seek vengeance? Which switch did he turn on to convert bitterness into forgiveness? Could it be because his daily job mandates his looking about the welfare of other mentally-challenged people why he is so far ahead of many of us in this regard? I may never know the answers. But he has truly given me hope in an otherwise dark situation. It is said that the best way to measure a man's character is not in the time of calm but in the time of tragedy, and indeed Paul C has passed those tests with flying colors. Just remember that whenever you forgive others, you are opening up the door for more blessings.

"Finally, all of you, live in harmony with one another; be sympathetic; love as brothers, be compassionate and humble. Do not repay evil with evil or insult with insult, but with blessing, because to this you were called so that you may inherit a blessing." – 1 Peter 3:8.

ISOLATE AND FORGIVE

IF YOU'RE having a hard time forgiving somebody, find it in your heart to isolate something – even one small thing – that is positive about that person. Culture it. Dwell on it. When you have brought it to a place of perfection, then gently put it back onto the seat of your heart. At that time it will envelop your being for you to love unconditionally. See it like a bad kidney in need of a transplant. Without remedying that bad kidney, it could potentially bankrupt your whole system. Once a new kidney is in place, the blood will begin to flow normal again.

I read some years ago about a mother who was pregnant with twins. She had some complications because one of the babies had gotten ill. Doctors performed a C section, took the injured baby from its mother's uterus and operated on it. After the condition was remedied, the other baby in his mother's womb went on to develop to its full term, while his sibling stayed in intensive care. Had that sick baby been allowed to stay in his mother's uterus, he not only could potentially damage his own life but those of his brother and mother's.

One good example to drive this point home is a mother abandoning her child. If that child were to be told the truth about his abandonment when he grows up, there is bound to be enmity between him and his birth mother. That child would ask a thousand questions as to why his mother would abandon him, and with each question comes bitter daggers. And if that child is not careful, those same daggers could turn around, pierce his body and poison him.

I was one of those boys. I struggled for years asking a thousand "whys" without getting any concrete answers. The more I questioned, the more bitter I became. One day after questions and answers eluded me, I started to examine myself in a positive light. I challenged myself to think of a few positive things I could tell my mother thanks for, and that was a stretch of the imagination.

As I wrestled with those thoughts, suddenly nouns like womb. Breast milk. Medicine. Cuddle. Caregiver, and diaper, began popping out of nowhere like fireworks. I was stunned. I thought about how I had made a grand entrance into the world at birth, after nestled for nine long months inside my mother's warm and nutritious womb. I pondered the medicinal and nutritional values of breast milk. It is said that the first three days after giving birth, the clear fluid (*colostrums*, also known as "liquid gold") that a mother produces from her breast is umpteenth times more powerful than penicillin. I radiated a smile for being the recipient of such a blessed gift. I cherished the cuddling my mom must have given me, even for a few times. I became thankful for the nights she stayed up when I became colicky, and the amount of soiled diapers she had to wash. By hand!

After I examined myself for some time, the albatross of unforgiveness that weighted down my heart for years was chased away. Its webbed feet of encumbrance that held my heart captive was no more. In a flash the gentle dove of forgiveness released me, and filled in those grooves with love and appreciation.

I further began to think about the millions of people who have benefited from breast milk. How they, too, have missed major illnesses and gained multiple benefits even for years to come. So, if you only had breast milk for five days out of your life, then thank God and your mom for that privilege. If you still cannot bring yourself to this stage, think back on some of the wonderful people who have impacted your life.

You might have come from a very abusive and dysfunctional background, but look around you today and see the people whose lives are positive because they benefited from their caring mothers' breast milk. Today some of those people are your wives, husbands, teachers, and managers. They are your postal workers, your bankers, pastors, and rabbis. They are your imams and best friends. The oncologist who has given you a clean bill of health from cancer perhaps survived early childhood from various diseases that were offset because of the medicinal properties from his mother's milk. Every time you say thanks to him, you are saying thanks universally to mothers as well. Give it a universal platform. See it from that vantage point, and slowly you will begin to find that indirectly, you have benefited from breast milk in one way or the other. Once you have fully realized the power of that concept, start thinking about the warm feeling of love. Empty out that love into your heart, and use it to start loving your mother unconditionally.

Think about the daddy who you have only spotted two times in your life. Some of you have never ever met him. But by applying the universal love of fatherhood, before long it will blunt the edges of your disdain for men in general. Fathers in your world will not only be seen as good-for-nothing dead beats. Because of somebody else's good father, you were able to find a good husband. Because of Mr. Beal's good father, you were privileged to have him as the best math teacher ever, who eventually became a father figure to you. Because of your best friend Regina's good dad, you, a single mother, are now raising your own sons to be better fathers for generations to come, just from his examples of how he raised his children.

Don't speed up the process. The incubation period for everybody varies. However, you should see it through to completion. And what a reward awaiting you once you can replace that abyss of bitterness with a mountain of love!

No sight warms my heart better than that of a grown man playing around with his mother, or a young mother caring for her little children. Even though I did not personally get those treatments from my own mother, vicariously I see myself in those scenarios. And instead of feeling sad or sorry for myself, I celebrate those blessed children and mothers. I know that their future will be a lot healthier than many of the abandoned children around today.

In order for this method to be effective, selfishness has to be kicked through the door forthwith. You have to get beyond the "why me"/poor me" syndrome. How else could you stand the sight of a daddy walking at the beachside, while stroking his daughter's hair? How will that deep-seated feeling ever go away if every time you see Mr. Porter, your friend's daddy, showing up to all of his son's basketball game, rain or shine, with your feeling covetous? Be happy for those people. The joy that emanates from those bonds will eventually start seeping into your heart.

How else do you explain a boy who grew up with no father becoming a good husband and father, contrary to what statistics say? Explain to me how an abandoned girl who was raised all her life in an orphanage, turned out to be the most loving mother in Anywhere, Across the World Blvd.?

THE WILD AND THE TAMED

I ALSO liken this approach to conditioning. Animals that were born and raised in captivity would have a hard time surviving in the wild, but over time, given the right coaching, that same caged lion or baboon will do what nature creates him to do. Gradually, he makes his first step away from the cage, then a second, third, and a thousandth step later, and voila, he is right at home in the wild among the best of them.

On the other hand, the animal in the wild, when taken captive, will have to undergo several changes before it can be transformed into a domesticated animal. Someday, she will be just like her other tamed brothers and sisters. One proverb asks how to eat an elephant. And the answer is one bite at a time. Merging the two frontiers is essential to bringing about wholeness to an otherwise sorry situation. Resolve to tame that unending venom of bitterness and unforgiveness today. Your life depends on it.

When I decided to rid myself of that bitterness toward my mother, it was very hard as I have mentioned before. I couldn't bring myself to write her a decent letter, but I did so on February 23, 2005. And what a blast I am feeling now writing these paragraphs. I can honestly say that I have not felt a shred of bitterness toward my mother ever since I sent her that letter. I can sleep in peace at last.

You, too, can let it happen in your life. Isolate your hurt and pain, deal with the questions then and clean them up. Don't make this a missing link. Like all good repairmen do, take it out; clean it up, and fix it. If a part needs to be replaced, do it but don't leave the slot empty.

"How could she betray me like that?" you grumble about your former best friend.

"The nerve of my dad to walk out and leave my mom with nine small kids!" you often murmur.

Frankly, those kinds of bitterness did not come about overnight, and I don't expect them to go away overnight. But if you begin to apply this approach, healing will come to your heart before long.

It must have been quite painful to love somebody when that

person has hurt you so badly. Are you that 50-year-old mother and wife who was physically and sexually abused by your father long before you even became a teenager? Were you the infant who made the evening news 35 years ago when your mother dumped you on the church steps in the dead of winter? Did your parents force you to marry that man at 14, when he was 25 years your senior just for the sole purpose of financial gains?

You can find something to start out with that will help you get on the road of healing. Try singling out something about the person that you once liked or treasured. Was it a name, smile, the breast milk the mother gave you as a child, the ice cream daddy once bought for you, the time you played horsey on his back? Did you hear family members speak about him in encomiums? Did they say that she was the pride and joy of her family before she changed?

Like the making of yogurt or culture in a lab, just start out with a little bit at a time. If you want to make quick yogurt, just get about one teaspoon of plain yogurt and add about one quart of milk to it. Before long, you will be getting a lot of yogurt. Similarly, to grow a tissue, scientists culture it, and then they're off to creating chemical/biological engineering.

Culture some of Mama's breast milk today, and let it expand into a vast pool of blessings for you, even though she has long been out of your life. Get that breast milk, separate it, dwell on it – think about all the positive things of breast milk: it gives life; it sustains life.

Sometimes little things can bring about big results. Ask a baker. Two ounces of yeast can increase the size of 10 pounds of flour. Baking powder and baking soda are some other rising agents. Why don't you isolate a particular item and bring it to perfection? Let's rise above our circumstances of hurt and pain and become the party of change.

See yourself today as that little bit of yeast, baking powder or baking soda. Inflate your way to freedom. Be the agent of change.

THE LOCK AND FORGIVENESS

I HAVE heard fabulous stories about the Panama Canal, but I've never been fortunate to see it at work. Nevertheless, there's a lock in a section of Seattle called the Ballard Locks, which does the same thing that the Panama Canal does: ferrying ships from one body of water to the next. The Ballard Locks are the closest I've ever gotten to a functional lock. To see the machination of a lock up close is mind boggling. As hundreds of big and small boats line up to cross from one body of water to the next on a daily basis, those locks work nonstop. One of the things that grab my observation every time I am there is how the water has to be constantly replenished in order for it to lower or raise a boat. For that boat to get to its desired destination, the water level has to be right, and that lock does take some time to fill up. Without having that desired water level, a boat could plummet more than 100 feet or an avalanche of water could sink it. Hence, water level is crucial.

I see a parallel between the locks and forgiveness. When you forgive, you are releasing those mental ships/boats and taking in fresh water. Your conscience needs to be set free, not tied up inside the lock chamber of bitterness. Water needs to change in order for the next set of boats to continue their journey. Every time you set a boat loose, you are freeing up the lock for another boat to set sail. So, what do you have tied up inside your locks? Set them loose today. Every time you forgive somebody, another person will find it in his heart to forgive you, too, and set you free.

If God forgives you, then it is only fitting that you should forgive somebody else. See Matthew 18:21-35 where Jesus gave the parable of the man whose debts were forgiven yet he was adamant in forgiving his friend/servant's debts.

THE UNWELCOMED NEIGHBOR

WHAT IS seen as punishment can turn out for your good. My dad told me about a Caucasian family in a predominantly white neighborhood in Brooklyn, New York, who sold their house to a black woman in order to punish their next-door neighbor. Some people in the community were up in arms over the black woman's moving into the area. But over time, their fears were allayed. Within a few weeks, the black woman and her neighbors became the best of friends. It turned out that they had more in common with her than with their former neighbors. Color became less of an issue.

The black woman was a registered nurse, and during her spare time, she took care of her neighbor's ailing father. For free. She cooked for them, house-sat for them, and over time, became the darling of the block. What was used to put a wedge between families, turned out to be a multiple of blessings to those who needed each other. I could just see that woman carrying a grudge among her unwelcoming neighbors for years, but she knew that forgiveness was the only option available to her if she wanted to live free of mental baggage. She had a big enough heart to forgive her neighbors and in turn found blessings at her fingertips, which she uses to bless them.

CONFESSION–A PREREQUISITE
TO BEING BLESSED

OUR BOYS have taught us many things, but one of the highlights of their teaching us is when they get into the mode of confession. Sometimes confessions are done inside the car, around the dinner table or inside the park. Jevaughn would go through story after story regaling us with how he covertly disposed of that piece of salmon or how he put on extra pieces of clothing, unbeknownst to us, to show off at school. Jason would pipe in, contributing his pieces as a partner in crime. Many times, Mr. Goody-Too-Shoe,

Jevoy, would be the last to get onboard. But once he gets going, he'll put a parakeet to shame.

Our garbage disposal in the kitchen sink has always malfunctioned. Because whenever they want to get rid of every shred of evidence, the garbage bin will not do. It is the disposal that becomes their best friend. It is the burial spot for chunks of meats, pints of beverages, and oodles of noodles.

While we laugh whenever these boys confess, often time there's an air of freedom that emanates from those confessions. They would say sorry for doing it, and pledge not to do so again. Well – until they find another route to dispose of food and drinks since we already know what they're up to. Yvonne and I would feel a sense of relief after hearing the boys confess and say sorry for their youthful indiscretions. And all of us are healed as a result of those open discussions. How could we possibly hold those things against them when we did some of the same things as children? Hence, for us, forgiveness is the only option.

We saw the healing of a nation after Nelson Mandela took office as president of South Africa when he created the Truth and Reconciliation Commission. It was set up to put post apartheid aches and pains behind the nation. Policemen and civilian alike came together in public confessions. While it was a bitter experience for victims and loved ones to listen to the traumas of yesteryear, there was great relief and healing from those forums. Confession, fused with forgiveness, gives you a new lease on life. It is a catharsis. It has the power to open up the way to greatness for you.

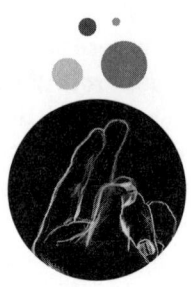

CHAPTER EIGHTEEN

WHY BAD THINGS
HAPPEN TO GOOD PEOPLE

Every now and then my family and I would go out to feed the homeless in Pioneer Square, downtown Seattle. We often cook food and make drinks from scratch. Fresh. It never ceases to amaze me how much more delicious those meals would taste versus the ones we regularly cook for ourselves at home. I just have to attribute that to the extra love imparted as the added ingredient.

On Memorial Day 2004, we went out as usual, setting up the food and drink in place, the plates and cups, etc. Men and women started coming from every which way to form the labyrinthine assembly. Before long, a man about in his mid 30s demanded, "Give me my food now; I can't wait!" I calmly said to him, "Sir, in a few minutes we'll get to you." He was irate. I would later budge and give him the food, bypassing those who were waiting patiently to be served. Within minutes, he came back, uttering, "I want some more!" I turned to him and said, "After we say the grace, Sir, I will give you some more."

I barely finished my sentence when he went into a rage:

"You? You are cursed! Watch out and see for the next few months how your life will go downhill. You will be cursed," he blurted out, his finger pointing at me, before he walked off.

I immediately remembered Jesus' saying: "Bless them that curse you." If I were to tell you that I was not shaken or taken aback with such vitriol, I would be lying to you. For weeks and months, I played that man's words over and over in my mind. "Why would he curse me when all I wanted to do was to bless him and other displaced homeless men and women with food, a word of cheer, and to show them that, yes, somebody cares?" I asked.

Granted, Memorial Day is the day when all grills are cleaned up, making parks and backyards teem with barbecues. As a matter of fact, we turned down several invitations just in order to do our mission. So that statement really boggled my mind for a long time. The only temporary relief I had that day while I continued to serve were the ubiquitous "thank you"; "God bless you"; "You really do this for us?" from grateful homeless men and women who were touched by our selfless dedication to them. Some came with tears in their eyes, brimming with emotion.

The months that followed were trying times. I started to experience some monumental struggles like never before, which put me in the dumps. Could it be a mind thing? I still cannot give you an answer as everything seemed to take a turn for the worst. I called a friend of mine in New Jersey one evening, telling him about the incident, and he rebuked me for taking that man's word seriously. I was somewhat relieved. Nevertheless, the real windfall came one morning when I stumbled onto a sage advice found in Proverbs. 26:2 – "Like a fluttering sparrow or a darting swallow, an undeserved curse will not come to rest." What a relief! That one sentence alone was worth a million dollar to me. I could now go on living my life. The mental paralysis that had crippled me for months was gone. Deliverance had come at last.

I have since considered the consequences of blessing and curse. Some people argue that curse is just a state of mind. They say that it has no place in people's lives. But you be the judge. My quest to put that haunting pronouncement to rest has given me a few more encouraging thoughts along the way. And I am very proud to say that I am more emboldened in my faith today more than ever as it relates to blessing and curse. I now know that no fly-by-night person can curse me if God doesn't permit it. The next passage will tell you why.

FAKE TOKENS DON'T GO ANYWHERE

IN THE summer of 2006, I walked up to the "token-booth" inside a Manhattan subway station, and confidently asked the clerk, "Can I get two tokens, please?" as I pushed in my $10 bill underneath the miniature window. She looked at me as if I were some relic of the past.

"Sir, I can see that you have not been in the New York City subway for years. We no longer sell tokens. We now use cards."

We joshed about the incident, and then the essence of the token got me going. Before I left New York City for Seattle in 2001, you could either use tokens or cards, but over time, the tokens were phased out.

When I first got to New York City in the mid-1980s, I used to be mesmerized by the use of tokens throughout the city's mass transit system. In order to enter the subway, you had to deposit a token in the slot, which gave you clearance to go through the turnstile. It's amazing how many people had tried to fashion other cylindrically-shaped metal pieces to mimic the subway tokens. But alas, those objects did not work. It is simple. Even though those other metals shared some of the same commonalities of tokens, they failed to do the job of a "real" token. If somebody deposited a nickel, dime or penny, it would go through the slot, but the turnstile would not give clearance for her to enter the subway. Why not? Because the metallic object was not coded to complement the design of the turnstile in order for the rider to gain ingress to the trains.

I use the token analogy to shed some light on blessings. If someone speaks curse or blessing over your life, God will see to it that only the blessings make it through to the spiritual realm. Blessing, like the subway token, will go to the reservoir of other blessings; it will open the gate. And curse, like the fake token, will be bombarded, unable to be effective. It cannot enter the blessed portals of your life. So at the end of the day, blessings will be salvaged while curse will be discarded. If you deposit a token (blessing) mistakenly in the slot, the turnstile will not refuse it. And if you fail to enter the subway, all you are doing is just opening the path to give the next passenger a free ride.

So, again, don't bless somebody if you don't mean it. Saul pronounced all kinds of blessings on David while still pursuing the future king to kill him. Obviously, he did not mean what he was saying, but David became more blessed, nonetheless. You cannot take back your blessing. It will find its way in the repository of other blessings on your behalf. And if you utter curse (non-token), it will not go anywhere because only tokens (blessings) were made for the slots.

Don't just take my subway analogy to position yourself for blessings. In Numbers 23, we see how Balak tried to inveigle Balaam to curse Jacob and his people, and how it backfired. "How can I curse those whom God has not cursed? How can I denounce those whom the Lord has not denounced?" said Balaam. In verse 20 of that chapter, Balaam went on to say, "I have received a command to bless; he has blessed, and I cannot change it."

Begin to see yourself as a blessed and highly favored person today. You cannot be cursed when it's God's will for you to be blessed. Always remember that fake tokens don't go anywhere, while "real" tokens will open many turnstiles in life for you. Continue to believe this.

BLESSINGS VS. CURSE

THE OPPOSITE of blessing is curse. Yes, a lot of people don't want to hear this part. It never ceases to amaze me how some of us, with good intentions in mind, manipulate even Bible verses to suit ourselves. One typical example is Deuteronomy 28. ". . . I will bless you . . . you should lend and not borrow. . . ." I cannot tell you the amount of times I have heard those passages quoted – sometimes verbatim – until I had a chance to read the Bible in its entirety for myself. I was shocked beyond belief when I stumbled upon its accompaniment – the section after verse 14, detailing the curse.

"How come I've never heard this preached from the pulpit?" I marveled at myself. Well, all those good blessings from the earlier verses are contingent on people's following certain laws/precepts. And if those laws are not adhered to, then curse will ensue. We are a society that wants the quick fix – the microwave generation, if you will. We want to get the smoky flavor of barbecued chicken yet our hands should not be blackened with charcoal. Granted, you can be assured of quicker, cleaner barbecue, namely, by way of the electric grill, but the taste will not be as authentic. In order to fully get the authentic taste of barbecued meats, the coal grill, hands down, will do the job. Nevertheless, be prepared to get your hands dirty, put out the fire, and clean out the ashes. Thus, there's no free lunch in life. Nothing for nothing. Everything comes with a price.

BAD THINGS SOMETIMES HAPPEN TO GOOD PEOPLE

DEATH IS never a welcome visitor for a lot of us. Even when Granny Pearl lived to the ripe old age of 110 years old – far outliving even some of her own grandchildren – and dying a week later, we are tempted to shed a tear or two. Why? Because we truly miss her. In May 1981 when Bob Marley died of cancer at age 36, I recall an irate man saying how life was a paradox, with the "untimely" passing of the international reggae icon. He was very hot under the collar:

"Life is so unfair. Look at a young man like Bob who had every-thing going for him. He had money; he had fame, and yet death has to come for him so soon. Meanwhile, look at those old street people who have nothing to live for. They can't find their next meal, yet you would have to stone them in order to kill them as they never seem to die," he said.

Phew! He ranted and raved to what seemed like no end. His sentiment sent shivers down my spine. But it got me thinking. Like that man, many of you are asking that question as well. You, too, are saying life is not fair. You are asking out loud why you have to suffer so severely in life when others flourish so much. Many of you are asking why did God have to take your Baby Sharon, your cutest baby girl, at just two months old. Why couldn't He allow her to live until at least she was married and give you a few grandchildren? Nobody knows those answers except God himself. The ongoing question, though, is why do bad things happen to good people and vice versa? Deuteronomy 29:29 says, "The secret things belong to the Lord our God, but the things revealed belong to us and our children . . ." Sometimes God's explanations come years later. It is by design that we don't know certain things.

I still hear people bragging about being unscathed by the monstrous Hurricane Katrina in New Orleans. Even ministers run with this bragging right saying that they were impervious to the hurricane or any disaster for that matter. I am not a messenger of doom, but all I can say to those individuals is to pray one more time. Thank God with a few octaves up above the rest. It is nice to rejoice but not at the expense of other people's demise. Hospitals were not spared; devout people of God were killed as well as vagrants and criminals. Churches and synagogues were damaged as well as prisons and bordellos. The big storms that wiped out large swaths of holdings before Katrina, spared a lot of churches more than 50 years ago, but during Katrina, some of the churches that escaped those prior hurricanes were now in ruins beyond repair. You can rejoice now, but can you predict what will happen in the next three years?

THE PASTOR WHO
SHUNS MEDICAL TREATMENT

THERE IS a book out with a pastor saying that he didn't believe in going to the doctors. He deridingly wrote that when people asked him who was his doctor, he told them that his wife was his doctor. He claimed that he didn't have any need for doctors. He had no use for hospitals. Frankly, when I read that book at first, I felt a little disturbed about his stance, wondering how many people would fall prey to his opinion and not seek much needed medical attention for goiter, colon cancer, lupus or other maladies.

Sadly, however, a few years later, he came down with a disease that nearly took his life. After months of rigorous chemotherapy, his emaciated body caused a stir among his congregation. Members started to question his health in silence. After his treatment was successful, he began telling his members to do everything necessary to be in good health — whether it was via the medical community or through herbal medicine. I was relieved to hear his new stance. Today he is hale and hearty, and continues to be a powerful force in his ministry. I truly thank God for his restoration because indeed he's a beloved pastor who has done a ton of good for his adherents over the years.

Many of you are sick but are afraid to seek medical treatment because you don't want to run the risk of bumping into Sister Gloria-Jean from church as you walk through the doctor's office. You don't want her to rebuke you, telling you, "Where is your faith, Chile?" It's not like you are buying *moonshine* in the Deep South or rum from speakeasies during Prohibition. For God's sake, it's your health folks!

Friend, it is not my intention to bring out the gloom and doom of life on you. I don't wish to scare you to death. And I certainly don't want to burst your bubbles, but in case you are not aware of it by now, bad things sometimes happen to good people. Look at Elisha. Only a few people in the Bible performed the amount of healings and miracles like he had. Remember the powerful King Naaman, stricken with leprosy, whom he told to dip in River Jordan seven times? Well, you got it, he is the same Elisha. With the power of God working in his life, he did them all and more, yet he died a sick man in the end.

Some questions many times don't have ready answers. And that is one of them. I still ponder over that one every time I read the passage in 2 Kings. Kathryn Kuhlman, the powerful evangelist who saw thousands of people get healed through her ministries, died with cancer after suffering for years. Evangelist Billy Graham reached more people worldwide with the Gospel, than thousands of pastors combined, and currently he's suffering from the dreaded Parkinson's disease. What is the crux of the matter here? Did they have faith for other people but not for themselves? We may never know. What did they do to bring on those calamities on themselves? The last time I checked, they had all been upstanding and God-fearing people; they possessed enough faith to shake Mount

Everest. Even the great prophet Jeremiah questioned God about why did the wicked prosper, a question many of us are still asking today. See Jeremiah 12:1

Therefore, it would behoove all of us not to pass judgment on our fellow brothers and sisters when tragedy strikes home. Often times the victims are people who love God wholehearted like Job, yet disaster after disaster come home to roost. Do not traduce people when they are down and out – give them mercy. Instead of criticizing them, find it in your heart to pray for them, because you never know when the pendulum might swing the other way. Instead of volunteering to draw the noose tighter around the victims' necks, again, just whisper a word of prayer on their behalf, being constantly reminded of these words: there I go but for God's grace and mercy. We ought to extirpate cold-heartedness from our midst and replace it with love.

I will never champion or wish sicknesses or adversities on my worst enemy as those things not only affect the individual but could have far-reaching consequences for their loved ones.

Telling people that their Christian walk after a 10-year period should yield them a Rolls Royce or a private plane is nothing more than a setup. You said that those who paid $500 for a piece of wool dipped into Jordan River didn't have enough faith when that piece of cloth in their possession failed to materialize into the promised bounty. It is good to be prosperous. Who among us would not want to have good health and strength, enough money to travel at his beck and call; to not ever rack her brains again to pay the monthly bills?

But prosperity has come to mean only material wealth. Planes. Luxury cars. Yachts. The 10,000-square-foot homes. What about the plethora of missionaries overseas who have labored long and hard to change lives, living among the poor and suffering? All some of those people possess are a mud hut, a paucity of food and clothing, and a lot of love and kindness to spread around. Are those people prosperous or not? Did they do something wrong for not amassing God's prosperity? Don't feel sorry for those missionaries. They have what it takes for them to be there. Just pray for their continued strength to run their races.

If you tell somebody from Mali, West Africa that the weather in Cheyenne, Wyoming never drops below 50 degrees at anytime, you are certainly setting up that person for some major damage. Should that African travel to Cheyenne in mid December without any warm clothes, he would be devastated, and could possibly freeze to death if he/she's not in the right housing. Just picture the shock that poor man/woman would feel.

Perhaps we cannot help it. We like to hear the good things. "Spare me the bad stuff," you say. But like rain and sunshine, sowing and harvesting, good sometimes accompany bad: 10 large puppies with one runt in a litter; the great soccer player with an acute case of *foot-in-mouth* disease; the Ph.D. candidate who has been blind since age 5.

Pastors in authority should tell people about the goodness of doctors. Modern medicine can cure/heal through God's divine power. I have seen the wonderful fusion of the two coexisting side by side harmoniously. Take, for example, Ben Carson, a devoutly religious man, yet a top surgeon in one of America's prestigious hospitals. He is the doctor most noted for separating conjoined twins from all over the world. For the record, I do believe in divine healing. Thus, I believe the words of Isaiah 53.

Many pastors deliberately tell their congregations to shun medicine for even major illnesses like cancer, heart diseases, and chronic depression. However, when things don't work out the way they had hoped, they are the first to send their members back to seek doctors' help. But, alas, many times it's too late for remediation. One old song in the church goes: "I don't need no doctor to heal me when I'm sick; I don't need no grocery man to give me my bread and meat . . ."

Tell people that there will be dark days. There will be rainy days and sunny days. Tell them that at times their lives will be blanketed by snowstorms and thunderstorms. But before long, the sun will rise again. Tell them, too, that without warning, their sun-drenched day could plummet to sub-degree temperatures in their finances, their health, their friendship, among coworkers, but that the sun will rise again. They will have no control over these events.

We should always expect the best in life, but prepare ourselves for the worst because bad things happen to good people. Among the World Trade Center victims were many devout religious people. Some served as Peace Corps officers for years in Africa and Asia. Some were upstanding citizens in their communities. But as we saw, they, too, perished among the thousands of victims.

So, don't go about looking down at your sister in church who always sits in the front pew taking copious notes from the pastor's message, when her 19-year-old honor student was gunned down in a drive-by incident. Don't indict her for her lack of faith or less-than-spiritual standing for running a liberal household devoid of prayer. That could not have been further from the truth. In fact, she holds family devotion every morning with her children and prays for them before they go off to school. She stresses helping others every chance she got around the dining table. Her children have caught the vision and have been heeding her every word.

Her son, Michael, had just finished volunteering, packing trailers for shipment to go overseas for disaster relief, even though his college homework had backed up. He thought his pitching in a helping hand was more important than his backlogged homework. He was heading to the bus station to go home when the racecar, coming like a bat out of hell, singled him out of a group of 10 people, and killed him on the spot. You ask "why" a thousand times, and I say bad things do happen to good people.

Again, pastors, exhorters, motivational speakers, please cushion your subjects by presenting them with a balanced picture of life. Talk all you want about the dream house to come or the $100,000 business venture as part of their quest for abundant prosperity, but please let them know, too, about the potential culprit lurking out there.

I don't believe that God handpicks people for tragedies and curse. If you are not convinced, just watch your local evening news for about 10 minutes each evening or read your daily newspapers: the middle-aged lady who fed the homeless three times weekly for 30 years who was shot and killed for $2 in her purse. The avuncular Sidney Brown who gave up his cushy job for mentoring runaway teens in the projects, and who was now strangled to death by the same people he had helped get their lives back on track. The family's SUV that lost control, killing eight people on the spot.

If you are battling a deep sense of misfortune and a life of curse today, don't despair. The redeeming value in all of this is that all is not lost. There is hope because God's mercy qualifies the disqualified; in other words, His mercy can undo a lifetime of curse just like that – in the twinkling of an eye. His mercy can repeal laws and render your judgment null and void. Grace is God's ability to restrain from us what we do deserve. There was a popular song that goes, "Surely goodness and mercy shall follow me all the days of my life. . . ." Believe that it is so today in your life. Make your way to God's happy family. Start by finding those blessings at your fingertips. Find out what that grace and mercy did for me.

WHEN TERMITE FAILS, CALL A DAWG

WHEN I was 16 years old, I was walking home from church at about 12:30 one morning, when my life flashed in front of me. There was a state of emergency throughout the Kingston metropolitan area for the upcoming elections, but a lot of us skirted that edict whenever we could get away with it. About four blocks before I reached home, I noticed that three of the streetlights were smashed out near to Mr. Wright's house. I walked by as usual, but this time a rope was drawn across the road. Out of nowhere emerged a character armed with an M-16 rifle.

"Hey, bwoy, tonight you a go dead," the character declared. "It's about time you come and help us wid de struggle . . . No more time for church!"

As the cold gun mouth cocked to my forehead, I was frozen in time. In all of his ramblings, I literally felt no fear. Was this the precursor of death? I pondered. What should I feel? Would I be experiencing the dark tunnel so many people who recall near-death experiences feel? Was death this simple? It didn't take long for another man to cross over from the other side of the street to us. He was an intermediary of sorts.

"Why you troubling de youth man? Mek de youth go 'bout him business," said my divinely-sent peacemaker.

A verbal altercation ensued, and moments later a struggle began. My agent of mercy, nicknamed *Dawg*, had just moved from the country to the neighborhood no less than three weeks earlier. To this day, I have not known his real name. I'm assuming that he, too, took on the sobriquet like many others hanging out on the street corners: Presser Foot, Suckling, Man-o-yard, just to name a few. There was something different about Dawg, though, from the other street toughs, which I couldn't put my fingers on. I would always nod at him, and he gave me the utmost respect. Frankly, I had no problem with the other guys either on the street. And prior to that night, Termite and I had never had any bad word exchanged between us. Therefore, it was quite shocking when he tried to take my life.

While the men argued, my thoughts drifted to some of the people who I could call out to, but they couldn't help me at that time. They were dead asleep. Diagonally across from Mr. Wright's gate were Miss Mary and Mr. Ellis. They would be happy to say a good word on my behalf. Miss Della and Mr. Smith, too, would gladly oblige to spare me from the deadly hands of Termite's rifle. You could tell that he really wanted to let off a few rounds of bullets, and I seemed to be the ideal candidate for that moment. The only life forms on the road then were dogs who seemed relieved to be away from their homes. For a change. I knew some of them by name, too: Lassi, Lion, Rover, Cootie, Boon, and Vietnam. But they were not willing to take an M-16 bullet for me. I was on my own! The war of words was still in high gear between the two men, with neither man willing to budge.

"Should I kill you instead?" asked the trigger-happy Termite, to Dawg.

Dawg tried to wrestle the gun away from him as I looked on bewildered. "Youth man, go 'bout your business," he said.

Termite finally relented, and I calmly walked away without saying a word to them. The last thing I heard from Termite was, "Hey, bwoy, tonight you better sleep on de same side you sleep on last night." In essence, he was saying that I should count my lucky star for being spared those deadly bullets.

I finally reached home, and straightaway went to bed. I did not alarm anybody, preferring to wait until daylight. But before I could get a chance to tell somebody about my ordeal, Miss Nerisa, Termite's aunt, preempted me. In a primal scream that pierced the neighborhood, she held her belly and was wailing most bitterly. People were opening up their windows, and ladies jumped out of bed in their nightgowns, just to find out what was going on.

When I inquired about the commotion, I was told that Termite was shot and killed by soldiers when he tried to open fire on them as they patrolled the area. His head, I was told, was riddled with bullets. For days his marrow plastered the walled fence where he was gunned down. An eyewitness alleged that a stray cat ran away with one of his eyeballs.

My heart went out to Termite's family, the loss of a son and brother, but I will be eternally grateful to Dawg for intervening on my behalf. Again, I believe that it was divine intervention that I was saved that night. Even though those evil fingertips were on the trigger to blow my brains into smithereens, God was able to send fingertips of blessings, through Dawg, to wrestle that gun from Termite. I also gain confidence whenever I am in the dumps to remember that if God is for you, no evil will overtake you. I believe, too, that whomever God blesses, no man can curse. I am a living witness to that.

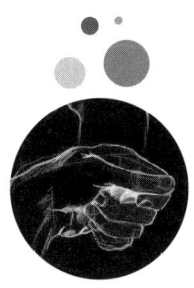

CHAPTER NINETEEN

RADIOACTIVE MONEY

MY FIRST PASTOR, DR. V.T. WILLIAMS, when giving the right hand of fellowship to new members of the church, would implore them about certain do's and don'ts. With regard to money coming into the church, he said that proceeds from the sale of a dog, or money by way of prostitution, were forbidden to enter the church. Youthful indiscretions would have me and my peers busting up laughing each time that line came around. Since I didn't know of any working courtesans in my time, and stray dogs were available dime a dozen, with nobody buying or selling one, I hardly believed that was ever an issue for our church. I didn't know whether or not if he had a scripture to back up his stance, but about two years ago while reading through the Bible, I stumbled on a verse to back up his tenet.

"Thou shall not bring the hire of a whore, or the price of a dog, into the house of the Lord thy God for any vow; for even both of these are abomination unto the Lord thy God." – Deuteronomy 23:18 (KJV).

Over the years, I've pondered long and hard about some of the other forms of "bad monies" that crept not only into the church but into our own personal lives. Among our families, and into our homes. One sore point for me is drug money. If somebody were to knowingly give me $1 million from the sale of drugs today, I would rather to live in abject poverty for the remainder of my life than to accept that money.

About three months after I arrived in New York City, I ran into a young man whom I had known before.

"So, what are you driving?" he asked, in a disparaging manner.

I didn't feel badly as most New Yorkers didn't drive. I told him that I commuted by trains.

"You are wasting time, man! Look out there," he said, pointing to a shiny, tinted BMW parked beside a bodega (grocery store). "By the way, I have three more, too."

I sensed that he was trying to recruit me for the weights and measurements business, but no sparks emitted that day. I wasn't tempted the least to covet him.

I have seen or heard about people in the past who allegedly were dealing in drugs, sometimes owning multimillion-dollar real estate holdings, yachts, service stations, laundromats, among other money-making entities. Today, most of them are either dead, serving life sentences in prison, or are dirt poor. Many of them appear as though a penny has never changed hands with them ever. They are flat out broke!

A few years ago, I read a story about a New Jersey family, which still sends chills down my spine whenever I think about that tragedy. The article appeared in one of the New York City daily newspapers. It featured a very prominent Wall Street executive who succumbed to the use of illegal drugs. The story tracked the man's daily route from his New Jersey home to the Port Authority bus station where he changed from bus to train connection en route to work. He bought crack cocaine from drug dealers inside the station, and before long, he started skipping work. His drug use escalated more and more, with his graduating to other forms of drugs, a habit which later led to his getting fired from his cushy job. Within months, he died from an overdose. His wife and children had to leave their comfortable home and moved into public housing because they could not afford the mortgage.

Again, I cannot help to think about this family's pain every time I hear about illegal drug sale/use. For everybody involved, it boils down to present satisfactions but future regrets. That poor man is dead and gone, and I'm sure those drug dealers' wallets were fat with the money they siphoned off from him and his family. But justice will be served in the spiritual realm. Those children's tears will not go in vain. That wife's heavy heart will be soothed, but wherever that money goes, destruction is bound to follow. What about the scholarships those children could have had? What about a warm embrace from a daddy every now and then to those poor children? All I can say is that somebody will pay for those children and wife's tears.

How can someone be blessed with that kind of money? Their success will be like what salt does to snails or heat to butter. Building a mansion with drug money is akin to building it with sea sand or using seawater for mixing the mortar. One way or the other, it will crumble. Some of you will argue, "Well, at least Melvin only sold drugs for three years then he stopped, and has used his money to build his dream home, start a business and help his family." But not so fast. In the eyes of God and man, that is nothing short of blood money. It cannot be justified. By no means was that New Jersey husband and father an isolated case. Thousands of families are broken up because of drug use. But justice is not one sided. The ones who profit from that trade, too, will have to pay the consequences.

David said, "I was young and now am old, yet I've never seen the righteous forsaken nor his seed begging bread." Do you fit that mold? Your holding onto "bad money" or "blood money" can be quite the reverse of David's observation.

Do you purchase "hot" items after midnight on the street from crack addicts? Most times those items were paid for by toil and sweat, but a crack addict would not think twice to sell his mother's plasma TV just for a quick fix. Friend, stay clear of this. Don't reap this bad blessing.

I am told that in certain school of thoughts, drug dealers often times believe that if they give some of their earnings to the church, that God would sanction whatever they're doing. I was shocked to learn that some dealers give their mothers money (if the mothers are in church) for offering or tithes. They contend that doing so would give them divine protection and favor.

Some years ago, one lady told me that her baby's father took off his four brand new, state-of-the-art tires and rims and gave them to a pastor. Indeed, he had good intentions, saying that men of God should have the best of everything. He felt, too, that giving those precious items to the pastor would bide him security from rival bullets. But alas, it was not to be. Her baby's daddy was killed, she said, a few years later. When I probed as to whether or not the pastor knew of the murdered man's drug dealings, she said no. That young woman is now a Christian – serving the church in various ministries.

DRUG MONEY IS RADIOACTIVE

I HAVE seen families from all walks of life die off one behind the other through sicknesses or sudden death. Often times, no gunshots are involved. They just wasted away. The bottom line is that their money is toxic. It is radioactive. Who wants to walk around with this spiritual Chernobyl around their necks? To be empowered spiritually and financially, find blessings at your fingertips and give back that money; give up that house or car that you knowingly purchased with drug money, and get the blood and tears of countless orphans off your shoulders. Don't blight your life or your children's future. The Bible says that it's better to hang a millstone around your neck than to touch one of my little ones. Indeed, their voices are crying out. Be made whole again. Start to sleep sound again. Have a heart again. Get back your conscience. Do the right thing. Job said, "My conscience will not reproach me as long as I live." Can you who indulge in this practice say the same thing? Know that there's no escaping this wrath unless there's full repentance, brushing your hands clean of those radioactive assets. Turn them loose; rid them from your camp.

For the person who is fed up of working minimum-wage salary, don't give up. The best is yet to come. But for the sake of your future and your children's future, stay clear of that leprosy called drug money. Again, it is radioactive. Even if you haven't taken an iota of drug, it will still bring you down. Resist the temptation to decorate your house with its proceeds, or buy the latest jeep. You will regret it. Remember, it's present satisfaction but future regret. Friend, do not be tempted to take bad monies. If you were given the choice to work $7 an hour for a week's pay or a $100,000 gift where you know comes directly from drugs proceed, opt for the $7 an hour pay until your change comes. I know that is a very hard decision to make for some people, but do not be tempted by drug money.

Your minimum wage job will stretch over time to take care of your needs. What $3,000 a week couldn't do, $300 a week will do. God will make a way for you. Another Scripture goes, "My father has cattle on a thousand hills." I heard a pastor in prayer once importuning God to sell some of those cattle and give him the money from those sales. You never know, God can do just that. Just remember, nothing is impossible when you put your trust in Him. Get the pseudo blessings out of the way and see God work in your life. Real blessings are awaiting you, but you have some housecleaning to do.

If that commandment, "Do not covet your neighbor's . . ." didn't make sense to you before, now is the time to put it into practice. Do not go off complaining why God can't make you live like the Blackwoods around the way, or the Browns near to the golf course. Do you know what they are doing to earn their money? For the little girl's graduation from kindergarten, the Browns rode in style in several limousines to celebrate, and you wish you could do the same thing for your son, Horace, who will be graduating in a few weeks from college. You will have to ride the bus or take the train to his graduation, but don't despair. God is in control. The last thing you want to do is mixing up your blessings in the wrong account. Every meaningful real estate broker knows the penalties that come with commingling of funds. Don't shortchange yourself. You have run your race well. Now, go for the prize. It's not far away. It's a hard thing to turn away money when you are broke financially, but find the courage to say no.

In the 1980s, former First Lady, Nancy Reagan's pet project was telling American kids to say no to taking illegal drugs. But today, some mothers and fathers need to be saying no to taking easy cash from drug proceeds. Grandma needs to confront her grandson about his expensive gifts to her. What about that 29-year-old man who never worked a day in his life yet he can pass on expensive gifts to Mama, while she asks him no questions but look the other way? Does she throw her offering from this money with a clear conscience? What about the latest outfits Sandra bought you for Mother's Day, which you now show off to your sisters at church as they fuss over you? The bling-bling, the pearls. Pastors need to sniff out this stench from the pulpit. Sound the alarm once and for all.

Drug use poisons the body, but its money poisons the spirit. Some of you might argue that the money is clean. A five-year-old one-dollar bill perhaps has gone from a stripper to a cocaine snorter, and from a butcher to a 12-year-old lemonade vendor. Universally, the law of money won't render that one-dollar bill unusable. If you spit on it and trample it in the U.S., it will still be of value to somebody in Iceland or Fiji. Hence, it is not the money, it's how you come by that money.

If you were to see an old lady tumble from a sidewalk with the content of her purse scattered out, you would not want to take her cash but help her get up. Taking her money will give you temporary relief, but if you have a conscience, that same money will haunt you for life.

I don't know many people who would readily turn over a $100 bill blowing aimlessly on a desolate road with nobody in sight. I would gladly say those people who find that money should consider it a blessing. Buy yourself a treat. However, seeing that same $100 bill with a nervous mother in pursuit of it, the best thing you can do is to help her arrest that bill.

Thus, the money you get without knowing the source will not be a curse to you. But if you knowingly accept bad money, be prepared for a downward spiral in your life. The opposite of that could yield you a windfall of blessings. Read the next story to see what I mean.

I just cannot resist recalling those good ol' newspaper stories of my youth. In one of our daily hometown papers, there used to be a column entitled, *Tell Me Something Good*. Stories from all walks of life flooded that newspaper weekly. One of them stood out in my mind even to this day.

A man had returned from the United States to make funeral arrangements for his mother. He was running all around town meeting with hospital and funeral home personnel, florist, among others. Before long, he found out that he had lost the wad of cash he was roving around town with. He began to retrace his steps to the various places he had been, not fully knowing where this money was.

That was the only money he had for his transactions. As a result, he panicked for awhile. But when he checked back at the funeral home and asked around, a worker presented him with the cash – every last dollar in place. He was overcome with emotion.

But before he left the island, he took the young lady's particulars. Over time, they began to correspond. The *mensch*, as my Jewish friends would say, who gave up the cash, was a single mother of about five children. She and the children were barely eking out an existence from her meager salary. Well, it pays to do good! And as the scripture says, don't get weary in doing good.

That man who sadly returned home to bury his mother the year before was now coming back a happy man to marry his betrothed – yes, that same woman who returned his money to him – the love of his life. He adopted her children and everybody found a new life in the great country called the United States of America. All because of honesty. Taking that man's "good money" for her personal use could perhaps stop a gap in the short term, but no doubt it could have caused a lot of misfortunes stemming from "bad money" for her and her children. I strongly believe that was a spiritual test, and that woman passed it with very high marks.

THE TELEVISION AND THE TELEPHONE

IN SEPTEMBER 1988, before the advent of cell phones, I bought a "phone number" from a street hawker for $10. He said that telephone number would allow me to talk to anybody around the world. One caveat, however: I should only make the calls from public phones. Well, I bought it that Friday evening, and I made calls to people everywhere and then some. That Sunday night after I made my final call, I rushed home to turn on my newly-purchased television to watch the evening news. I clicked the remote as usual, and in less than a minute, the screen went black. Right there and then a voice said to me that I will have to pay back every penny I used in making those telephone calls. I was convicted by my conscience. When I went back to the store to discuss my store warranty on the TV, the store manager said that I was one day over the limited warranty. I then had to pay to fix it on my own. I paid $128, plus transportation to and from the repair shop, for that TV. From that day forward, no deal is ever so sweet where you would catch me paying for "hot" items.

Frankly, I didn't know that the number was illegal. I thought I just got a good deal. It was while talking to other people over the months and years following the incident that they informed me that it was an illegal practice, where people steal other people's telephone numbers and sell them back on the street. My lesson came with a price. It shows that what goes around comes around. I am glad that I am somewhat redeemed, having paid back the charges in a roundabout way.

Friend, resolve today never to tarnish those precious fingertips with illegal gains and drug money. Don't block your blessings. I doubt very much that my counsel will ever be as effective as these few words found in Proverbs 13:11: "Dishonest money dwindles away, but he who gathers money little by little makes it grow."

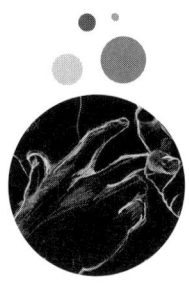

CHAPTER TWENTY

HE SMELLS LIKE SHEEP

HE OPENS THE PASSENGER'S DOOR FOR THE 6-foot 4, strapping man who is slowly hobbling along to be seated inside the sparkling, welcoming black Mercedes Benz. The contrast is stark: one man is well groomed, while the other seems to just throw some articles of clothing together, just for the sake of it. The smile is still etched on the man's face as he leans over to keep the door open for his celebrated passenger. The distance from the lobby to the parking lot is not long, but it seems to be taking the man forever to get to the chauffeured car. He finally reaches his destination. Relief, no doubt, is his favorite word right now. He is jockeying for space to fit his long legs. And he barely succeeds.

It is Easter Sunday, and Dr. Andre Sims, senior pastor of the Christ the King Bible Fellowship Church, is taking the homeless man to his house where he and the rest of the Sims family will host a few other homeless people for dinner.

That's when it all became clear to me. Now I know why a few months earlier when Yolanda, a Brooklyn visitor to our church, made that comment about Dr. Sims. She and her friend, Cory, a gospel rapper out of the Bronx, were hosted by the Simses for a few days. And while addressing the congregation that Sunday morning, she spoke about how well they were treated by the family. And soon, she was at a loss for words. That's when she blurted out, ". . . All I can say is that he smells like sheep."

After seeing him in action with that homeless man and other down-and-out, displaced people, it is not hard to see why he would smell like sheep. Very often.

For many pastors and counselors, sometimes they have to smell like sheep in order to reach a broken teenager. Many times they have to be prepared to smell like sheep in order to save a marriage. Smelling like sheep can help them slay some Goliaths. Smelling like sheep comes with added favors. Smelling like sheep has the ability to leapfrog your way into greatness as in David's case.

Shepherds sometimes step into soft matter on the ground, which they did not bargain for. But instead of complaining, they gladly wipe it off from their sandals and move on. Sometimes shepherds' services merit their cutting wools that have grown too long. Sometimes they have to nurse back a sheep to being healthy. Other times they have to carry an injured lamb to a place of safety. He cannot always guarantee their safety, but many times a shepherd's sleep is predicated upon his ensuring that his sheep are safe — that they are safely put away in their folds, and out of the reach of voracious animals. Sometimes the cologne or perfume which was splashed on an hour ago is now overpowered by musky sheep scent. Thus, it is impossible for shepherds not to smell like sheep.

THE SIMSES BENEVOLENCE

WELL, NICENESS cannot be locked up inside of a bottle forever. No wonder why Mary Magdalene had to break her perfume bottle in order to display her niceness or generosity. Niceness can be cultivated. And many times you don't have to look far to see the roots of it.

Long before Christmas one Sunday morning, the keyboard

player at our church handed me a bag as soon as I walked inside the lobby. He said that our pastor's parents, Drs. Joe and Connie Sims, told him to give it to us for our boys. They were going out of state, and would not have been back for the holidays. The package was neatly wrapped and we took it home, stashed it away into a safe place until weeks later when the Christmas tree was up. On Christmas morning, when the package was opened, the boys found three of the most beautiful sweaters/shirts from those two angels on earth. They were elated beyond description.

We later wrote the Simses to tell them thanks for their generosity. A week later, I ran into them, and they, too, were grateful for our thank-you card. Dr. Joe took me aside and asked me how could he and Dr. Connie become more involved in the boys' lives.

"I would love to play the role of a grandfather, an uncle, a mentor, or in whatever capacity you will allow me to play in the boys' lives," the avuncular figure said.

One week after that conversation, Yvonne called to tell me that Dr. Joe had called her at work to ask her again for the boys' clothes/shoes sizes, as he was planning to shop for them again. We were both speechless for a good minute.

Wow! We considered the Simses' gestures blessings on top of blessings. To avail themselves voluntarily spoke volumes to us. For these former college professors to become so selfless and look about the well-being of others only spurs me on to continue to do good to others. Their open arms and hearts mean a lot to us, especially in the area of familial relations. We are nearly 3,000 miles away from the nearest blood relative, and so the boys would gladly welcome such a gesture in the area of a surrogate grandfather/grandmother, uncle, aunt, etc. We are richer to have had their acquaintances.

Our family had gone over to see Dr. Joe on a Tuesday evening, and Dr. Connie read our boys' thank-you cards to him for their birthday gifts he had bought them a few weeks earlier. He implored them to stay in school, and to always reach for the stars. Sadly, however, just a few days after his 70th birthday in February 2007, Dr. Joe passed away the following Saturday evening. We truly missed that wonderful, big-hearted man. He, too, definitely smelled like sheep.

THE CALL ON THE CHURCH

I READ a line somewhere, which states, "Every church was perfect until you and I got there." Is it me or is it just the signs of the time? I have noticed for the last five years or so that you will hear a lot more about multimillion-dollar expansions on church properties, but nary a voice about helping the poor and downtrodden. Some pastors seem as though they're on the last leg of their furlong to beat out the other pastor 10 miles away to launch the biggest and most expensive edifice in that city. They brag about this at conferences. Going to some of these conferences is like going to some Fortune 500 companies general meetings, $20-million projects dedicated to this and that. Some churches will spend millions of dollars sprucing up their vestibules but not a penny to rehabilitate drug addicts or domestic violence victims. It is a sorry state of affair in Christendom when we allow this to go on unremedied.

Over the Thanksgiving 2006 holiday, I listened with pride to a radio call-in program how common, blue-collar workers were stepping up to the plate to donate money for meals during Thanksgiving and Christmas. Children, too, called in, emptying their piggybanks to lend support to those displaced people, but ashamedly, some churches didn't budged.

One lady talked about how she went days at a time without eating. She went on to say that she had to steal baby formulas at nearby supermarkets, even though she knew it was wrong, just in order to feed her famished baby. She was giving praise to the mission that was spearheading the food drive, thanking them for coming to her rescue. May all those people who contributed to the myriad of food drives to bless others be blessed themselves.

I want to make it clear that I am not singling out any particular church for shunning their community or religious obligation because God knows there are thousands of churches out there today doing more than their fair share to give hope to millions of unfortunate people. Some churches have been castigated for hosting the homeless population on their church properties, but that doesn't faze them. One of the perennial churches that have given selfless services over the years is the Glide Church in San Francisco, California. They feed upward of a million people, primarily the homeless, annually. Those people get nothing but people's utmost admiration and respect. The loyal volunteers who work selflessly and assiduously year after year are a godsend to their communities. You people know who you are. Stand up and take a bow. God will bless you and your family a hundredfold for being wonderful stewards to these seemingly abandoned, forgotten people.

TAKE OFF THE MASKS

THE SUNDAY morning youth service at the ending of October was seeing an unusual turnout since the summer break. After all, it should be no surprise to anybody since the visiting youth pastor/ comedian from Dallas, Texas, Jason Earls, had them and the grownups in stitches months earlier. I was ready for a hearty laugh. And, yes, I did get a few in, but somewhere out of left field, the genial minister segued into his topic for the day, "Take Off the Masks."

People started to straighten up in their pews. And the smiles were slowly vanishing from the faces when the young preacher lambasted the hypocrisy inside a lot of our churches today. He spoke about people who were undergoing pain but would just mask their feeling by reciting, ". . . Oh, I'm blessed and highly favored," when asked how they were doing.

Brothers no longer confide to other brothers about their struggles. Married couples who seemingly had it together were all fearful of asking for help, even in intimate settings among their peers. People feel better going to a coffee joint by themselves than to talk about their grief with someone who cares for them. Many are so enjoined to this secret society of Grin-and-Bear-it, that they have placed a fence between them and their fellow brothers and sisters. It is by faith we confess that we are blessed and highly favored, and hopefully that will be the case after the dark clouds have cleared. But for a young mother who has an 8-year-old daughter in a coma for the last three months, she needs your prayers, not your judgment. Therefore, whenever she's unable to say, "I'm blessed and highly favored," every time you run into her, don't beat her over the head for being "faithless." God is able to supply her needs, but help her out with some bus fares; put some gas in her car; tell her to hold on and be strong, but don't verbally beat up on her. In her heart she knows that God still cares for her, but for now, she is asking a thousand questions by the minutes. She will get it together before long. But for now, just pray for her.

How do you expect a brother to say blessed and highly favored when only one of the 10 brothers he had asked for a helping hand when he was moving showed up? He's still wobbling from the sprained knee he suffered while he struggled to lift the chest of drawers all by himself. His hands are callused from the extra work he had to do by himself.

Take off the mask from your face. Don't come grinning ear to ear in your 3-piece suit talking that talk, blessed and highly favored, when you failed to be your brother's keeper.

MEGACHURCHES VS. SMALL CHURCHES

THE ELDERLY widow whose legs have been amputated for the last two years is now going through deep depression. You blamed her for her lack of faith. You also said that no rightful child of God would ever be dealt this fate in life, but you forget those poignant words found in 1 Peter 1:6, "In this you greatly rejoice, though now for a little while you may have had to suffer grief in all kinds of trials." See also 1 Peter 5:8-11: "Be self-controlled and alert. Your enemy the devil prowls around like a roaring lion looking for someone to devour. Resist him, standing firm in the faith, because you know that your brothers throughout the world are undergoing the same kind of sufferings. And the God of all grace, who called you to his eternal glory in Christ, after you have suffered a little while, will himself restore you and make you strong, firm and steadfast. . . ."

That widowed amputee, too, is having a hard time saying she's blessed and highly favored. In fact, she used to sing on the senior choir. She tithed regularly. And, yes, once upon a time she used to regale you with fine dinners in her home. But ever since her husband died and she lost her legs, a few members only visited for the first two weeks. There are no telephone calls. Nobody to ask, "Can I cook you dinner this evening?" "Can I help you with laundry?" The audacity for us to dress up in our Sunday best, walk around pushing out our chests, saying "we are blessed and highly favored."

What about your hurting sisters and brothers? Stop and think about them for a moment. Many people who have volunteered their services for years in various ministries of the church are so disillusioned with church now. But who could blame them? They had been gone for nearly a year now without anybody missing them. There was never a call from a pastor, a deacon, an usher to inquire about how that brother or sister was doing. "We haven't seen you around, what happened why you haven't been to church?" No such telephone call. Nevertheless, the church never fails to call whenever there's an upcoming event – a request for that brother or sister to volunteer their time in a conference or concert, with no mention of how those individuals had been feeling spiritually and otherwise. You see, those disgruntled folks feel as though they were on somebody's list but not in their heart. It is high time that the church turned away from that sore blight on Christendom.

I was so refreshed and charged with what that pastor had to say that I hurried to search myself, and pledged never again to fall victim to that hypocrisy. So, after the service ended that Sunday afternoon I wanted to make sure that I was making a difference in somebody else's life. I wanted to get those rubber masks back to the melting stage. They could serve some other purposes like shoes and gloves. I felt that it was about time some faces got freed up and get some well needed breeze on those dimples and clefts. I soon called up one of our acquaintances and asked him if there was anything he would like us to do for him. He had a simple request, and I prayed with him via the telephone. I asked him whether or not there was something he didn't like, and if there was any animosity that abound since I wanted to make things right there and then. I am talking about a mask-tearing moment here.

Phew! He lambasted me for about half an hour without my saying a word. I listened intently. But after his rebuke, the strange thing was that there were no solutions to the changes he would have liked to see from me and Yvonne. I felt like Job when his friends ganged up on him, blaming him for something he didn't have any control over. The insults that spewed forth would grow hair on a bald pate. After being dragged through the mill and heaped over the coal, I felt so condemned; so wounded. I agonized greatly over that conversation. But I'm glad that I made that call. I had an option: Instead of being bitter, I got better.

I prayed about the matter and asked God a lot of "whys" all day Monday. Tuesday morning Yvonne pointed out a section in Job where she was using as part of her devotion. How his friends had come down hard on him, even though Job was pleading his case, to no avail. I had not said anything to her about the conversation between me and that young man the day before. But her showing me that passage had truly brought about healing and confirmation that God still cares about everything that concerns us.

What a difference a few days can make. By Thursday evening, I received an email from a police officer and youth leader from church, someone who was fairly new to our acquaintance. The email had a video with a man walking with all his might to get somewhere. But every time he journeyed to a certain distance, a whale of a hand, out of nowhere, would just grab him and place him back to where he had first started. It read: "GOD IS IN CONTROL. Always Encourage Those Who You Love and Care For. There will always be people in life who try to do this to you . . . ! [Keeping you back]. But just continue to be strong, and keep moving forward! I just want to let you know that even though it sometimes seems as if for every step we take forward, we're pushed back 10 steps. Just stay strong and we will get where we are destined to be. And never forget that what God has for you is for you. Continue to trust God . . . The steps of a good and righteous man are ordered by the Lord. So order your steps in His word."

I felt like a million dollar after reading my brother's kind words. It doesn't take much to bless others. When we do, all of us can rightfully say we're blessed and highly favored.

Down and out people who pop into your church will leave over time when the masks are forever fastened to your faces. They will feel as though they are the skunks at the party, and since they don't want to stink up your pews, they gladly take their flight. That could have been your first and last time to reach him or her, but because of these masks, you chased them out. Because of this mask church has become a byword for hypocrisy to them. Nobody is real anymore? Nobody wants to show his true emotion.

It's not all doom and gloom out there, though. Enough caring people are spread out all across the globe. You will find them in Japan, England, Peru, Trinidad, and Mali. You will find them in megachurches and storefront churches.

The very pregnant Dorothy was weighed down with a pan of lasagna perfuming the church vestibule with its mouthwatering aroma. In her other hand was a huge cake that could feed the Chinese army. I offered to lighten her load, and I had a newfound admiration for her physical strength. That pan was heavy! When I inquired as to what was the occasion, she simply said that there was nothing special going on. People just wanted to bless her with some food. I was astounded. I thought that those kind deeds had long been dead with my great-grandmother, but the successful attorney told me that acts of kindness were commonplace among her fellow congregants.

She went on to say that people would often times purpose themselves to drop off food for her, sometimes enough to last for a whole week. Some dropped by to do laundry, and still others came by to clean her house. Her husband had suffered injuries from a car accident months earlier, but that hardly posed a setback to them. In fact, one of the co-pastors at his church volunteered to take him to his doctor's appointments for the duration of his treatments, while others promised to cook them dinner for a month.

Dorothy confessed that it was hard at first to accept those treats, since she and her husband were always on the opposite end of the pole. It was a wonderful feeling, she said, to give away things to people, but taking things from them was something she had to train herself to get used to. Her husband said that they started feeling more comfortable taking gifts and services from people when he came to the realization that reciprocity was a godly act. He further stated that he didn't want to block those people's blessings by refusing what they were offering.

Now, Dorothy and her husband don't have to think twice about God's favor on their lives. And all those kind folks who gave of their time, talents, money, and otherwise, must have felt good doing those things. Without a shadow of doubt, everybody, both givers and recipients, can truly say, "We're blessed and highly favored," without rendering that term a mere platitude.

What a heartwarming reminder of how we should all act among ourselves! In Acts 2:44, it say, "All the believers were together and had everything in common. Selling their possessions and goods, they gave to anyone as he had need. Everyday they continue to meet together in the temple courts. They broke breads in their homes and ate together with glad and sincere hearts." But not all the time that exhortation holds true for a lot of us as you will see again. Now they must have all smelled like sheep.

One Saturday afternoon I called up a friend in Georgia, and the conversation drifted to his telling me about a member from his church who weekly wrote a check for one of the ladies of the church who was out of work. She did that for months without anybody knowing. It would have remained a secret, but at a sendoff reception, the recipient brought the matter to light to the astonishment of everyone present. What a blessing! The irony is that a lot of churches would readily give to a mission in Asia or Africa, while their own members could be suffering right under their noses, and fellow members, pastors and deacons would not turn a blind eye.

What are the forces that make some churches become champions of the poor and outcast, while others remain stoical about their conditions? That question would be quite debatable, as there are megachurches that truly care about the spiritual and physical well-beings of their adherents. There are cell groups in place to bridge greater connections. Their pastors donate thousands of dollars to overseas missions, while giving in like manner to local food banks. I'm even told of a megachurch in Atlanta, Georgia, whose pastor has made it his duty to personally visit new converts at random. Yes, you are reading correctly – a modern-day pastor making house calls!

Some of these churches sponsor Thanksgiving and Christmas dinners, specifically for those who would not have otherwise had a meal. Some round up homeless people by the busloads and put on Christmas cantatas for them like the Brooklyn Tabernacle. Reeking or not, these homeless people are warmly welcomed.

But sadly, there are those megachurches whose only mission is to swell their pews at all costs, in the hope of gaining bragging rights regionally and nationally. Some pastors are constantly in search of the new wave of membership. They will cajole new converts to get onboard, but once those people are in, the honeymoon is over. They are on their own. As a result, those new kids on the block soon found out that there is nobody in place to shepherd them. Over time, those wayward, forlorn men and women just drift away without anybody even missing them. There would never be an altar call for them should they be hurting. Nobody calls out from the pulpit sicknesses, financial struggles, and loneliness. After all, the higher-ups contend, those needs are only reserved for people who don't know God. They would tell you that if you are in God's will, then those things will not beset you. You should always be blessed and highly favored and sickness and poor finances have no lot and part in that realm.

But by and large, a lot of small churches are not given the credit due to them. Many of them carry the lion's share of a community's burden. They are more accessible more often than their megachurch counterparts. Many of them serve faithfully as the spiritual fulcrums of their communities. Their pastors wear several hats at a time: teacher, counselor, father, attorney, just to name a few. They are called any hour of the night for everything from praying for a distraught mother to posting bail for a delinquent juvenile.

A lot of today's megachurch pastors had their humble beginnings at many of these small churches. Often times, it takes gusto to pastor these churches, a number of pastors have told me. Some beat up on themselves for not having the star power to attract increased membership. And because of this, some of their members vacillate from their small churches to megachurches. As a result, there's no stability in membership, and this shows up in the bottom line.

Financially, many of them are breaking at the seams. There is that ongoing quest to measure up to the megachurches with their latest technology-savvy equipment. Some have gone over budget trying to pattern their sets to those they see on TV, with overhead cameras, large-sized screen, and all the trappings of a megachurch, even though only 70 members have been coming for the last two years. One pastor confessed to feeling discouraged when he tried in vain to attract a decent-sized crowd.

CHURCH AND BANKRUPTCY

I WAS talking with a gentleman at a reception recently, and while we chatted, the conversation drifted to his leaving his church. When I probed further, he said the church was foreclosed on. A mass exodus ensued and members are now splintered all across the city. A small group, along with the pastor, is currently meeting at a school house. It is alleged that the pastor lives inside a gated community in a house valued at nearly $2 million. Now, is that a travesty of justice or what?

Mismanagement of finances in some churches is the order of the day. There are no checks and balances in place. Hence, whatever Pastor says, goes. That is flat out wrong.

This church was a huge church, courting many of that city's well-heeled residents as its adherents. Many are sad and forlorn, and asked quietly how could such a thing happen right under their noses.

It is a sad day in Christendom when pastors wanted to become a TD Jakes or a Joel Osteen overnight: They would stop at nothing to make their church like the Pottter's House and Lakewood without going through the fire and flood. They want the 5,000-member congregation last year. And in pursuit of that, they forget their purpose.

I strongly believe in growth, and I celebrate increase, but not at the expense of breaking the backs of your members.

One pastor in Los Angeles, a friend told me – was very upset with his members for having him still driving a car when every pastor who was worth his weight in gold owns a private plane. He told his congregation that it was about time that they bought him a plane where he could fly about in style.

I have seen more interviews about churches filing for bankruptcy in the last three years than at any other times. Perhaps church bankruptcies were always ongoing but that the television magazine programs were not giving them any attention. One notable broadcast I recall was a pastor who suckered members to put up millions of dollars on a shoddy real estate scheme, under the guise of church building fund. The pastor himself admitted that he wanted to copy

Joel Osteen's Lakewood Church in Houston, Texas. The church was to boast a swimming pool and several high-end restaurants. But alas, it was not to be. The contractors ran away with the money. Members lost their lifesavings, and the church finally lost its property to foreclosure. Again, the few members who remained were now meeting in a high school for weekly service.

How can men of the cloth subscribe to greed when their cardinal book – the Bible – lists it as one of the deadly sins? Do they misinterpret greed and envy to mean something else?

Contrast this. Non-religious groups are going to Africa and Asia in droves, giving their money, time, and services. Sometimes they go for two months at a time digging wells, building schools, sewing school uniforms, etc. Wake up church! Oprah Winfrey, Bill Gates, Bono, among other private individuals, God bless you!

Where is the church going into hospitals and nursing homes visiting the sick and shut-in? I was speaking with the entertainment coordinator of a nursing home some time ago, and she said come December each year, people literally run over each other trying to give food and gifts to the residents. Choirs compete among themselves to wow the seniors with their stellar performances, but come January, the seniors are once again ensconced in that winter wonderland of solitude from no visitors. The cherubic soprano voices from the middle school ensemble no longer fill the room. The warm lilt of the cellos no longer wafts down the hallways effortlessly. Seniors no longer get their faces rubbed by complete strangers.

While it is commendable for anybody to take time from their busy schedules to help bring cheers to seniors, it would behoove the church as a whole to stagger their visits to at least a few times per year. Don't bottleneck your way in December trying to compete with the high school choirs, the café employees, the engineering middle managers from across the street, and a few performers from the local circus in town. Purpose yourself to make this a part of you. Many times those seniors don't demand a lot. Some of them want to play board games with a few unfamiliar faces. And still others need to be touched by people aside from their caregivers.

If you are one of those small church pastors, who are out on a limb, be encouraged today. You might not have the latest, high-tech cameras in your congregation, but keep heart. You are doing a thousand good deeds for your members. You have a role to play in your community. So don't look at what you don't have. You can reach that young man or that young woman who perhaps would not have been privileged to meet a pastor from a megachurch. You don't have a praise team or a 50-piece orchestra in place, but God is still with you. He inhabits your praises. Don't watch your less-than-desirable, Spartan office space. God will be doing a new thing for you. Just be faithful. Continue to dole out blessings at your fingertips.

Many of us tend to associate big churches with being uncaring. We tend to believe that anything too big is never good. But that is not always the case. There are legions of men and women of God who are making a difference from the pulpits of megachurches. They touch and kiss AIDS babies – not just when the camera lights are on them for photo ops. They agonize over the members they are unable to talk to personally on a one-on-one basis. But their love can be felt throughout their congregations.

AN OPEN LETTER TO PASTORS:

Dear Pastor,

I love to hear about Brother John's testimony when he landed the $12-million government contract for his software company. I also love when you feature Sister Grace when she made it to the top of her Fortune 500 corporation. It warms my heart, too, to hear Brother Gary – the NBA Forward's testimony for the twentieth time, but please, I cannot stress it enough, please, diversify the testimonies coming from your pulpit.

There's a Brother Calhoun, a grandfather of 10, who once ran with a gang, waiting in the wings ready to tell the world about how he overcame cocaine and heroin addiction after battling the habit for more than 30 years. Hundreds of lives can be made whole by his testimony. There is Sister Greta who cannot keep her heels quiet because of the urge to tell others how God delivered her from a life of prostitution, where she's now a missionary for the last 15 years. You perhaps don't know this but she's building a halfway house for teenage runaway girls in Bamako, Mali in West Africa.

And how can I forget Brother Manny Rodriquez. Remember him, the brother who always shows up to park the cars rain or shine; the one who visits the prisons twice weekly to counsel inmates? Yes, the same gentleman who makes coffee and mops the floor whenever he's called on to do so. He wants to tell you about his years of gang-banging, and how God has cleaned him up and given him a wonderful wife and five beautiful children.

In fact, he, too, started an office-cleaning company where he made a whopping $500,000 last year. You wouldn't know it, but he doesn't want to brag about it. He prefers to share his testimony, though, among his brothers and sisters in a primetime Sunday service like Brother Gary and Sister Grace. Will you please give them a chance to be instruments of blessings to others? Thank you for your time.

I remain your faithful member,
—Brother Neville Nelson

Dear Rev. Murray:

Yesterday I was so joyful, and then it dawned on me that it was the 15-year anniversary of my being free from drug and alcohol abuse. I wish to thank you for never giving up on me. You saw something in me that I could not see. Remember when my life was so wasted that I didn't even know my own self? Being a teenage mother of two children with no father around, you and your wife rescued me from the dreaded streets of Chicago, and brought me to your home, even when others were telling you not to do so. You fed me, clothed me, and paid my way through college, while taking care of my babies. Today, I am an immigration attorney and happily married to my wonderful husband, Josh. You truly live what you preach. What a blessing you are to the world!

Bright beginnings,
Telsa Jackson-Pugh

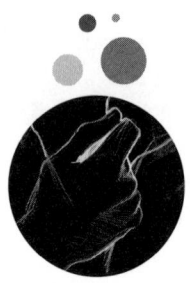

CHAPTER TWENTY-ONE

BEING NICE IS A PRECURSOR TO BLESSINGS

WHY DO WE RUN TO STRAIGHTEN UP THE living room when strangers are coming over, yet week-old pizza boxes are strewn about the floor when nobody knocks us up? I strongly doubt that many of us set out to do this, putting our loved ones in second place. But if we're not careful, practice can become perfect over time.

We must learn never to take those closest to us for granted. For everybody who has worked for me on a particular job, I've always purposed myself to write them a thank-you note, acknowledging my gratitude for her work. A kind deed never goes unnoticed by me, but several times when Yvonne would help me out, there was never any thank-you card to tell her how much I truly thank her for her hard work as well. I would do it sometimes, but I am now committed to do it always.

A popular Jamaican saying goes, "Learn to dance in your yard before you dance aboard." In other words, practice your dancing moves at home first before taking them to strange places. If you don't practice to be nice at home to your family, then you will not be nice to strangers on the street.

One afternoon I was writing up a few thank-you cards, and after I finished writing up those cards, I realized that there were none for Yvonne and Jevoy, not that I didn't mean to write them cards as well. I told myself that I would tell them personal thank you's, but the outsiders were more important in this regard than my family. For that function, we worked our tails off. I am indebted to Jevoy for his Herculean strength. He often badgered me to come with me on assignments, and that particular day was one of those times. Yvonne actually took a day off from work just to be there. So it was only fitting that she should be praised as highly as the others, but it was not so.

I have a few socks, T-shirts, and sweat suits from the time God said "let there be light," and for some reason, I have not parted with them. I sometimes put them on around the house, but I would never be caught outside the house with them. If the doorbell rings, I wouldn't face a stranger that way. But I have no reservation in doing it around my family. Some of you might argue that being comfy around the house is relaxing, but why is it okay with your family but not okay for the man in the street? Am I the only one who has this problem? I often wonder.

Some wives give their husbands the stocking cap, pulling the wig from their head until they are ready to go through the door again, all dolled up. Their best friends would never see them like that, but husbands and kids get the worst of them. Collectively, we ought to change in this area by giving the best to our families. We should never take our loved ones for granted.

Some pastors' wives and children to this day are estranged because of the pastors' treatment to their families. Brother Pastor spent so much time looking about the affairs of others that his family suffers over time. Some of you spent hours doing church work but not a minute to take your kids out for ice cream. Remember, family is one of the highest forms of ministries in the church. If you cannot be effective to your own family, then how can you be effective to your congregation? Priests, in biblical times, were given a year off when they got married. See Deuteronomy 24:5. Young and old, leader and laity, all must utilize this form of respect.

Let's all dump those old clothes and bring a fresh start to our families. Some of us feed our children poor nutrition, but save the best for our guests. We make the living room off limit to our kids for days, while visitors have the run of the space to themselves. Remember again, charity begins at home. Start loving your loved ones from home, not only when you're out in the mall or at public functions, when you cannot get your hands off each other. And whenever you get back home, one person goes east while the other one goes west.

ONE COUSIN'S DEEP REGRET

SOME YEARS ago I was inside an internet chat room where a woman was having a hard time coming to terms with the death of her cousin. The two women grew up together in Jamaica, and one emigrated to America. When the cousin visited Jamaica for the first time after being away for many years, she described her running to meet her cousin, and as she neared her, both of them just broke down and wept. Even though they were face to face, neither one could bring herself to hug the other, since they had never done so growing up.

The cousin talked about returning to America and within a year after her visit, her cousin died. She was having a hard time dealing with her passing, but the biggest guilt she harbored was that she did not hug her cousin, even though she wanted to do so badly. One good, however, came from that saga: She forced herself to hug her husband, children and other loved ones every chance she got. And she started saying more I love you's.

Don't take your loved ones for granted. Find it within yourself to hug freely and without reservation. You will be a blessing as well as being blessed. Celebrate your children, husband, wife, friends and other loved ones. And just remember, whenever you are tempted to start taking them for granted, do yourself a favor. Do some soul searching, because indeed it starts from within.

TAKE HOME YOUR BREAD

As CHILDREN, like clockwork, my dad never came home without some treats for us. He seemingly had a gift for choosing the largest and juiciest fruits like soursops, bananas, mangoes, oranges, etc. I can still smell his oversized boxes oozing with a thousand scents, and the joy it was for us to open them and spot some of our favorite things. But it wasn't always like that. Many times when those boxes reached home unopened, most likely it would be late evening.

Once neighborhood kids spotted him along the way, you could bet that half the time all he would have left was one or two fruits to share among his children. Some of the children would still show up at the gate begging for more treats. And whenever food was out, he would give them money. The sight of those children coming around would get me so mad. Many times they would come to our gate to taunt us – eating those same goodies my father gave them and smirking. Just to get us upset.

One boy in particular, Raymond Polson, was the main culprit. I might have been 10 years old or so, but one afternoon, my dad, after making it home with one fruit, turned around and gave it to Raymond, while my siblings and I looked on with tears in our eyes. I had had enough! And all I could do then was to get a handful of sand, and with full force, I tossed it in his face. He yelped so hard that I felt sorry for him afterward, but not before my father gave me the beating of my life. My dad is that person who personifies kindness to a fault. He would give up his last penny and do without.

Even stray dogs had a way of making their demands known, too, when he was around. This is still a family classic, and my sister, to this day, tells it with rib-hurting laughter. About six houses from our home, Phyllis, a woman who was hardly ever home, had a dog. That poor dog would get so hungry that he passed the time just barking at anything that moved. But for some weird reason, he always had a bone to pick with my father, even though he would drop off scraps of food for the dog at times.

My dad used to love buying a loaf of fresh bread daily. One morning, while he was walking back home with his bread in hand, the dog started to chase him, and he thought up this grand idea of breaking off a big chunk of bread just to appease the mad mongrel. He thought that he could bide himself some time while the dog ate, but as fast as he could break off another chunk of bread and throw to the dog, the hungry mutt would gobble it up and give chase. My dad couldn't keep up with this demand. Since there seemed to be no way out of that dilemma, my dad decided to make a mad dash home from the dog. Finally, when he made it about half way home, with no bread left, it was said that he took off like a bullet, with the dog behind his heels. The dog tried to bite him, but he soon dis-covered that all along the old, hungry mutt had no teeth. Well, you would think my father would not be kind to such a dog again now that the sting of fear was gone, but quite the contrary. He became even kinder to that dog until it died.

Every now and again my sister ribbed him on that incident, much to his chagrin. That passage in Matthew 15:26 where Jesus said, "It is not right to take the children's bread and toss it to the dogs," takes on a whole new meaning for me, which brings a smile to my face whenever I read it.

A NIGHTINGALE SINGS IN NEW YORK

YOU WOULD see her pushing her cart among the horde of genteel partygoers, Wall Street executives, and rank and file folks. Come rain or shine the cart is full. Of what I don't know. But some of the items looked as though they were salvaged from the Mayflower or the Titanic. The one tooth, which jutted precariously from the left side of her lower lip, appeared to have been on a race to touch her nose. Her lean face fought in vain to tell a story of yesteryear about this proud woman, one no doubt which was a life of elegance. But her droopy eyes belied that chance. She didn't beg and she didn't bother anybody. She remains nameless to this day. And I regretted not getting to know her some more. But I will never forget her sense of gratitude as long as I live.

She was one of the thousands of homeless men and women who traipsed up and down the vast expanse of New York City on a daily basis. She sported a bag of dreadlocked (matted hair) under a knitted hat. But she was a nightingale. You would find her in SoHo, Upper Broadway, Washington Heights – just but everywhere throughout the city. The first time I spotted her, she was belting out the most melodious rendition of *Day Oh*. After the song ended, I knew I had been hooked! I walked over and dropped some money inside her cup, and the most unexpected thing happened: She presented me with a stem of roses, followed by a gummy smile – the kind which has the power to melt a tyrant's heart. I was blown away! I doubted very much that she got those roses for free. I am sensing that she used part of her handout to purchase flowers as a way to say thank you to her generous donors.

Ever since that day, I never passed that woman without asking her to sing for me. Whether she was huddled underneath her bundle of bags and pans at midnight, she would break free from her load to sing me a line or two of that song, with extra effort to reach the descant where her soprano voice twirled like a figure skater in high gear.

One evening I saw her inside a subway station in Washington Heights – Upper Manhattan. She was in a corner as usual minding her own business, and there were quite a few people waiting for their train on the platform. I walked over to her, and you could see the eyes following me. I chatted with her briefly, and finally made my request. She said that she was not in the mood to sing, but I coaxed her anyway, and she obliged. As she belted out the sonorous tune, it cascaded throughout the cavernous walls effortlessly. When she was finished, I gave her some money as usual, and before long, people were marching lockstep to fill her cup. And as usual, each one walked away with a rose in hand and a smile. You could see the shock on people's faces when they got those roses. Many of those people's eyes brimmed with tears. She took them by surprise.

Every now and then, I think about that woman, and recall the beauty in her heart, voice, and the rose despite her being homeless. One of the reasons why I think she did not beg for money, was that she wanted to keep her dignity intact.

Another thing I discovered as I interacted with the chanteuse was that at times, all it takes to create an impact in society is one person. I've walked with friends, and whenever I stopped and talked to her, they would be a mile away from us. They would later say I have a heart to stop and converse with the homeless. Over time, they would tell me that they spotted the woman and because of my bravery to talk with her, they, too, have come to like her singing. And when they are drawn to her, other onlookers feel braver and toss their pride aside to give the woman a few bucks. That gesture has paved the way to their doing more volunteer work for the less fortunate people, and in turn they are blessed. They swallowed their pride in order to let another human being feel special and worthy. Since blessing is not one sided, you never know what kind of blessings you are releasing in your own life whenever you purpose yourself to be nice to others.

A BLESSING AT THE FUNERAL

In January 2006 Michael and Wanda Carter, along with their 13-year-old daughter, Ashley, were dropping off some cakes at their church, while a funeral service was going on. As they were about to leave, somebody grabbed them and asked them if they could stay around to help. There was no organist or pianist, and Michael volunteered to play the organ while Wanda sang two solos. Ashley was instantly placed at the door as an usher. As Wanda put it, "we were a hot mess" since they weren't dressed for church, but they felt compelled to do a worthy cause.

The Carters were looking to buy their first home, and had their eyes opened to any reasonable leads. Wanda chatted with the limousine driver for a brief moment, which led to the driver's talking about selling a condominium. The unit was on the market for more than eight months without anybody showing an interest to buy. Within a week's time, the limo driver turned over the keys to the Carters and began referring to the unit as theirs. Some financial setbacks crept up, which would seem to erode their hopes, but they pressed on. And the owner kept referring to the unit as theirs. Michael spent three months out of work on sick leave, but they were able to move into their condominium four months later. Today they host every chance they got, and you cannot find a warmer home anywhere this side of town.

The Carters are living proof that when you give of yourself self-lessly, you will be rewarded abundantly. Blessings were right there at their fingertips, and all they had to do were to bring them home. The last place anybody would be looking to talk about a business deal was at a funeral service. But when they least expected it, God had it all worked out with one of his stewards – the limo driver. Their passing the test was imminent, and they did so with 100 percent.

I have been exhibiting this so-called *madness* for some time now. When the freezer/refrigerator or cupboard is full, I am grateful, but over time, I cannot wait for it to get empty again so as to trust God for more. In times like those, I would go out of my way to cook and serve the homeless, give away to families who are experiencing financial constraints. And what a joy it is to see those cupboards, refrigerator, and freezer filling up again.

The thing is, when you bless others, you are bound to receive blessings. Reciprocity is a sure way for God's richest blessings.

THE JOY OF GIVING BACK PAYS OFF

IT WAS after four on the snowy Wednesday evening. I had gone to the doctor's office for the two younger boys' appointments, but it was closed early because of the snowstorm in Seattle. Yes, believe it or not, snow in Seattle. Not rain this time; the real stuff! Even though it was my third time seeing the Emerald City transformed into ice in my five years living here, it had caused quite a nightmare on the roadways for motorists over the last few days of November.

As we journeyed home, one of the boys suggested, "Why don't we go shopping for Mom?" In a split second, everybody was in on it. I thought they were talking about doing an early Christmas shopping for Yvonne, but they flatly said no. They just wanted to surprise her for that day with impromptu gifts. Pretty soon, I, too, was in on the deal. When I suggested a few stores where they would like to go, they finally chose a dollar store outlet. They bought a mug, a teddy bear, and a hand lotion. When we got home that evening, they hustled and bustled to their room to hide the gifts. From the car, they had decided that they would give her the treats around the dinner table.

Another countered that the best way would be to give her each gift in a 10-minute sequence. They agreed to adopt the latter. When Jason walked out with his gift, Yvonne screamed and asked what was the reason, but he just said that he wanted to surprise her with something nice. As she lolled away on the sofa watching the rerun of *Oprah* in the evening, Jevaughn came out with his gift. This time she yelped! She hugged him and told him a thousand thanks.

Jevoy made his grand entrance about 15 minutes later, and she was beside herself. She hugged and kissed him, oohing and aahing as he dashed to round up the other two boys, now busily playing their video games in their room. To see the million-dollar worth of joy that emanated from just a thought and $3 was quite a sight to behold. I don't think she will ever forget that kind gesture anytime soon.

Was it the snow that brought about a newness or freshness on our landscape? Did it trigger some kind of serotonin inside their brains to be super kind? By the look on their faces, I knew that they were immensely blessed as was the recipient – their mom – Yvonne.

Don't ever discount the thought of a gift. Somebody could be on a beach in Thailand and pick out a triangular-shaped stone, traveling thousands of miles just to bring it to you as a souvenir. Don't curse her out after she leaves. Don't murmur to your friend that the cheapskate of a woman didn't buy you some T-shirts, but only that good-for-nothing stone. Don't discount that gift. Perhaps that three-sided stone could start off your thinking in a different light altogether. You could start seeing things on a trilateral level. It could teach you that when one door is closed, at least you have two more left to push open.

GIVE UNCONDITIONALLY

I AM always skeptical whenever somebody is only nice to me. I had a supervisor once, and she was the nicest person you would ever want to meet. She would reward me for every project I turned out. She invited me to expensive breakfasts, and always had a positive word for me. I took advantage of those treats while looking out from the corner of my eyes to see whether or not her generosity was across the board. Over the months, I soon learnt that by no means was I unique to her niceness or her largesse. She was the same with females. Old. Young. Whites. Blacks. Asians. Americans, and non-Americans. Frankly, I had never met another individual like that up to that time.

Because of my uncertainties and insecurities, I was missing out on my full blessings. However, once I realized that my supervisor's intentions were pure, I just went headlong into those perks. The breakfast would not only involve me but the entire department. Everybody's birthday was celebrated. There was love and acknowledgment for everybody. Looking back now, I am so grateful for my life touching that of a warm and caring human being. It would later pave the way for me to give back to others unconditionally.

I was at my neighborhood library when a young woman – about 17 – of Asian descent, walked over to me and asked if I could help her with her essay. I was flattered that a complete stranger, who could be my daughter, would want my help. After giving her a few pointers, she was very appreciative, and offered to buy me coffee. I told her it was okay, and that she didn't have to reward me for my service.

She asked me for my telephone number or email address where she could send me her work from time to time for me to look them over. I wondered what would her parents say should they discover a strange telephone number in their child's address book. I was hesitant in doing so, but I just remembered my female supervisor and her kindness; how her giving back to people was not corrupt but pure. I wanted to follow in this vein – helping people without looking back for any remunerations from them.

Mission was accomplished that day at the library. Some of her friends, both male and female, were around while I was going through certain steps with her. They seemed anxious, seemingly wanting to know more about this reservoir of blessings. Some of them are very bright, taking on challenging calculus or physics. But for a lot of them, English is a challenge. I cannot wait to be of some help across the board for that young lady and her peers. If not for anything else, I owe it to my supervisor.

KINDNESS WILL ALWAYS BE REMEMBERED

DAVID REMEMBERED the crippled Mephibosheth, his friend, Jonathan's son. He ate from David's table like one of his sons. See 2 Samuels 9:1-12; also 2 Samuels 10:1-2. Do good always. It will yield a ton of rewards later on for you.

"Render more and better service than that for which you are paid, and sooner or later you will receive compound interest on compound interest from your investment. For it is inevitable that every seed of useful service you sow will multiply itself and come back to you in overwhelming abundance.

"Put your mind to work. Access your ability and energy. Who could use your help? How can you help? It doesn't take money . . . all it takes is ingenuity and a strong desire to be of genuine service. Helping others to solve their problems will help you to solve your own.

"The most successful people are those who serve the greatest number of people." – Napoleon Hill.

THE TWIN TOWERS TRAGEDIES

I HAD been privileged to work with a few law firms inside the towers at the World Trade Center in New York City. The walls of some of those attorneys' offices were bedecked with degrees and awards from many of our country's most prestigious universities. Expensive artworks from renowned artists were commonplace in boardrooms. Many of those offices had breathtaking views overlooking the East River, the Hudson River, George Washington Bridge, and the heart of Times Square. It took a lot of prodding to get a visitor out of those offices. The views were so captivating! I had not been inside other offices such as those on other floors, but I would assume that they were equally impressive. Multimillion-dollar deals were closed around lavish dinners atop the Windows on the World restaurant. That was the life!

But despite such opulence, given the chance again, many of the deceased occupants of those posh offices would give up every cubit inch of those areas and views to live in poverty for the rest of their lives with their loved ones. And many of the survivors, too, would gladly have their loved ones back sans the "good life."

While mangled steel and concrete rained down on the streets of New York City on that fateful morning of September 11, 2001, with precious lives in tow, those cushy offices were no more. They had ceased to be. It is so eerie whenever I'm scrolling through my organizer for a contact address and stumble upon One World Trade Center, with telephone numbers and everything intact. As if the place still exists.

As mentioned in an earlier chapter, I had relocated from my beloved New York City to Seattle just five days prior to that tragedy. And that Tuesday morning, as I watched the interminable broadcast on television, I resolved then and there that I would always love my family, friends, and neighbors more – not things. I started saying more *I love you's*, writing more thank-you cards, etc. I've come to realize that the coveted titles, dream houses or cars can go, but your loved ones are irreplaceable. How else do you explain workmen expending hundreds of man hours round the clock, sometimes racking up millions of dollars in cost trying to extricate a Baby Jessica McClure trapped in a Texas well in 1987, or freeing trapped coalminers in West Virginia in the early parts of 2006? Those wells and mines perhaps cost millions of dollars to replace or rebuild, but things are not important – people are.

KEEP YOUR WORDS SWEET

I HEARD somebody once say that one should always keep his words sweet, because he will never know when he'll be called upon to eat them. I found that to be quite true for me. In January 2007, I had gone for some consultation with a colleague. He seemed to get so many things accomplished in any given day: chambers of commerce meetings, Kiwanis meeting, this group and that. He had to go for dental appointment, pick up his children from school, among other errands. I was just amazed at how he could possibly get so many things done in his day. What was he doing right? I didn't beat around the bush to ask him how he did it.

"Man, you are asking me that? I learned from you. Remember you were the one who was always networking with chambers of commerce and other meetings? You are the man who got me so involved."

I was speechless. I couldn't believe what I was hearing. I had been so bogged down with so many things to do, it was hard at times being focused. I soon had flashbacks of my days doing the circuit. But had he not reminded me about those days, I would not have remembered my days going hither and yon for business prospects and other go-getter activities. He spent the next 45 minutes fleshing out my contributions to his life that I had long forgotten. My encouragement for the day were some of the same recycled words I had encouraged my colleague with in the past. I was so driven and alive after I left that meeting.

A few months later I met with my accountability partner from church, and frankly, I was not up to going to our scheduled meeting that day. I was having a severe headache, and was feeling out of sorts. I was prepared to encourage him, but the role was shifted that day. It was déjà vu all over again. I could hardly get a word in. Like my earlier colleague, my accountability partner hammered me with the Word that day, which baffled me for days. He, too, used some of the same words I had used to encourage him in the past. And hearing those recycled words could not have been sweeter to my ears that day. The anecdotes he shared with me were right on point, while I nodded in assent. I walked away taking those words, "keep your words sweet," to heart.

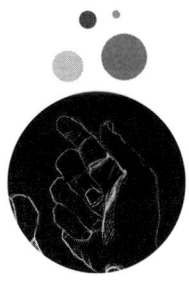

WHAT PEOPLE ARE SAYING
ABOUT BLESSINGS AT YOUR FINGERTIPS

"... Thank you, Nandell, for honouring your teacher, Miss Martin, and paying tribute to her. You have become a wonderful, generous, compassionate and caring person. That in itself is a reward for her efforts. God bless you."

—Archbishop Desmond Tutu, South Africa

"In today's world with our always on the go, 24/7 lifestyle, we need to stop every now and again to count our blessings. We have so many of these blessings hovering about us without our even realizing them. Read Nandell Palmer's Blessings at Your Fingertips and you will be inspired, grateful, driven, and at peace with all that you are blessed with. This book unequivocally is a winner!"

— Patrick Snow, bestselling author of Creating Your Own Destiny

"Your life will be touched — at best changed — as a result of reading Blessings at Your Fingertips. Nandell Palmer has used very personal and unique stories to teach us that there is a blessing in even the simple things we do. Thanks, Nandell, for being one of those blessings at our fingertips!"

— Devon Harris, 3-time Olympian; Captain of the Jamaican Bobsled Team, which inspired the Disney classic, Cool Runnings

"Nandell Palmer is a truly remarkable human being, as proven by Blessings at Your Fingertips. He inspires with simple, down-to-earth stories that transcend culture and nationality, showing us the importance of a kind word and generous heart. His concept of extending blessings is powerful, and demonstrates how each one of us, no matter how insignificant we feel, can indeed make a lasting difference."

—Alesa Lightbourne, Ph.D., Chapman University, author of The SALSA Solution

"Nandell Palmer uses personal stories and deep insight to challenge his readers. Inspirational, uplifting, and thought-provoking, Blessings at Your Fingertips will inspire every reader to re-examine their own lives and drastically change their view of power of the spoken and written blessing."

— Mark L. Brown, World Champion of Public Speaking, Toastmaster International

"Blessings at your Fingertips is a strong and refreshing reminder of the importance of making every day and every moment count in the lives of those around you. Nandell Palmer reminds us to have a heart. Chapter 15 is a most powerful chapter. What a story. This is a great read!"

— Mike Schindler, author of Operation Military Family

"I've just finished reading Blessings at Your Fingertips, and I am inspired. Inspired to give my life more purpose. Mr. Palmer has, through his writing, caused me to rethink my attitude about money, food and personal relationships. For a first book, this is a masterpiece, and I can hardly wait for his next one."

— Brenda Burke, Cascadia Law Group, Seattle, Washington

"Blessings at Your Fingertips is the best inspirational book I've ever read. It has answered so many questions I've often asked myself, and has brought a certain peace and calm to many feelings and thoughts I've had. This book is thought-provoking; encouraging; self-empowering, and self-atoning. Buying this book bears no regrets whatsoever."

— D. Pierre Francois, Poet

"I have read Palmer's Blessings at Your Fingertips and am very impressed with his quite scholarly but simplistic style of writing. Encouraging and eye-opening words indeed! I am convinced he has been inspired by a Higher Being, and startled at his memory of every child in his 4th-grade class! If you are seeking inspiration, grab your copy! Great work, Nandell!"

— Derry Lyon, Cayman Islands

"Blessing at Your Fingertips is an easy, folksy, well-written book. While the book is about our bettering ourselves and others through positive steps, it is at the same time a book about one person's values and the paths he has taken to where he now finds himself. Towards the end, you'll realize that the first "blessing" is right at your fingertips because you're holding it."

— Bob Flannery, Tacoma, Washington

". . . You will feel exhilarated about the opportunities and blessings you have at your fingertips everyday. The stories are compelling and unique. You can almost picture yourself sitting down and having a conversation with Palmer as you read through each chapter."

— Jason Coleman, Corporate Executive